P9-BHY-447

13.60.

slimmer

POPULATION
EDUCATION
A Knowledge Base

POPULATION

EDUCATION

A Knowledge Base

WILLARD J. JACOBSON
Teachers College, Columbia University

TEACHERS COLLEGE
COLUMBIA UNIVERSITY

Copyright © 1979 by Teachers College, Columbia University. All rights reserved. Published by Teachers College Press, 1234 Amsterdam Avenue, New York, NY 10027.

CAMROSE LUTHERAN COLLEGE
LIBRARY

Library of Congress Cataloging in Publication Data

Jacobson, Willard J
    Population education.

    Includes bibliographies and index.
    1. Population — Study and teaching (Secondary)
2. Interdisciplinary approach in education. I. Title.
HB850.J3   301.32'07'12   78-13398
ISBN 0-8077-2533-1

Designed by Dennis J. Grastorf   /27, 139

First Printing, 1979
10 9 8 7 6 5 4 3 2 1

Manufactured in the U.S.A.

Contents

Foreword by Sloan R. Wayland   xiii

Acknowledgments   xv

Introduction   xvii

1 Population and Education   1

   Characteristics of Modern Problem Situations   2

   Definitions   5

   Goals and Assumptions   6

   Inquiry Approach   8

     Defining the problem   8

     Values and valuation   8

     Problem contexts (systems)   9

     Frames of reference   9

     Multiple factor causation   10

     Identifying universal laws or principles   11

     Suggesting possible solutions (hypotheses)   11

     Logical consequences of suggested solutions   12

Testing proposed solutions   13

What can I do?   13

Conclusion   14

Selected References   15

2 Populations and How They Change   16

Basic Terms and Concepts   17

Population size and census taking   17

Births and birth rates   19

Death rates and life expectancy   19

Migration   20

Population growth rate   21

Mathematical concepts   22

Exercise: A practical demonstration of growth rates   25

Exercise: Population size after a given number of years   27

Projections and Predictions   28

Age Structure of Populations   29

Population pyramid   30

Exercise: Studying population pyramids   31

Exercise: Constructing a population pyramid   31

World Population Growth   32

Exercise: A demonstration of population growth   34

Population Distribution   35

How Populations Grow   36

Growth Patterns   38

Pattern of stabilization   38

Pattern of rapid growth and rapid decline   40

Human Population Growth Pattern   41

Stabilization model   41

Rapid growth and rapid decline model   43

Discussion: Implications of different models   44

Conclusion   45

Selected References   46

3 Population Regulation   48

General Hypothesis: Feedback Control   49

  In physical systems   50

  In biological systems   50

  In social systems   51

Population Regulation in Animal Populations   52

  Growth limited by food supply   52

  Growth limited by disease and accumulated wastes   53

  Territoriality and population regulation   55

  Social organization and population regulation   58

  Feedback model of self-regulation   60

  Exercise: What factors regulate the size of a
    population?   61

Population Regulation in Human Populations   61

  Technologically undeveloped societies   62

  Demographic transition theory   63

  Exercise: Stages of demographic transition   64

  Theory of change and response   67

  Discussion: How can developing nations achieve
    population stabilization?   69

  Education and culture feedback model   70

  Man's destiny   72

Conclusion   73

Selected References   75

4 Families and Population   77

The Family   78

Human Reproduction   80

  Reproductive capacity   80

  Process of human reproduction   83

Exercise: What are the critical stages of reproduction
in other organisms?   86

Birth control and contraceptive methods   87

Menstrual cycle and conception   87

Preventing the union of sperm and egg   88

Inhibiting release of the egg   89

Creating an environment unfavorable to conception   90

Voluntary sterilization   92

Termination of fetal development   93

Discussion: Abortion   93

The search for better methods of birth control   94

Social Factors That Influence Family Size   96

Age of marriage and of bearing first child   97

Intervals between births   98

Number of children   98

Discussion: What factors influence family size?   100

Changing normative roles of women   100

Widowhood, separation, divorce, and abstinence   102

Young People and Their Futures   102

Some consequences of teen-age childbearing   104

Discussion: Family size, population growth, and
quality of life   106

Family Planning and Public Policies   107

Kinds of public population policies ·   108

Discussion: Effects of population policies   114

Conclusion   115

Selected References   117

5 Population and Space to Live   118

What Is Crowding?   119

Exercise: The population density of your community   122

Population Density versus Population Size   122

    Exercise: Density or size — which is more important?   123

    Exercise: Effects of population density and
         population size   125

Population Density and Social Stress   125

    Effects of population density on animal populations   125

    How relevant to man are animal population studies?   128

    Discussion: Relevance of animal population studies   130

    Effects of population density on human populations   130

    Discussion: Explaining results that seem
         contradictory   131

    Discussion: What factors might lead to crime and
         juvenile delinquency?   132

    Exercise: Multiple causation   136

Problems for Research   137

    Discussion: Research into population problems   139

A Concept of "Open Space"   139

    Questions of values and possibilities   140

    What is open space?   141

    Exercise: Open space — how much? how accessible?   142

    Exercise: Open space — how is it used?   143

    How much space do we need or want?   143

    Discussion: Questions about open space   145

How Do People Want to Live   146

    Exercise: Choosing a place to live   148

Conclusion   148

Selected References   150

6 Populations and Their Environments   152

    Concept of "System"   153

    Exercise: Example of a system   153

    Discussion: Aspects of systems   154

Natural Ecosystems   155

   Exercise: What is a natural ecosystem like?   156

Villages and Self-contained Agrarian Systems   159

   Exercise: Migrant workers in the community   161

Modern Farming Systems   163

Cities and Industrialized Urban Systems   167

   Exercise: The location of cities   168

   Discussion: Some consequences of urbanization   171

   Discussion: Education for the future   173

The Global System   173

   Population distribution   174

   Exercise: Distribution of the world's population   175

   Global environment   178

   Migration from the global system   179

   Discussion: Would migration to outer space be desirable?   180

Impact of Population Growth   180

   Discussion: Implications for government   184

Optimum Levels of Population   185

   Discussion: What would be an optimum level of population?   186

Conclusion   187

Selected References   189

7 Population and Resources   192

Application of Universal Laws   193

   First law of thermodynamics   193

   Law of tolerance levels   194

Food — A Necessity of Life   195

   Exercise: The foods we eat   199

   The sources of food   199

   Exercise: Example of a balanced system   201

Food pyramids 201

Exercise: Where on the pyramid are foods we eat? 203

World food requirements 203

Exercise: How the world's food supply is distributed 204

Increasing the production of food 208

Increasing acreage 208

Exercise: Growing more food 209

Improving plant and animal strains 209

Mechanization 210

Increased use of fertilizers 211

Irrigation 211

Control of weeds and pests 212

Food from the sea 213

Improving technology and education 213

But . . . greater sophistication, greater risk 214

Materials and Life Styles 215

Exercise: The kinds of materials we use 215

Material resources in limited supply 218

Discussion: Limited resources and future policy 221

Access to material resources 222

Energy and Standards of Living 222

Exercise: The ways we use energy 223

Exercise: Income per person throughout the world 225

Conclusion 226

Exercise: Seeing the whole as well as the parts 227

Selected References 231

8 Population, Values, and Education 233

Clarifying Terms 235

Exercise: Differences in meanings 235

Approaches to Valuation 235

General goals 236

Exercise: Analyzing issues in terms of general goals 238

Basic Values 239

Exercise: Analyzing proposals in terms of basic
values 241

Issues Related to Population 243

Should population control be *imposed?* 244

Discussion: Population control 245

Should young people be taught birth control? 246

Discussion: Access to birth control methods 246

Group interests and population policies 247

Exercise: Role imagining 248

Survival: A Question of Responsibility 250

Discussion: Some ethical dilemmas 250

The ''right'' to self-location 252

Discussion: To grow or not to grow 252

Discussion: The illegal aliens problem 254

The use of world resources 255

Discussion: Basic values and the use of resources 255

The limits of concern 256

Conclusion 257

Selected References 259

Glossary/Index 261

Foreword

THE WORLDWIDE CONCERN about population issues, symbolized by
the designation of 1974 as World Population Year by the United
Nations, has evoked varied responses by public and private agencies
around the world. Population education has emerged as a significant
curriculum innovation. This innovation, which was first developed
in the late 1960s, is moving ahead rapidly in a number of countries,
particularly in Asia.

Population issues, like most areas of public concern, do not fall
neatly into one of the instructional areas around which school curricula are currently organized. Furthermore, the knowledge base for
the cognitive aspect of the curriculum development process nor-
mally available for established areas has not been systematically
developed for this field.

This book is designed to provide the curriculum developer and the
teacher with a single systematic formulation of the knowledge base
for a population education program. At the present time, teachers
can find a large number of documents but few that are addressed to
their needs. Some of these documents are highly specialized references focusing on one portion of the field. Others are popularly
written articles or books usually intended to persuade their readers
to a particular point of view. Natural scientists writing on population
matters typically do not pay systematic attention to the perspective
held by the social scientists, and vice versa. Reports of public de-

bates and symposia tend to emphasize the distinctiveness of the positions held by the participants, rather than provide a basis for synthesis.

In this volume, the author has prepared a text for teachers that provides a pattern for integrating concepts and data from the various disciplines relevant for an understanding of population issues. Any effort to bring together concepts from different academic disciplines is a difficult undertaking and is subject to criticism by specialists from the various fields concerned. In the process of developing this book, the author has had the benefit of comments by professional educators and academic specialists from several fields. The dialogue involved in the process is reflected in the content, and it is hoped that publication of this volume will provide a basis for extending that dialogue to others who are interested in developing the knowledge base for population education programs.

This book has been written primarily for teachers of science and social studies at the middle and junior high school levels, and the suggestions for classroom activities are in general geared for students and teachers at these levels. However, since the basic intent is to provide a knowledge base for this new field, rather than a formal teaching guide, the book should be of value to teachers at other levels in dealing with the cognitive aspects of population education.

SLOAN R. WAYLAND
Professor of Sociology and Education
Teachers College, Columbia University

Acknowledgments

THE WRITING of this book was encouraged by the Commission on
Science Education of the American Association for the Advancement of Science as part of its Science in Society Series. As often in
the past, I have benefited from discussions with my mentors and
colleagues in curriculum development, John Mayor and Arthur
Livermore.

This book developed out of discussions in a seminar in population
education conducted at Teachers College, Columbia University. The
clash of ideas in this seminar was often sharp but always illuminat-
ing. We all struggled to learn from one another. While I have no hope
that any member of that seminar will agree with all of the ideas
presented in this book, I am deeply indebted to them for help-
ing me to see where I had not seen before. Among the participating members of this seminar were: Donald Cook, Michael Davidson, Hazel Hertzberg, Carolyn Iyengar, John McLoughlin, Ward
Morehouse, Betty Mueller, Audrey Roberts, Ramesh Sharma,
Stephen Viederman, Sloan Wayland, and John Youngpeter.

I and all members of the Population Education Project are indebted to the Population Council for its support and for its understanding of the problems we encountered. I am grateful to Teachers
College for its sabbatical leave policy, which gave me a period of
time free of most other responsibilities that made possible the completion of the manuscript. I also wish to acknowledge the help of the

libraries and librarians of Columbia University; I made many demands upon their rich and unique resources.

My students have patiently tried out the various activities suggested here. A number of their suggestions and variations have been incorporated into the final draft.

Steve Viederman has made more contributions than he may realize. His encouragement and support were helpful. But even more helpful were the questions he raised that turned my mind to matters I had not thought of before.

I am especially indebted to Ramesh Sharma who was a member of the Population Education Seminar and has written a companion volume relating to India. It was rewarding to be able to learn and work together.

Sloan Wayland gave generously from his long and extensive experience in population education. We have worked together in several undertakings and, as always, he gave more than any colleague should be asked to give. This book could not have been written without his wise counsel and generous help.

Authors require technical assistance. I am indebted to Barbara Tholfsen for the illustrations and to Mary Allison of Teachers College Press for wise counsel and generous help in the final stages of completing the book.

My secretaries, Grace Messina and Marcela Lorenz, helped coordinate the difficult task of completing various drafts of the manuscript. The unknown heroes of our typing center deserve credit for managing to decipher my difficult penmanship. I am indebted to Claudia Pomponi for her skillful typing of the final draft.

As always I am indebted to my wife Carol. Without her understanding during moments of perplexity and her support during too frequent "lows," I would not have had either the stamina or fortitude to complete this task.

Willard J. Jacobson, Codirector
Population Education Project

Introduction

THE PROBLEMS associated with population may be among the most critical facing mankind. The ways that we do or do not deal with these problems will certainly affect our lives and those of future generations. Some believe that physical survival, or at least survival with some vestige of human dignity and civilization, may hinge on how this generation and the next resolve issues associated with population. It has been said that this generation may be the last to have any options with regard to population.

Any humane and effective approach to many of the problems associated with population will need to have education as a significant dimension. It cannot be just any kind of education; it will have to be education in which young people are enlisted in this important undertaking, in which they study and deal directly with critical population problems. Since our students have the greatest stake in the resolution of these problems, they deserve an opportunity to prepare themselves to analyze the issues.

In this book a knowledge base for population education has been delineated. This knowledge base has been drawn from mathematics, philosophy, the humanities, and many of the natural and social sciences. No attempt has been made to draw territorial boundary lines around the field. Instead, the aim has been to indicate directions in which further investigations, probings, and explorations might be undertaken. There may be disagreement about the directions charted or the aspects emphasized; but it is hoped that these directions and these emphases will at least be considered.

This volume is intended to be a source book for population education that contains background information on problems associated with population, and practical suggestions for teaching. Among these practical suggestions are analogues designed to help relate abstract ideas to more concrete and familiar situations, and "role imaginings" that permit consideration of controversial issues in the way that others may view them. Throughout, these practical suggestions are indicated by distinctive type.

Experiences in population education can be developed within subject areas that often are included in school programs. Throughout this book, for example, there are background information, discussion of issues, and suggestions for teaching that can be useful in social studies, the natural sciences, mathematics, health, home and family life, and literature. All these are important avenues for developing the study of population, and in many cases the study of population can provide examples and applications for work undertaken toward other objectives in these subject areas. There is much to be said for approaching a problem area such as population from the perspective of the different curriculum areas that are already a well-established and familiar part of school programs.

Another approach is to devote some blocks in the curriculum to the study of population as a subject in itself. Then, rather than trying to fit various aspects of population studies into the subject areas that happen to be represented in the school program, whatever subject area is useful can be used as and when it is needed to explore and inquire into the problems and issues associated with population. It may be that such an approach is more conducive to the development of a generalized approach to problem areas. If it is education that matters, then specific allotments of time in school programs should be devoted to the study of such major problem areas as population.

POPULATION
EDUCATION
A Knowledge Base

CHAPTER 1

Population and Education

We show respect for the child in school, not by indulging or coddling
him, but by enlisting him in significant undertakings that result in the
development of his resourcefulness as a human being.

John L. Childs

THIRTY BRIGHT, energetic young people saunter into a ninth grade
classroom early in September. They have hopes and fears, yearnings
and desires. They were born of parents, may have brothers and
sisters; live in a community; go to school; are citizens of a city, state,
and nation; they are fellow travelers on the third planet away from
the sun. We may hope they will live their three score years and ten
with as much happiness and no more sorrow than their 4 billion
fellow Homo sapiens. Many of them will leave offspring who will in
turn leave offspring, all of them destined for their "time in the sun."

In many ways these 30 youngsters are more fortunate than those
who have lived before them. They will live longer; in the United
States girls have an average life expectancy of 75.3 years while boys
on the average will have to settle for 67.6 years (1977). They will
have fewer debilitating diseases and probably enjoy better nutrition
than any of the generations who lived before them. They will be
better educated, have access to more cultural resources, and be

1

more widely traveled than many of their predecessors. Certainly, they will have the companionship of more fellow travelers on Spaceship Earth.

But probably no generation enjoys the distinction of being "most favored," and these bubbling, bustling youngsters will also have to face problem situations of unprecedented complexity, full of dire possibilities. Hanging over their heads is the Damoclean sword of nuclear warfare, which, if ever unleashed, might threaten the survival of all life on the planet. It is strange that, although this is a problem of overriding importance for the future of the human species, it is seldom studied or discussed in our schools. There are environmental problems — problems of pollution and of environmental desecration — that certainly threaten the quality of the lives they will be able to lead. Unlike nuclear warfare, the problems of the environment are much discussed and sometimes studied, but there is usually more discussion than action to deal with the problems. There are problems of limited resources. Inventive people can devise substitutes and we can certainly make better use of what we have, but there is a limited supply of some essentials; and, while we may have enough of many resources, someone will begin to suffer when we run short of some critical essential. Then, there are more people on the planet than there have ever been before; the young people in our classrooms will have to deal in some way with the problems associated with an already large and still rapidly growing global population. These are the kinds of problem situations that face our young people, and they have several common characteristics.

CHARACTERISTICS OF MODERN PROBLEM SITUATIONS

Many of our modern problem situations are in part the result of cultural, scientific, and technological developments. Most people have applauded the conquest and near eradication of such scourges of mankind as malaria, diphtheria, tuberculosis, smallpox, and polio. If it had not been for these advances in the medical and health fields, most of the 30 youngsters in our imaginary classroom would not be there; most would have died before the age of four. These developments are major factors contributing to the rapid growth of the human population. During the lifetimes of these students something will probably have to be done about this rapid growth if calamitous situations involving large numbers of people are not to arise.

The scope of many of these problem areas is unprecedented, and we have had limited experience in dealing with them. The world population (1978) is about 4.2 billion people; it has never before been so large. Even more important, world population is growing in an unprecedented manner. For millennia, there was probably only a small gradual increase in the human population. About 300 years ago the population of the earth was probably only about a half billion people. It has been increasing very rapidly in the last 100 years. For most of the 3 million or so years that man has been on the planet, the population growth rate has been no more than 2 percent per thousand years, but now it is almost 2 percent per year — an increase of almost 1,000 percent in the population growth rate. Homo sapiens, "the wise one," has never encountered this situation before; if nothing else, it gives the wise one something to think about.

Many of the problem areas are essentially global in nature, and we have had only limited experience and success in dealing with problems in the global system. For example, while migration from dense to sparsely populated areas is a possible outlet for population pressure, this will not be a viable response if the entire world becomes densely populated. Large-scale migration from our planet does not seem to be a likely alternative in the near future. Hence, people everywhere have a stake in what happens in terms of population growth in different areas of the world. While there may appear to be difficulties in approaching the population problems of independent political units, in these systems there usually are social and political mechanisms through which problems can be discussed and acted upon. People throughout the world have had very little experience in dealing with problems on a global level, and certainly the political mechanisms for considering such problems and acting upon them are inadequate. U Thant, former Secretary-General of the United Nations, expressed the need for the development of a global civilization:

> The inevitability of the development of the first global civilization and the necessity for its conscious, directed growth has not yet been grasped or sufficiently appreciated to provide the motive power for the great advances which mankind must take in the very near future or perish — if not with the "bang" of a nuclear holocaust, then with the "whimper" of a species and a civilization which ran out of air, water, resources, and food.[1]

Hopefully our young people can begin to work toward a global civilization as they study and consider such issues and problems as those associated with population.

A disconcerting and frustrating characteristic of modern problem situations is that there is *no complete and final solution* to most of the problems. Because of the increasing distribution of fissionable materials, the widespread knowledge of how to make nuclear weapons, and continuing nationalism, there is little hope of finding a "final" solution to the problem of nuclear warfare. Similarly, even if some way could be found to slow down population growth and perhaps achieve a stabilized world population size, this would not be a "final" solution. The potential for renewed explosive population growth will remain. Many of our modern problem situations can be resolved in completely acceptable ways, but we probably will not be able to find final solutions to any of them.

Most modern problems require the willing cooperation of many if continuing and acceptable resolutions of these problems are to be achieved. Obviously, population growth is a result of human reproduction. When births exceed deaths, there is population growth. If population growth is to be checked without coercion or the cruel environmental checks that eventually arrest the growth of any population, cooperation on a broad scale will be necessary. For example, under the conditions that exist in the United States, the fertility rate for replacement and eventual population stabilization is about 2.1 children per family. Those who believe that voluntary cooperative action can lead to a replacement fertility rate have been heartened by the drop in the fertility rate in the United States to a level slightly below replacement rate (1977). Even so, because of the large number of young people reaching the age of childbearing, it will take about 70 years of birth rates at this level before the population can be considered stabilized.

To achieve this stabilization will require widespread awareness of the problem, a realization of the broader implications of the decisions and actions of individuals and families, and a general knowledge of the ways individuals and families can limit the size of their families. If we consider population worldwide, then similar kinds of knowledgeable, voluntary cooperation will be essential on a global scale. This dependence upon widespread voluntary cooperation is one of the reasons that education is of such central importance in efforts to resolve modern problem situations.

The resolution of most modern problems requires a concerted educational effort in which many people have an opportunity to inquire into the problems.[2] If rapid population growth is to be checked without coercion or the cruel Malthusian checks of famine and pestilence, it cannot be done unless large numbers of people become aware of the problem, decide that they want to do something about it, and learn how they can contribute to a resolution of the problem. If our experience in other problem areas is germane, then propaganda, advertising, and sophisticated persuasion techniques probably will not be sufficient to sustain the long term effort needed for a resolution of the population problem.

Much more likely of success are educational efforts in which young people have a chance to inquire into the problem area, try to determine what the real problems are, examine and evaluate some of the ways that the problems might be resolved, try to deduce the logical consequences of various proposals, and come to some kind of proposed resolution on the individual, family, community, national and international levels. In many modern problem situations, there are those who think they know the answers, but in most cases effective resolution involves the cooperative action of many. Since everyone, and particularly the young, eventually has a stake in the resolution of these problems, everyone has a right to inquire into these problem areas, to learn how she or he may be affected, and to find out what can be done. This is education in which young people learn to grapple with the momentous issues of our times and through which they may have some possibility of resolving problems that touch us all. Thus, education assumes more than its traditional role of acculturation: it becomes a way by which everyone tackles the problems that touch human well-being and possibly threaten its survival.

DEFINITIONS

A population can be defined in terms of the biological species, geographical region, or political unit. From a genetic standpoint, a population is composed of all individuals whose genes can combine. All these individuals are members of a species and can interbreed. Since the genes of all humans, regardless of race or ethnic background or any physical differences can combine, all such individuals belong to the population of humans.

Populations are sometimes defined in terms of geographical regions. This is especially useful when analyzing the resources available to support a population. For example, the agricultural resources of the Indian subcontinent can be analyzed to try to determine how large a human population that geographic area can support. Considerable attention in population studies is given to comparing the dynamics (patterns of change) of population in various developing regions of the world.

Often, population is defined in terms of such administrative and political units as cities, states (or provinces), or nations, since much of the information about populations is collected in terms of such units. Whatever the level of the unit, information about the size and nature of the population is essential for wise planning.

Population education is the study of populations in their environments. It deals with the interactions within populations and with the interactions between populations and the environments in which they live. Within a population, there may be growth or decline in size, migration, shifts in age composition, and changes in population density. These in turn will be influenced by social interaction. For example, the number of children a family desires to have is affected by the social and cultural mores of the society in which the family lives. The interactions of a population and its environment are also important and a part of population education. A population needs food, water, energy, and other environmental resources. Also, each individual and family needs a certain amount of living space if a desirable quality of life is to be achieved. In the words of Sloan Wayland, population education "stresses the interrelationship between population and other aspects of life, and uses materials which contribute to the understanding of that relationship, rather than the population phenomenon as such."[3]

GOALS AND ASSUMPTIONS

There are three major goals to be achieved in population education:

1. To enable young people to *participate intelligently in decision making* related to population issues. The policies we develop and the actions we do or do not take with regard to population will certainly affect the quality of life in the future. An aim of population education is to foster the ability to participate intelligently and effectively in decision making as members of a family and as

members of a community, a nation, and the world community. The decisions that are made now and in the near future will have very long-term consequences.

2. To develop an *operational understanding* of some of the basic concepts and processes relating to population: reproduction, birth control and population regulation, the interactions between populations and their environments, the development and use of resources, and the role of values in all of these aspects of the problem. Such operational understanding provides a framework for approaching phenomena associated with population and the intellectual foundations for responsible action. As Stephen Viederman has stressed, "The goal of understanding is not purely intellectual. It is rather to provide the intellectual underpinning for responsible action."[4]

3. To foster the *ability to inquire into problem situations* associated with populations. This "inquiry" goal usually involves such processes as defining the problem, taking account of the social and cultural values involved, considering the problem as manifested in various systems, viewing it from various frames of reference, suggesting possible solutions, and analyzing the possible consequences of those solutions.

The following assumptions are made in this approach to population education:

1. Education can be a *profound* and *powerful* undertaking. Too often, education is a vapid experience, patently inconsequential — and students, teachers, and members of the community sense it. While we cannot hope to find "final" solutions to population problems, education will be an essential element in arriving at resolutions that are morally acceptable to most people.

2. Young people have a great stake in the future. Thus they have a *right to know* about the problems associated with population, which inevitably will have great impact upon their lives.

3. Man is both a *cultural* being and an integral part of the *biotic* world. To gain an understanding of the problems associated with population we need to study both their cultural and their biological dimensions.

4. The *inquiry approach* is an appropriate and effective method by which to study and teach about population. Population education should not be an attempt to indoctrinate or coerce; it should be

characterized by systematic investigation into some of the problems associated with population.

INQUIRY APPROACH

Education that deals with the problems and issues of our time can enable students to develop a generalized approach that can be used to analyze other problems at other times.[5] If students have experience in using such an approach in one area, say population, they will be equipped with the intellectual tools to tackle other problem areas throughout their lives. They will know some of the kinds of questions to ask; they will have a framework for analysis.

Defining the Problem A problem situation is a state of affairs in which one has the feeling that there is something wrong, that the situation is not as it might be. We sense that, unless something is done, we may be faced with more serious problems. There are many who believe that rapid population growth constitutes this kind of problem situation.

Problem definition is the process of identifying and delineating specific problems within a problem situation—A problem clearly stated is a problem half solved. There has been a great deal of discussion of "the population problem," but what precisely is it? How large a population can our environment and resources support? or, How can we check the rapid increase of the human population? or, How can we find and develop the resources to sustain a rapidly growing population? or, How can we utilize the earth's resources more equitably so that there will be enough for everyone? Perhaps there are many problems at many levels: How large a family would we find most satisfying? or, Should the state of ————maintain its present population size or aggressively try to attract new industry and with it probably more people? or, Should our nation stimulate population growth or try to stabilize its population? Problem definition is usually the most difficult operation in dealing with problems. Probably no one ever completely masters this operation, but if students have experience in probing and discussing the steps involved in problem definition, they will hopefully become more adept at it.

Values and Valuation Values are the criteria by which we make judgments of worth, of right or wrong, of what actions we should or should not take. What is of greatest importance to us?

What do we value most? When our values conflict, what criteria do we use to judge and choose between them? Intricately interwoven into all population issues are some of our most deeply held values. In considering the issues, it becomes essential to examine and clarify our values and the implications of those values for possible actions. Thus, developing effective approaches to valuation is an important aspect of a generalized inquiry approach to problem situations.

Problem Contexts (Systems) A problem must be considered in its context — large or small. Population problems are generally considered in the context of a system — again, large or small. Many people, for example, tend to define population problems in terms of the global system. It is the world population and its growth that they are primarily concerned about. But some population problems can best be analyzed in terms of developing or developed countries, national systems, regions, cities, communities, or families.

Usually, it is advisable to consider which system will provide the most useful context for purposes of analysis. To complicate matters, there are often interactions between systems. Certainly, there are interactions between family systems and national systems; a nation's population can be seen as the sum of the families within that nation. But, however closely they are interwoven, it is useful to delineate the systems that are involved.

Frames of Reference Frames of reference are the various points of view from which phenomena and problems can be considered. The child who searches for safe paths on which to bicycle will probably view that problem from a perspective different from a distraught taxpayer anxious to keep his tax bill from rising still higher. Both are important frames of reference. Most problems can be viewed from differing, sometimes diametrically opposed, frames of reference. Viewing a problem from a reference frame other than one's own can be useful in seeking more generally acceptable solutions.

While perhaps recognizing population problems in a broad context, some groups feel that they must maintain or increase the size of their particular group in order to maintain parity with competing groups. Such views are especially prominent in such regions as the Middle East, where there is intense rivalry between competing groups, but there are occasional flickerings of such views in most places. It may be difficult to "see the larger picture" when one's own group seems threatened. Similarly, a majority group may have difficulty in seeing matters from the perspective of a threatened minority.

Many problems appear different when viewed from a different reference frame. It is useful for students to try to see and describe problems as they might appear to others. This is not easy. To try to "put on another thinking cap" is a formidable undertaking, but it can help to generate fresh ideas about problems, and certainly it can help to achieve a better understanding of the views of others.

Multiple Factor Causation
Many social and biological phenomena are very complex, and a variety of factors may be associated with an effect. The relative weight of various factors may be difficult to ascertain. Students of such phenomena are understandably reluctant to ascribe a particular effect to any single cause. On the other hand, the failure to act upon a cause, even though it may be only one of several causative agents, can have much worse consequences than waiting until further investigation clarifies the influence of that factor relative to others.

Does population density lead to crime, juvenile delinquency, and other social pathologies? Undoubtedly many additional factors — poverty, lack of education, broken homes, poor housing, lack of recreational facilities — are also linked to these pathologies. So, there is not one cause but many — one of which may be high population density. In chapter 5 it is suggested that population density may be a condition through which other factors take effect. For example, a lack of recreational facilities may not be as critical for the children and young people living in an uncrowded area as it is for those living in a highly congested area. Under conditions of high population density, a lack of recreational facilities is more likely to become a causative factor of social ills. Thus, there may be interrelationships among causes. The presence or absence of one factor, such as population density, may affect the relative influence of other factors, such as lack of recreational facilities.

Some of our most critical problem situations involve multiple factor causation. While there may be inherent limits to the degree of precision with which we can determine the relative weight of various contributing causes, it would seem especially important that young people begin to have experience in analyzing such complex situations. In terms of the ancient dictum, students need to learn to see both the forest and the trees and to recognize that there are many kinds of trees in the forest.

Identifying Universal Laws or Principles   There is a very basic drive in the sciences to find laws that hold true at all times for all situations, that is, laws that follow the "principle of universality." If a principle or law can be shown not to hold for *all* situations and *all* times, then the search is for a principle that will at least have general application. For example, there is a drive to find general principles that will hold for all populations, including human populations. General principles simplify inquiry, in that one does not need a separate law or principle for each different situation — and simplicity is greatly valued in the sciences.

The "law of mass production" holds that populations tend to reproduce at such a rate that they eventually outgrow the resources needed to support them. This law seems to hold for many plant and animal populations. Does it hold for man?

There is considerable controversy as to whether the patterns of population growth that seem to hold for many other populations also hold for the human population. The controversy probably will not be resolved until we can see more clearly the growth pattern of the human population. However, if we merely stand pat and wait to see whether or not the law is universal — whether or not the human population, like other populations, is tending to reproduce at a rate that will outgrow the resources needed to support it — we will eventually be faced with a catastrophic situation. But humans differ from all other species in the extent of their ability to act rationally. If we clearly recognize the danger — the possible tendency for the human population to conform to laws governing other populations — then perhaps we can take rational steps to avoid that ultimate catastrophe.

Suggesting Possible Solutions (Hypotheses)   Proposing possible solutions is a very useful intellectual technique for dealing with problems. It provides a focus for observation, analysis, and the search for data.

It is important to come up with imaginative hypotheses that may point the way to possible solutions. The major difference between the plodding investigator and the brilliant researcher is in the quality of the hypotheses with which each sets out on his or her search. Certainly, students should have the freedom to suggest imaginative, fresh ideas for the solution of the problems we face, and they should be encouraged to do so. The crackpot of one generation has often proved to be the genius of the next.

One of the problems discussed in the report of the Commission on Population Growth and the American Future, as well as elsewhere, is how the population of the United States can be stabilized. One of the suggested hypotheses is that an important step toward population stabilization would be the prevention of all unwanted births. Analyses can and have been made to try to determine whether the prevention of all unwanted births would actually lead to population stabilization. Specific programs can be suggested to prevent unwanted births, and the possible consequences of such programs can be explored.

Logical Consequences of Suggested Solutions It is desirable to try to predict or deduce the possible consequences of suggested solutions. Through investigation and education we can try to predict what might happen if a particular solution were attempted. Would the proposed solution really resolve the problem situation? What might be some of its side effects? How would various individuals and groups be affected? What are some of the uncertainties associated with various proposed solutions? What are the risks involved? One of the aims in education is to develop intelligence, and one of the marks of intelligence is the ability to think through the possible consequences of various suggested actions.

One of the proposals for achieving a stabilized population is to prevent the birth of unwanted babies. Investigations have been carried out to try to determine what percentage of babies born are "unwanted." Various groups, such as teen-age mothers and other unwed mothers, have been studied to find out the relative incidence of unwanted children among them. If the incidence were proved to be particularly high, then special efforts could be made to prevent unwanted births among these groups. What might be some of the side effects? It could be argued, for example, that some of the world's most brilliant and creative people probably were unwanted children and that there is a danger that by preventing unwanted births we might lose the contributions that such people make. Alternative proposals for achieving a stabilized population also need to be examined. Which proposals are most likely to achieve our aims? Involve the least risk? Be most compatible with the values we hold? An important dimension of population education is thinking through — investigating the possible consequences of — various suggested solutions.

Testing Proposed Solutions   Even the most careful prediction and logical analysis often cannot fully acquaint us with the consequences of proposed actions. Yet the possible consequences of such actions (or of inaction) may be so critical that we need to know them with as much certainty as possible before initiating those actions on a large scale. In the laboratory, hypotheses are often tested through *experimentation*. This, of course, is difficult, often impossible, in such social areas as those associated with population. However, *historical studies* or the study of programs recently carried out by others may indicate the consequences of similar proposals tried out under comparable conditions. Such studies may alert us to the difficulties and possible problems we may encounter. Sometimes, it is possible to carry out *pilot studies* to test ideas on a small scale, which reduces the risks involved.

In population studies, as in other areas, we have much to learn from the experience of others. Studies have been made of how population size and growth are limited in relatively primitive hunting and food-gathering societies. Other studies have been undertaken to try to find the biologic maximum of human reproduction among groups where there apparently are very few limits to reproduction. Experiments have been done to assess the effects upon animals of crowding and extremely high population densities, and such studies may afford clues as to the effects upon humans of extremely high population density conditions. Various nations have tried various policies for stimulating or limiting population growth. It would be unintelligent to institute population measures without considering the knowledge and experience gained by others. Thus, the study of population can provide students with experience in learning from the experience of others.

What Can I Do?   Too often, students may deem modern problem areas as abstractions having little direct impact upon them. Certainly they often feel that there is very little they can do about these momentous problems. It is true that no one individual can "solve the population problem." Like most other modern problem areas, the intelligent cooperation of many individual groups will be required to resolve the problems associated with population. But what we do, or fail to do, is likely to affect virtually every individual inhabiting the planet — and the impact will be greatest upon young people and upon their offspring. Also, while what one individual can do may not seem important, the concern and effort of many individuals are essential if we are to deal effectively with modern problem areas. While no individual may be able to move a mountain, mountains can be moved by individuals working and cooperating together.

CONCLUSION

There are three important focuses for the study of the phenomena associated with population and population growth:

1. *The potential effect on every individual,* especially young people and future generations, of rapid and unchecked population growth.
2. *What the individual can and should do.*
3. *What the society can and should do.*

In a democracy, these three aspects form the basis for democratic social and political action — since it is individual citizens and their concerns that shape the ultimate decisions. Population education should help individuals to participate in this process and thus try to ensure that the population policies developed by the society are the wisest ones possible for the individual, for the society, and for mankind as a whole.

FOOTNOTES

1. U Thant, quoted in *War on Hunger: A Report from the Agency for International Development* 5, No. 10 (October 1971): p. 7.
2. The proposition that education is an integral part of any conceivable resolution of many of our problems is one that I made more than a decade ago. See Willard J. Jacobson, "Science Education under Challenge," *Teachers College Record* 65, no. 7 (April 1964): 627–34.
3. Sloan R. Wayland, "Population Education: Orientation for the Teacher," *Intercom*, no. 72 (May 1973): 4.
4. Stephen Viederman, "Population Education in Elementary and Secondary Schools in the United States," in *Aspects of Population Growth Policy*, ed. Robert Parke, Jr., and Charles F. Westoff (Washington, D.C.: U.S. Government Printing Office, 1972) p. 455.

5. The possibility of developing such a generalized approach was first proposed by me in 1968: See Willard J. Jacobson, "Education and Societies in Transition," vice-presidential address to Section Q of the American Association for the Advancement of Science, Dallas, Texas, later published in the Indian journal, *Educational Trends* (March 1970): 1–16.

SELECTED REFERENCES

Bussink, Tine; Van Der Tak, Jean; and Zuga, Connie S. *Sourcebook on Population.* Washington, D.C.: Population Reference Bureau, 1976. 72 pp.
A comprehensive, annotated listing of the major population-related books, monographs, reports, and bibliographies issued in the English language between 1970 and the summer of 1976.
Callahan, Daniel, ed. *The American Population Debate.* Garden City, N.Y.: Doubleday, 1971. 380 pp.
A collection of articles written by noted authorities; they discuss some of the most important issues related to population.
Carey, George W., and Schwartzberg, Julie. *Teaching Population Geography.* New York: Teachers College Press, 1969. 134 pp.
Of special interest are three case studies of changes that have occurred in populations and their environments.
Horsley, Kathryn, ed. *Environment and Population: A Sourcebook for Teachers.* Washington, D.C.: National Education Association, 1972. 112 pp.
A collection of source materials that are valuable for teachers of subjects related to population at the junior and senior high school levels.
Interchange. Washington, D.C.: Population Reference Bureau.
A population education newsletter distributed to educators several times a year.
Teaching Notes on Population. Appleton, Wis.: Lawrence University.
Issued occasionally; contains articles of particular value to those who teach population at the college level.
Viederman, Stephen. "Population Education in Elementary and Secondary Schools in the United States." In *Aspects of Population Growth Policy,* edited by Robert Parke, Jr., and Charles Westoff. Washington, D.C.: U.S. Government Printing Office, 1972. pp. 433–458.
A status report on population education in the United States.
— — —, ed. *Population Education.* Washington, D.C.: National Council for the Social Studies, 1972. pp. 323–466.
A special issue of Social Education *devoted to population education.*
— — —, ed. *Teaching about Population.* New York: Center for War/Peace Studies, 1973. 70 pp.
An issue of Intercom *devoted to population education. Contains an article by Sloan Wayland, "Population Education: Orientation for the Teacher," and a condensation of the pamphlet* Population *written by Valerie Oppenheimer.*

CHAPTER 2

Populations and
How They Change

If Americans now and in future generations are to make rational, informed decisions about their own and their descendants' future, they must be provided with far more knowledge about population change and its implications than they now possess.

Commission on Population Growth
and the American Future

WHAT ARE SOME of the important characteristics of populations in general? How can we gain a better understanding of changes that take place in populations? How do populations grow? How is the human population growing? Are there generalized patterns of population growth, and, if so, what are they? What may be the pattern of future human population growth? Some of these questions can best be discussed in terms of the systems for which the data about the populations are collected. However, some of the most profound questions about a population can only be considered in terms of the entire population; in the case of human population this means in terms of the global system.

Human population policies should be based on the best possible information. The reliability of information depends largely on how it is collected and how it is analyzed. In some cases, information that would be very useful is not available.

BASIC TERMS AND CONCEPTS

Certain basic terms and concepts can help us to achieve a better understanding of a population and the changes that are taking place. In this section these terms are defined and discussed, using the population of the United States as an example.

Population Size and Census Taking
Population size is the number of individuals living in a given area. For example, the population of the United States (1978) is estimated to be about 218.4 million people. A *census* is an official count of all the people living in a defined area. Population size is determined through periodic censuses. In the United States, the Constitution provides for a national census every 10 years. Ideally, every individual should be enumerated. Practically, in modern censuses an attempt is made to contact at least one adult in each household. Ideally, the census should be carried out in one day. Practically, the census takes several weeks, but a certain day is specified as the date of the census.

Governments are usually the only agencies with the authority to undertake the extensive interviewing involved in a census. The United Nations has developed a manual that attempts to standardize procedures in census taking. In many nations, census results are checked, and additional information is acquired by obtaining data from a relatively small, scientifically selected sample that is representative of the total population.

Serious questions arise about the census data for many parts of the world. In populations where there is a high rate of illiteracy, it is difficult to obtain information from much of the populace. In some countries portions of the population live in remote and inaccessible areas. In such cases, part of the count is sometimes based on aerial surveys, which count the number of villages and make assumptions about village size. Some nations do not publish the methods used in conducting their census, and this casts doubt upon the reliability of their census data.

In the United States a census is taken every 10 years by the Bureau of the Census. An attempt is made to reach every household and to account for every person living in the household. This census is checked and supplemented by surveys of scientifically selected representative samples. To obtain data more frequently, a monthly nationwide survey is made of a scientifically selected sample.

The population size of the United States on April 1, 1970, was 203,211,926. Certainly the population of the United States has grown. The following statistics show the population size of the United States at 30-year intervals:

1790	3,929,214
1820	9,638,453
1850	23,191,876
1880	50,155,783
1910	91,972,266
1940	131,669,275
1970	203,211,926

As we shall see, many factors have led to this growth in population size. Nevertheless, the population of the United States was more than 50 times greater in 1970 than it was 180 years earlier.

In addition to finding out the population size of the nation as a whole and of many of its subsystems—the states and cities—the U.S. census collects data on the sex, color or race, age, and marital status of each individual; the size of the household; and the nature and size of its living quarters. In the 1970 census a procedure called "self-enumeration" was used, in which forms were mailed to households to be completed and mailed back by the householder.

There are many difficulties involved with taking a census. There is the problem of making sure that everyone is included in the count, and this is particularly difficult in the case of people who are not members of households. Self-enumeration, of course, is dependent upon all possible respondents being literate — and responsible. In the 1970 census, an estimated 5.7 million persons were missed, and about 2.1 million of these were of races other than white. This is actually a small percentage error, but it is of considerable importance in the allocation of funds and the apportionment of representation in legislative bodies.

In the United States, there are a number of very important uses for census data. Representation in the House of Representatives and in the Electoral College is apportioned according to population. Similarly, census data are used to apportion representation in many state legislatures. Funds for education, housing, health, highways, sewage treatment, and many other categories are allocated, at least in part, on the basis of census data. Of great importance is the use of census data to plan policies on the local, state, and national levels.

Births and Birth Rates The term *births* usually refers to the total number of babies born in a year. While this statistic is valuable, the *birth rate* (or crude birth rate) — that is, the number of births per year per 1,000 population — is often more useful. It is also useful to know the rate at which women of child-bearing age are having children, and this is shown by the *general fertility rate* — the number of births per year per 1,000 women aged 15 – 44 years. The *age-specific fertility rate* is the birth rate for women of specific age groups in a population. For example, the age-specific fertility rate in many populations is highest for the 20 – 24 years age group.

The total number of births in the United States in the year 1970 was 3,718,000. This, then, is the size of that particular age group (or cohort) in the United States. By 1975 or 1976, most of these children were entering school. By 1983, about half of them, the girls, will be reaching the age when they, in turn, can bear children.

Thus, the number of children who will enter school in a few years time and the number of children who will be born in the future will be influenced by the number of births occurring now.

The crude birth rate for the United States in 1970 was 18.2 (i.e., 18.2 births per 1,000 population). There has been a decline in the birth rate since the years immediately following World War II. In 1950, for example, the crude birth rate was 24.1. In 1978, the U.S. birth rate of 15 was considerably lower than the world birth rate of 29. The birth rate in Asia was about 30 and in Latin America it was 36. In Europe, the birth rate in 1978 was also 15.

The general fertility rate in the United States in 1970 was 87.6 (i.e., 87.6 births per 1,000 women aged 15–44 years). This rate has also declined since the years following World War II.

Death Rates and Life Expectancy While all mortals eventually die, the rate and age at which they die is an important factor in population and population growth. If deaths exactly equaled births and there were no migration, the population would be stabilized. The birth rate, and consequently population growth, is greatly influenced by the number of people that survive to the age of reproduction. A very important factor in the rapid population growth of the world has been the decline in the death rate of infants and children and the consequent increase in the number of individuals who survive to the age of reproduction. The nature of a population and its physical needs and social concerns are considerably affected by the age distribution within the population.

The *death rate* (or crude death rate) is the number of deaths that occur in a year per 1,000 population. The *age-specific death rate* is the death rate for each age group in a population. For example, the age-specific death rate of children 0–4 years is quite high in many populations. Age-specific death rates are important in calculating *life expectancy* —the average number of years a person can expect to live. While life expectancy can be determined for individuals at any age, it is usually stated in terms of a child's life expectancy at birth.

There has been a steady decline in the U.S. death rate: In 1910 it was 14.7; for the year 1970 it was 9.4. The 1978 U.S. death rate (9) is considerably lower than that for the world (12), Africa (19), and Asia (12). However, Canada (7) and some other countries have even lower death rates.

Life expectancy at birth in the United States in 1970 was 70.8 years. Females had a considerably higher life expectancy (74.6 years) than males (67.1 years). With the decline in death rates there has been a correspondingly steady rise in life expectancy. In 1920, for example, life expectancy in the United States was 54.1 years.

Migration The population size of a nation, region, or city is also affected by the movement of people in and out. *Immigration,* the movement of people into a given area, of course contributes to the population growth of that area, while *emigration,* the movement of people out of a given area, tends to reduce the population of that area. The United States and some other nations have absorbed large numbers of immigrants, and this has been a major factor in population growth. Other nations, such as Ireland after its potato famine of 1845, have experienced large-scale emigration. In the global system, of course, there has been neither immigration nor emigration; all the people that are born stay within the system until they die.

A system that experiences migration —in or out —is said to be an *open system.* One that experiences no migration is said to be a *closed system.* The global system is a closed system —unless and until we learn to colonize the moon or the planets. A nation that permits neither immigration nor emigration can also be considered a closed system. Most nations, regions, cities, and other subsystems are open systems — people move, with greater or lesser freedom, into and out of them. Thus, a closed system often has open subsystems.

A very important form of migration that seems to be a worldwide phenomenon is the large-scale movement of people from rural areas to urban or metropolitan areas. Certainly, an important cause of this migration has been the mechanization and general modernization of agriculture.

An important issue that is raised in a number of countries, including the United States, is whether immigration can be allowed to continue as it has in the past. Immigrants make important and creative contributions to any nation or region. On the other hand, large-scale immigration makes attempts at population stabilization more difficult.

In the United States, everyone—including the American Indians, who were the earliest immigrants to the Americas—is here as a result of immigration. Most Americans need not go back many generations to trace the ancestors who immigrated to America from somewhere else. From 1820 to 1971, 45,533,000 people immigrated into the United States. This immigration continues; 373,000 legally entered in 1970. This was an annual rate of 1.8 immigrants per 1,000 population.

There is also considerable movement of population *within* the United States. Between March 1970 and March 1971, 17.9 percent of the people in this country moved to a different house. One of the very significant movements of population has been from rural to urban areas. In 1910, 45.7 percent of the population of the United States lived in urban areas. By 1970, 73.5 percent of the population was living in urban areas. Since birth rates in urban areas have been lower than in rural areas, the increase in urban population is mostly the result of migration. In 15 years, from 1954 to 1969, about 10 million people moved from rural to urban areas. Certainly, this is migration on a very large scale.

Population Growth Rate
Population growth rate is the percentage of change in population size over a period of time, usually a year. It provides a useful picture of the rate at which a population is growing (or declining). As shall be seen later, it is also used to calculate the rate at which a population is doubling.

$$\text{Growth rate} = \frac{\text{population at end of period} - \text{population at start of period}}{\text{population at start of period}}$$

Using the United States as an example:[1]

| U.S. population (1969) | 202,677,000 |
| U.S. population (1970) | 204,879,000 |

$$\text{U.S. growth rate} \quad \frac{204{,}879{,}000 - 202{,}677{,}000}{202{,}677{,}000} = 1\%$$

Population growth rate can also be calculated directly from birth rates, death rates, and net migration rates. Since these rates are given per 1,000 population, they have to be divided by 10 to yield a percentage rate.

$$\text{Growth rate} = \frac{\text{birth rate} - \text{death rate} + \text{net migration rate}}{10}$$

Again using the United States as an example:

U.S. birth rate (1970)	18.2
U.S. death rate (1970)	9.4
U.S. immigration rate (1970)	1.8

$$\text{U.S. growth rate} \quad \frac{18.2 - 9.4 + 1.8}{10} = 1\%$$

U.S. growth rate can be compared with that of the world:[2]

| World birth rate (1970) | 33 |
| World death rate (1970) | 13 |

$$\text{World growth rate} \quad \frac{33 - 13}{10} = 2\%$$

Mathematical Concepts *Doubling time* is the length of time it would take a population to double at a given growth rate.

A rule-of-thumb method to calculate doubling time is to divide the percentage of annual growth rate into 70. For example, in the United States:

| Population growth rate (1978) | .6% |
| Doubling time | $70 \div .6 = 117$ years |

The annual population growth rate for the world in 1977 was 1.8 percent. What is doubling time for the world population? *(Answer: 39 years)*

Mexico has one of the highest growth rates in the world: 3.3 percent in 1977. At this growth rate, how long will it take for Mexico's population to double? *(Answer: 20 years)*

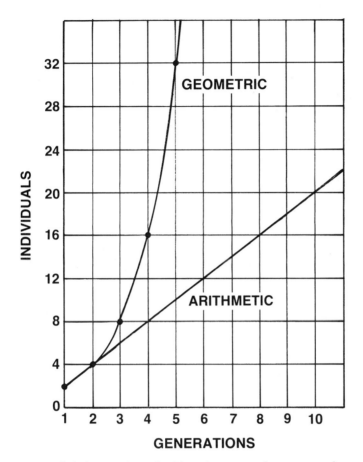

Figure 2-1 Geometric and arithmetic progression compared.

Arithmetic progression is a series of numbers that increases each time by the same amount, e.g.:

$$2, 4, 6, 8, 10, 12$$

is an arithmetic progression in which each succeeding number is *2 larger* than the one before. A population that increased only by the immigration of the same fixed number of people each year would increase by arithmetic progression.

A series of numbers that increases by multiplying the preceding number each time by the same fixed number is said to increase by *geometric progression*. For example:

$$2, 4, 8, 16, 32, 64$$

is a geometric progression in which each succeeding number is *2 times as large* as the one before. Since individuals who are added to a population usually have offspring who, in turn, usually have offspring, population growth tends to follow a geometric rather than an arithmetic progression.

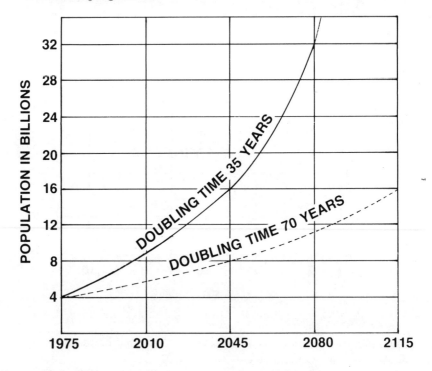

Figure 2-2 Exponential growth: A population doubling time of 70 years compared to one of 35 years.

In geometric progression the numbers increase very rapidly. In a classic anecdote, a king's life was saved by a soldier of fortune. As a reward the king offered the soldier anything that he wished, including the hand of his daughter. Instead, the soldier spread out a chessboard and asked that the king place one grain of rice on the first square, 2 on the second, 4 on the third and so on. This was geometric progression. The sixth square required 64 grains of rice. But, the fortieth square required a million million grains of rice. And there probably was not enough rice in the whole world for the sixty-fourth square.

Exponential growth occurs when a quantity increases by multiplying the total periodically by a number (such as a percentage) and adding the increase to the original quantity. This is the way money in a bank grows by compound interest. For example, if $100 is deposited in a bank at 5 percent compound interest, at the end of 1 year it will increase to $105, at the end of 2 years the increase will be 5 percent of $105, or $5.25, so that the total is $110.25. Each year a new, increased base is used to calculate the new increase. The original amount will increase even more rapidly if it is compounded at shorter intervals, such as every day or every minute.

Exponential growth seems to be a common natural phenomenon, and it is also a characteristic of many economic and technological activities. Our use of materials ranging from fertilizer to fuel oil seems to be following an exponential growth pattern. When some of the limits of growth are removed, populations of organisms, including man, seem to grow exponentially.

Perhaps the clearest way to understand and explain exponential growth patterns is in terms of doubling times. The population of the United States is increasing at a rate of .6 percent per annum (1978), and its doubling time is about 117 years. The population of the world is increasing at a rate of 1.7 percent per annum (1978), and its doubling time is about 41 years.

A critical, but often unappreciated, characteristic of exponential growth is that small changes in growth rate are greatly magnified over several growth intervals. Where population growth rate is 1 percent, doubling time is 70 years; where population growth rate is 2 percent, doubling time is 35 years. However, after 140 years the population whose doubling rate is 35 years will be *four times as great* as the one whose doubling time is 70 years.

Exercise: A Practical Demonstration of Growth Rates It is possible to demonstrate with practical examples a comparison of arithmetic progression, geometric progression, and different rates of exponential growth, using a quantity of some small object, such as seeds or paper clips. In the following examples, the factor 2 is used but any other number could just as well be used.

Pile A will illustrate *arithmetic progression.*
    The time span will be 60 seconds.
    Time intervals will be 15 seconds.
    Begin with 2 objects in the pile. At the end of each 15-second interval, *add 2 objects to the pile.*
    After 4 intervals (60 seconds), how many objects are there in Pile A? *(Answer: 10)*

Pile B will illustrate *geometric progression.*
    The time span will be 60 seconds.
    Time intervals will be 15 seconds.
    Begin with 2 objects in the pile. At the end of each 15-second interval, *double the number of objects in the pile.* (The number of objects to be added after each interval will have to be calculated and counted out in advance.)
    After 4 intervals (60 seconds), how many objects are there in Pile B? *(Answer: 32)*

Pile C will illustrate *exponential growth leading to a doubling at each 70-second interval.*
    The time span will be 280 seconds.
    Time intervals will be 70 seconds.
    Begin with 2 objects in the pile. At the end of each 70-second interval, *double the number of objects in the pile.*
    After 4 intervals (280 seconds), how many objects are there in Pile C? *(Answer: 32)*

Pile D will illustrate *exponential growth leading to a doubling at each 35-second interval.*
    The time span will be 280 seconds.
    Time intervals will be 35 seconds.
    Begin with 2 objects in the pile. At the end of each 35-second interval, *double the number of objects in the pile.* (Again, the number of objects to be added after each interval will have to be calculated and counted out in advance.)
    After 8 intervals (280 seconds), how many objects are there in Pile D? *(Answer: 512)*
    After 280 seconds, which parallels 280 years, how many more objects are there in Pile D, which doubled every 35 seconds, than in Pile C, which doubled every 70 seconds? *(Answer: 480)*

This practical demonstration is a dramatic way to illustrate different kinds and rates of growth. While the logistical problems of amassing some of the object piles are quite challenging, they are obviously minuscule compared to the logistical problems of providing all the resources needed for the support of human populations that grow at comparable rates.

The above demonstration can be repeated using a larger number as the base, say 3 or 4, instead of 2. While this will present even greater logistical problems, it will illustrate the accelerating growth effects of starting with a larger numerical base, paralleling the growth patterns of very large populations, such as those of China and India.

The various rates of growth can also be illustrated graphically. The number of objects in each pile after each interval can be plotted and a curve drawn to connect the dots. In the case of exponential growth curves, there are twice as many intervals in a given period of time when there is doubling after 35 seconds (years) as when there is doubling after 70 seconds (years). Figures 2-1 and 2-2 illustrate the various types and rates of growth discussed here.

If the size of a population and its growth rate are known, the same exponential growth formula that is used in compound interest calculations can be used to determine the size of future populations. If the carrying capacity of the environment is not approached, no catastrophe ensues, and other factors do not enter, then future population size can be calculated using the following formula:

$$N_t = N_0 e^{rt}$$

where

N_t = future population size after a given number of years
N_0 = present population size
e = 2.7183 (the base of natural logarithms)
r = annual rate of increase in population in decimals
t = time in years

Exercise: Population Size after a Given Number of Years Students can carry out calculations, using the compound interest formula, with the aid of hand calculators that have an exponential function key or with printed tables of exponential functions.[3] For example, the following is the calculation of world population size in 25 years based on a 1975 world population of 4 million and a growth rate of .02:

$$N_t = 4,000,000,000 \times 2.7183^{(.02 \times 25)}$$
$$4,000,000,000 \times 2.7183^{.5}$$
$$4,000,000,000 \times 1.6487$$
$$6,594,800,000$$

The population of the United States in 1977 was about 216.7 million with a growth rate of .6. If the United States continues to have this growth rate, what will be its population in the year 2000? *(Answer: About 249.2 million)*

Teachers might wish to help their students find the present population of their own community and its growth rate. What is its population likely to be by the year 2000?

PROJECTIONS AND PREDICTIONS

A *prediction* is a forecast of what will happen. It is a calculation of future conditions based on knowledge of and observation about present conditions. For example, on the basis of present population composition of known growth rates, a school official might predict that in 1980 there will be — — school children of school age in Shadyside. Or, on a similar basis, a student of population might predict that the world population in the year 2000 will be 6.3 billion. A prediction has an air of precision about it.

A *projection*, on the other hand, is an extrapolation from a given situation into the future that takes account of the various elements in the situation — both those that are likely to continue and those that are likely to change. Thus, some projections have a qualifying phrase such as, "if conditions remain the same as they are now." But conditions may change. For example, there may be reasons for believing that the fertility rate will change. These anticipated changes are then taken into account when the projections are made. Often, it is very difficult to foretell what will happen in the future, and several projections may be made, each one based on a different assumption. For example, the United Nations has made "high," "medium," and "low" projections of future world population. Projectors hope, of course, that "high" and "low" projections will bracket the possibilities and that actual events will fall somewhere between these extremes. Most demographers tend to favor projections rather than predictions.

One of the reasons that both the prediction and the projection of future populations is so difficult is that small changes in certain vital rates can have substantial and long-term effects upon population growth rates. A slight change in the birth rate can have a considerable effect upon population size, and, since any increase (or decrease) in the number of children born means more (or fewer) potential parents in the next generation, future population growth rates are also affected.

It is very difficult to take into account all the sociological, psychological, and technological factors that may affect future birth rates. For example, who would have predicted in 1960, when birth control pills first became generally available, that by 1968 they would be used by 34 percent of the women in the United States practicing some kind of birth control and be the most widely used contraceptive?

The following are some of the factors that are sometimes used in making population projections:

1. The population size, or base, at the particular time from which the projection is to be made
2. The age structure of the population
3. Basic vital rates such as birth rates, death rates, and migration rates, as well as sex ratios
4. Estimates of possible changes in the vital rates during the period of the projection
5. General theories of population growth and regulation.

THE AGE STRUCTURE OF POPULATIONS

Life in a society is affected by the age structure of its population. Walk through various neighborhoods on a sunny Sunday afternoon when many of the people are outside, and you may see striking differences in the kinds of people that you see basking in the sun or strolling along the street. In some neighborhoods you may see mostly young parents and their children with very few older people around. In other neighborhoods you may find predominantly older people with few children or young people in sight. These differences in the age structures of populations can have considerable effect upon life in a society. They are also an important dimension of population study.

In a population where there is a large proportion of children and young people, many have yet to reach the age of reproduction. Many new families will be formed, and a rapid increase in population can be expected. There will be a heavy demand for education, child health services, children's clothing and toys, and all the other goods and services needed by children, young people, and their parents. On the other hand, in such a population the number of people who can work and help provide for the needs of children and young people may be proportionately small. In other words, there is a high *dependency rate*. This is one of the serious problems in developing nations with high birth rates. The children and young people who need health and educational services are a large percentage of the total population. High dependency ratios place heavy burdens on the people who are in their productive or working years.

In a population where there are many old people, there will be proportionately fewer people reaching the age of reproduction, and there probably will not be as rapid an increase in population. However, there will be a relatively heavy demand for nursing homes, geriatric services, and recreational facilities for those who have retired. Greater demands on pension plans and more money paid out in social security payments can be expected. In this population also, the proportion of people of working age may be relatively small, and they will have to bear some of the burden of providing some of the goods and services needed by older people.

Population Pyramid One of the ways to study the age structure of a population is to construct a *population pyramid*, that is, a bar graph showing the percentage of the population of various ages. Conventionally, the bars in a population pyramid represent 5-year time spans. Figure 2-3 shows 1970 population pyramids for the United States, the world, and a developing nation.

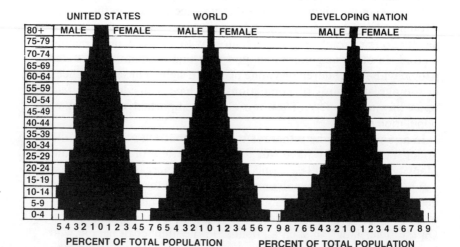

Figure 2-3 Population pyramids for 1970.

Exercise: Studying Population Pyramids In which of the three populations in Figure 2-3 would there be the highest percentage of young children who might be expected to enter elementary school in the next few years? *(Answer: Developing nation)*

Which of the populations has the highest proportion of people between the ages of 10 and 19, who are just beginning or about to enter the period of reproduction? *(Answer: Developing nation)*

What will probably happen in terms of population size in the developing regions of the world in the next few decades? *(Answer: Rapid increase)*

Which of the populations has the highest percentage of old people? *(Answer: United States)*

Which of the populations has the highest percentage of people between the ages of 15 and 65? By convention, people between these ages are considered to be in their productive years and able to support themselves. *(Answer: United States)*

What might account for the relatively low percentage in certain age groups and high percentages in others in the U.S. populations? *(Answer: Economic depression in the 1930s and World War II)*

Rises and declines in the sizes of age groups can have lasting effects. For example, a baby born in one generation can be expected to lead to another baby born when that generation reaches the age of reproduction. What shape would you expect the population pyramid of the United States to be a generation from 1970? *(Answer: Narrower base and steeper sides)*

Exercise: Constructing a Population Pyramid Students can gain further insight into how population pyramids are constructed and how they can be used to gain a better understanding of the nature of a population by themselves constructing a population pyramid. Students can take a census of the age and sex of individuals in their families and use this data to construct a population pyramid.

Have each member of the class write on a small piece of paper his or her age and sex—M for male, F for female. Then, have the students find out the age of each member of their families and write each one of these on a separate slip of paper—again designating F for female and M for male.

Using the information on all these slips of paper, have a small committee from the class make a horizontal histogram of the frequency at which various ages are represented in the families of students. It is suggested that 5-year age spans be used: 0–4, 5–9, 10–14, etc. (Note that this population pyramid will show the actual number of individuals in each age span, rather than the percentage in each. The actual numbers can, of course, be converted to percentages.) Figure 2-4 shows a population pyramid constructed by a fourth-grade class.

How does this pyramid differ from the population pyramid for the United States? *(Answer: Higher percentage 0–10 and 26–40)* What might account for these differences? *(Answer: Pyramid in Figure 2-4 shows only families of a class of elementary school children.)*

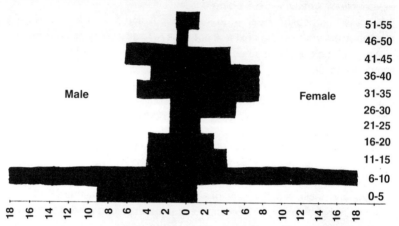

Figure 2-4 Population pyramid of the families of a fourth grade class. (I am indebted to Marilyn Cohen and her fourth-grade class of the Benjamin Franklin School in Yorktown Heights, New York, for this pyramid.)

What kinds of goods and services will be needed in the near future by the population represented in this population pyramid? *(Answer: All of the goods and services needed by children about to enter junior high school and their parents.)*

WORLD POPULATION GROWTH

After growing very slowly for a long period of time, the human population has recently been increasing very rapidly.[4] Two to four million years ago the first specimens of Homo sapiens, physically very much like modern man, emerged — probably in East Africa and possibly in other places as well. There were not very many of them. The human population grew very slowly, and the growth rate during much of man's time on earth may have been about 1 percent *per thousand years*. It is estimated that ten thousand years ago there probably were about 10 million human beings. By the year A.D. 1, the population may have been 300 million. From the year A.D. 1 to the year Columbus reached the Americas (1492) an average of about 130,000 people were added each year, resulting in a population of about 500 million. From 1492 to 1850 an average of 1 million people were added each year, resulting in a population of about 1 billion in 1850. Note that if 1 million people were simply added by arithmetic progression each year after 1492, it would take 1 thousand years to add 1 billion people. Instead, we have had much more rapid exponential growth.

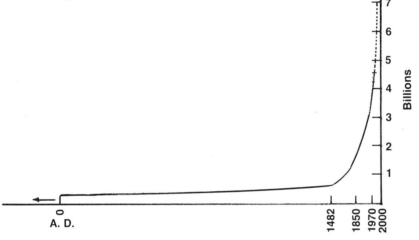

Figure 2-5 Generalized world population growth curve.

In the nineteenth century, the rate of population growth increased remarkably, to 1 percent *per year*. While the population in 1850, after 2 to 4 million years of man's existence on the planet, was probably about 1 billion, in the ensuing 75 years an additional billion was added, leading to a population of about 2 billion in 1925. Only 35 years were needed to add the next billion, so that in 1960 the population was 3 billion. The world population in 1978 was probably about 4.22 billion. It now takes less than 13 years to add a billion people to the world population. Figure 2-5 shows the pattern of increase in world population size during the period A.D. 1–1970, and as projected to 2000.

In the 1950s, United Nations demographers published projections for the world population that have had tremendous influence.[5] Operating with admittedly inaccurate data, they showed that, under almost any reasonable set of assumptions, the world was experiencing very rapid population growth. Their "high" projection assumed little decline in fertility. Their "low" projection assumed a considerable decline in fertility. In each of the projections it was assumed that death rates would continue to decline in developing countries. Following were their projections for the years 1970 and 2000:

	Projected population (in billions)	
	1970	**2000**
High	3.5	6.9
Medium	3.48	6.28
Low	3.35	4.88

In actual fact, world population in mid-year 1970 was about 3.6 billion, according to the United Nations, which was even higher than the "high" projection of 3.5 billion.

The increase that has taken place in the *rate* of growth is perhaps even more striking than the increase in population size. For most of man's time on earth growth rate has probably been about 1 percent per millenium. This means that population doubling time was about 70,000 years. By 1900 growth rate was about 1 percent per year, so that doubling time was 70 years. Now, growth rate is about 2 percent per year and doubling time is 35 years. If this growth rate continues, world population by the year 2045 will be over 15 billion. The nature of future population growth is certainly one of the great concerns of mankind.

Exercise: A Demonstration of Population Growth How has the human population grown? It is very difficult to conceptualize the long periods of time and the changing rates of growth. Again, a practical approach is to use an analog involving concrete materials such as piles of paper clips or other small objects that are readily available. A watch or clock with a second hand will be needed. And before the analog is begun, it is suggested that students count out sets of paper clips containing 1, 30, 20, 50, 100, 100, and 100 clips.

In this analog we will assume that man has been on the earth a little more than 3 million years.

1 paper clip will represent 10 million people.

1 minute of time will represent 1,000 years.

The start of the analog, say 9 A.M., will represent the emergence of man about 3 million years ago. At this point there are no paper clips in the pile.

50 hours later (11 A.M. two days later), place 1 paper clip in the pile to represent 10 million people added in 3 million years.

10 minutes (10,000 years) later, at 11:10, add 30 paper clips to represent an increase of 300 million people.

1½ minutes (1,500 years) later, at 11:11:30, add 20 more clips to represent an increase of 200 million.

21 seconds (350 years) later, at 11:11:51, add 50 clips, to represent an increase of 500 million.

5 seconds (75 years) later, at 11:11:56, add 100 clips, to represent an addition of 1 billion. 2 seconds (35 years) later, at 11:11:58, add 100 more.

How many clips are there on the pile at 11:11:58? *(Answer: 301)*

How many people does this represent? *(Answer: Over 3 billion)*

How many clips will there be by noon (1990)? *(Answer: About 520 clips or 5.2 billion people)*

Table 2-1 presents the analog in tabular form.

Table 2-1
A Practical Demonstration of Population Growth

Time by the clock	Time interval in years	(Approx. date) (A.D.)	Clips added	Population size
09:00	The emergence of man		0	Few
11:00 (2 days later)	3 million		1	10 million
11:10	10,000	(1)	30	300 million
11:11:30	1500	(1500)	20	500 million
11:11:51	350	(1850)	50	1 billion
11:11:56	75	(1925)	100	2 billion
11:11:58	35	(1960)	100	3 billion
11:11:59	15	(1975)	100	4 billion

POPULATION DISTRIBUTION

World population is not evenly distributed. Mainland China, with an estimated population of 930 million (1978) contains about one-fifth of the world's population. India has a population of about 634.7 million (1978). These two nations contain about one-third of the population of the world. Almost two-thirds of the people inhabiting Planet Earth live in Asia.

The developing regions contain almost three-fourths of the world's population, while the remaining one-fourth live in the industrially developed regions. Figure 2-6 shows the distribution of world population and the projected increases for different countries and regions. Not only do the developing nations have relatively large populations, but they also have high growth rates. India, with its population of about 634.7 million (1978) has a growth rate of 2.0 percent a year, which is considerably higher than the global average. Ecuador, which is one of the poorest countries in South America, in 1977 had an annual population growth rate of 3.2 percent. These growth rates can be contrasted to that of Northern Europe, which in 1978 was about .1 percent.

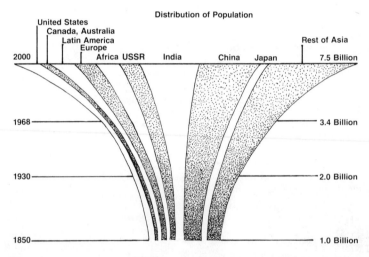

Figure 2-6 Population distribution and projected increases. (From World Population: A Challenge to the United Nations and Its System of Agencies, *Report of the National Policy Panel, United Nations Association of the United States of America [May 1969].)*

HOW POPULATIONS GROW

All populations of living organisms have an intrinsic capacity for growth. Except under the most adverse conditions, more young are produced than are needed to replace the preceding generation. We have only to look at a fluffy dandelion to see the large number of seeds produced by a single plant, and each of these seeds is a potential plant. Or, we can see the large number of eggs deposited in the backwater of a pool by one female frog. But how many survive, grow, and produce seeds or eggs of their own?

A major reason why populations have such intrinsic capacity for growth is that offspring beget more offspring. For example, beginning with a male-female couple, if each female were to have six offspring, half of whom were female, and they in turn were to have six offspring, there would be 18 offspring in the third generation (see Figure 2-7). If none of the individuals were to die, there would be a total of 26 living individuals by the third generation.

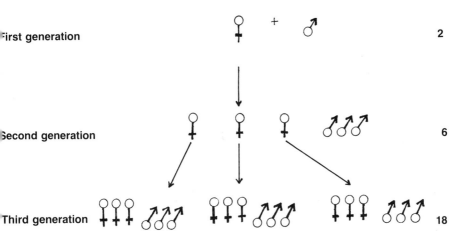

Figure 2-7 Intrinsic capacity for growth in populations.

If populations were to grow unchecked, some rather absurd conditions would ensue. Charles Darwin illustrated this with the elephant, which is one of the slowest breeders. If elephants start breeding at the age of 30, live to the age of 100, and each female bears six young, then, starting with a male-female pair, in 750 years there would be about 19 million elephants. Similar calculations can be made for other organisms, including man, and, if the intrinsic growth potential of such a population were to go unchecked, each population would overwhelm the space resources of the surface of the earth.

Populations do not grow unchecked. There are certainly not 19 million elephants on this planet, and no other species has completely overwhelmed the earth. How do populations grow? What are the checks on populations? How will the human population grow? What checks will probably operate on the human population?

Unfortunately, we have less than satisfactory answers to many of these questions. We know something about how populations of other organisms grow and the checks that tend to limit their population growth. We can also do experimental work with other organisms to study the influence of various factors on population growth or decline. But what about man? We can study population changes in the past, although the records are often scanty or nonexistent. But we may be in an unprecedented situation — there had never been 4 billion people on the earth before 1975, and the present growth rate may be one of the highest ever. So, when we ask these questions, the simple reply is, "We just don't know." Yet it would seem critical that we try to project answers to these questions, try to understand the possible consequences of proposed action or inaction with regard to population and population growth.

GROWTH PATTERNS

The growth of populations of living organisms seems to follow certain generalized patterns.[6] The human population cannot continue to grow indefinitely. If it continues to grow like Darwin's hypothetical elephants, there will eventually not even be "standing room only." Long before that, undoubtedly, the supply of some absolutely essential resource will be depleted, or some other limiting factor will check population growth. If we are concerned with the possible consequences of our actions or inactions, it is important to become aware of and consider possible growth patterns.

Pattern of Stabilization
In some populations, the pattern of population growth and stabilization follows a sigmoid or "S" pattern. In this pattern, there is a period of rapid population growth. Then, various factors begin to check population growth and keep it below the environmental support limit. Population then stabilizes at a size that can be supported by the environmental system in which the organisms exist.

About the year 1800, a few sheep were introduced onto the island of Tasmania. As shown in Figure 2-8, the sheep population in Tasmania increased very rapidly at first but was stabilized, around 1850, at about 1,700,000 sheep. There have been some fluctuations, which are believed to be due to climatic variations, but the population over a considerable period of time has remained essentially stabilized. This is an example of a population that has followed the sigmoid or "S" pattern of population stabilization.

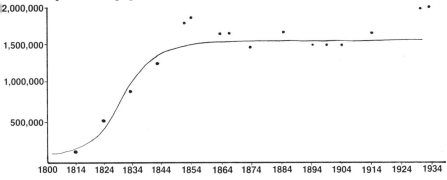

Figure 2-8 Growth of sheep population in Tasmania, 1800-1934 (an "S" curve) (From James Davidson, "On the Growth of the Sheep Population in Tasmania," Transactions of the Royal Society of South Australia 62 [1938]: 342–46.)

This pattern of population stabilization is followed by a number of organisms. While there may be some oscillation, population size in general is maintained at a particular level. Probably, a balance is achieved between the population and all the environmental elements that impinge upon its existence.

It has been suggested that the growth of human population may be comparable to the population growth that takes place when a species is introduced or migrates into an environment where there is little competition from other species. Through public health and sanitation measures, mankind has eliminated much of the competition that in the past curtailed human population growth. For example, through widespread control of the anopheles mosquito, large regions of the world have been rid of one of man's greatest scourges — malaria. Through vaccination, immunization, and chemotherapy, the incidence of death from such afflictions as diphtheria, smallpox, and pneumonia has been greatly reduced. Instead of moving into a competitor-free environment, man has rid himself of the ravages of some of his competitors in his existing environment. These are among the factors that have led to very rapid human population growth. A critical question is whether the size of the human population will stabilize and, if so, at what level.

Pattern of Rapid Growth and Rapid Decline Another general pattern is that of rapid growth in population followed by a catastrophic drop in numbers and, usually, periodic oscillation after that (see Figure 2-9).

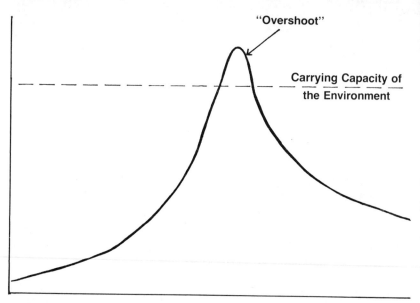

Figure 2-9 A pattern of rapid population growth and decline (the "J" curve).

In 1912 or 1913 a few moose crossed on the ice from the mainland to the Isle Royale in Lake Superior, where they had few natural enemies.[7] By 1930 the moose population on the island had expanded to between 1 and 3 thousand. The moose had migrated into a situation where there was limited competition. But in 1935 the moose population dropped sharply to 200 individuals, it rose to 800 in 1948 but declined again, to 500, in 1950. After the initial rapid surge, the population apparently began to oscillate within limits that are perhaps less than could theoretically be supported by the resources of the island.

The lemmings of Northern Canada and Scandinavia are another population that apparently follows a growth and decline curve. Probably because of pressure on the food supply, although the reasons are not completely understood, lemmings die in large numbers. They may tumble by the thousands over the cliffs of fjords and into bodies of water. The population that remains again multiplies, and in a few years the cycle is repeated.

HUMAN POPULATION GROWTH PATTERN

A central question in population studies is, "What will be the pattern of future human population growth?" There is general agreement that the human population cannot continue to grow indefinitely as it has been growing in the last 200 years. A number of limiting factors, such as available food and living space, will eventually limit population growth if other controls do not regulate population size. The possible patterns of human population growth, and conceivable actions to influence the nature of these patterns, are of central importance.

The growth curve of the human population (see Figure 2-5) has the features of an exponential curve, and it could conceivably be a part of either the sigmoid "S" curve leading to a stabilized population size or the oscillating "J" curve leading to a catastrophic decline in population size. The first would lead to a population stabilized at a level that can be supported by the environment. The second implies a rapid population growth beyond the support capacity of the environment and then a catastrophic decline in population size. Which will it be? There are projections that fit both patterns.

All human population growth projections assume that the world population will continue to grow for a number of years. One of the reasons for this assumption is the large number of young people in the population, who will soon enter their reproductive years. In 1970, about 37 percent of the world's population was under 15 years of age. In the developing nations, where about two-thirds of the world's population lives, probably about 42 percent of the people are under 15.

Stabilization Model[8] Population stabilization models assume a continuance of growth for some time, but then an eventual reduction of growth rate. They differ in their assumptions as to how soon the net reproduction rate (NRR)[9] will decline (see Figure 2-10):

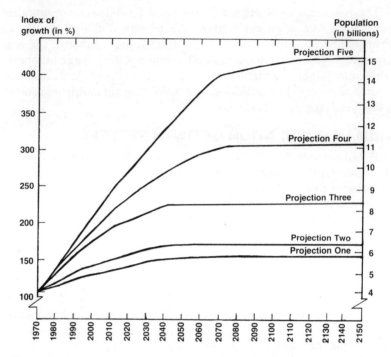

Figure 2-10 Population stabilization models based on various assumptions as to when NRR will decline. (From Tomas Frejka, The Future of Population Growth, Alternative Paths to Equilibrium *[New York: Wiley, 1973], p. 54.)*

Projection One, which assumed an immediate NRR decline, reaching 1 by 1975, is now unattainable. World population by this projection would have been at least 4.7 billion by the year 2000, and 5.6 billion by the year 2100.

Projection Two assumes that an NRR of 1 will be achieved in the period 1980–1985. This would lead to a population of at least 5 billion by 2000, and 6.4 billion by 2100. This also is considered unattainable.

Projection Three assumes that an NRR of 1 will be achieved in the period 2000–2005. This would necessitate a decline of average family size (worldwide) from the present level of about 5 to considerably less than 3. (This decline is typical of the present fertility pattern of the developed nations.) There would be a population of at least 6 billion around the year 2000. Population might stabilize by the middle of the twenty-first century.

Projection Four assumes that an NRR of 1 will be achieved by the period 2020–2025. This would result in a world population of more than 6 billion by 2000, growing to 10 to 11 billion before stabilization.

Projection Five assumes the most gradual decline in fertility, with an NRR of 1 achieved by the period 2040–2045. This would lead to a population of about 6.7 billion by 2000, and the population would stabilize at over 15 billion. (This growth pattern was followed by the present-day developed countries early in this century. For example, it is similar to fertility patterns in the United States between 1905 and 1940.)

Since an equilibrium status is so urgently desired, the Club of Rome has attempted to determine a set of policies that would lead to a stabilized system.[10] One such model calls for a slowed increase in industrialization until stabilization in 1990. There has to be a reduction of resource consumption and pollution generation to one-fourth of 1970 levels. A value shift is needed, away from material goods toward emphasis on such services as education and health. There has to be a shift of capital to food production, the recycling of urban organic wastes and other materials, and the design of better and more durable industrial equipment. The population has to be stabilized by bringing births and deaths into equilibrium as early as possible.

Rapid Growth and Rapid Decline Model

The rapid growth and rapid decline model also assumes that the human population will continue to grow. But, instead of stabilizing within the carrying capacity of the environment, this model projects an "overshoot" of the environment's capacity to support the population and an eventual catastrophic decline in population. This model is roughly equivalent to the "J" curve followed by the populations of some other species.

In the model shown in Figure 2-11, it is assumed that there will be no significant changes in human values or patterns of global population growth. The levels of consumption of raw materials, fuel, and food resources, and of such variables as industrial output, population, and pollution are plotted from 1900 to 1970 and extend into the future. All curves continue to rise until there is an "overshoot" and collapse due to the depletion of nonrenewable resources. The lack of nonrenewable resources causes the production base, including agriculture and services, to collapse. Rising death rates, due to a lack of food and other life-sustaining factors, lead to a rapid population decline.

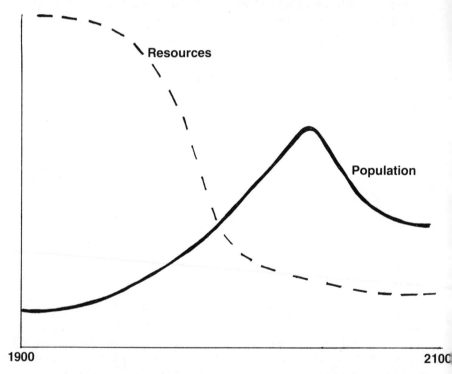

1900   2100

Figure 2-11 The rapid growth and rapid decline model: Shortage of nonrenewable resources leads to a sharp fall in population.

Discussion: Implications of Different Models   What are the implications, for individuals and for families, of the different models of human population growth? Of course, no one knows with much certainty which, if any, of these models is to be our destiny. However, we can examine the models and consider the possible consequences for individuals and families.

• Which of the models is to be desired? Why?

- What might be the consequences for individuals and families of an "over-shoot" of the environment's carrying capacity?
- How would the steps that are needed for population stabilization affect individuals and families?
- What are some of the ways that these steps could actually be implemented?

CONCLUSION

Birth rate and death rate, migration, and age structure are among the factors that influence the nature of a population and its patterns of growth or decline. Apparently all populations, including the human population, have an intrinsic capacity for growth. In the last two centuries, the growth of the human population has followed a geometric or exponential growth pattern. Possible models for population stabilization have been projected. But, if the human population is not stabilized, there may be a catastropic decline if the population grows beyond the carrying capacity of the environment.

FOOTNOTES

1. The vital statistics of the United States are based on the various publications of the U.S. Bureau of the Census. Many are available in *Statistical Abstract of the United States* (Washington, D.C.: U.S. Government Printing Office), which is issued annually. Statistics are for July 1 of each year.

   Most of the statistics for populations throughout the world can be obtained from publications of the United Nations. A convenient source is *World Population Data Sheet* (Washington, D.C.: Population Reference Bureau), which is issued annually.

2. More recent statistics are obtainable from the latest issue of the *Statistical Abstract of the United States* (Washington, D.C.: U.S. Government Printing Office) and from the *World Population Data Sheet* (Washington, D.C.: Population Reference Bureau).

3. A convenient source of exponential function tables is the *Handbook of Chemistry and Physics* (Cleveland, Ohio: Chemical Rubber Publishing Company), which is issued annually.

4. For a discussion of the history of world population growth, see Ansley J. Coale, "The History of Human Population," *Scientific American* 231, no. 3 (September 1974): 41–51.

5. United Nations, *The Future of World Population* (New York: United Nations, 1958).

6. For a more extended discussion of these population growth patterns, see Eugene P. Odum, *Fundamentals of Ecology,* 3rd ed. (Philadelphia: Saunders, 1971), pp. 162–233.

7. From L. W. Krefting, "What Is the Future of the Isle Royale Moose Herd?" *Transactions North American Wildlife Conference* 16 (1951): 461–70.

8. Several such models have been proposed, differing usually in the assumptions that are made. The ones described are based upon Tomas Frejka, *The Future of Population Growth, Alternative Paths to Equilibrium* (New York: Wiley, 1973), pp. 52–66.
9. The net reproduction rate (NRR) indicates the number of daughters born per woman surviving at least to the age that her own mother was at the time of the woman's birth. The NRR is an approximate indicator of the rate at which a generation is replaced by a future generation of potential mothers. To reach population stabilization, an NRR of about 1 must be achieved.
10. Donella H. Meadows et al., *The Limits to Growth* (New York: Universe Books, 1972), pp. 156–84.

SELECTED REFERENCES

Bogue, Donald J. *Principles of Demography.* New York: Wiley 1969. 917 pp.
  A basic textbook in demography.
Eisenberg, J. F., and Dillon, Wilton S., eds. *Man and Beast: Comparative Social Behavior.* Washington, D.C.: Smithsonian Institution, 1971. 401 pp.
  A collection of papers delivered at the Smithsonian Institution's Annual Symposium, 1969.
Frejka, Tomas. *The Future of Population Growth, Alternative Paths to Equilibrium.* New York: Wiley, 1973. 266 pp.
  Explores several possible paths to achieve population equilibrium. Includes a discussion of such demographic concepts as fertility, mortality, and reproduction rates.
Meadows, Donella H.; Meadows, Dennis L.; Randers, Jórgen; and Behrens, William W. III. *The Limits to Growth.* New York: Universe Books, 1972. 205 pp.
  A report to the Club of Rome of the first phase of the Project on the Predicament of Mankind. An examination of the basic factors, including population, that may ultimately limit growth, and an exploration of some alternative patterns.
Odum, Eugene P., *Fundamentals of Ecology,* 3rd ed. Philadelphia: Saunders, 1971. 574 pp.
  A basic text in ecology. Chapter 7, "Principles and Concepts Pertaining to Organization at the Population Level," deals with population growth as well as other aspects of population study.
Petersen, William. *Population.* New York: Macmillan, 1969. 784 pp.
  A basic text on population as a field of study.
Population Reference Bureau. *World Population Data Sheet.* Washington, D.C.: Population Reference Bureau (issued annually).
  Perhaps, the most convenient source of population data concerning countries, regions, and the world.
Study Committee of the National Academy of Sciences, *Rapid Population Growth, Consequences, and Policy Implications.* Baltimore: Johns Hopkins Press, 1971. 696 pp.
  A collection of original papers and policy recommendations. The paper by Philip M. Hauser, "World Population: Retrospect and Prospect," is of special importance for the topics discussed in this chapter.

United States Department of Commerce, *Statistical Abstract of the United States.* Washington, D.C.: U.S. Government Printing Office (issued annually).

A convenient source for much population data concerning the United States and its states and cities.

"The Human Population." *Scientific American* 231. 212 pp.

The entire issue is devoted to human population, with articles by some of the most distinguished students of population. "The History of the Human Population," by Ansley J. Coale, is especially pertinent to this chapter.

CHAPTER 3

Population Regulation

> How odd it is that anyone should not see that all observation must be
> for or against some view, if it is to be of any service.
>
> *Charles Darwin*

IF ORGANISMS have an intrinsic capacity for growth, how are the
populations of various organisms regulated? Given that the human
population grew very slowly for most of the 3 million or more years
it has been in existence, how was population size regulated for all
those years? How is population size regulated in nations that are
approaching or have reached population stabilization? What are
ways that world population stabilization might conceivably be
achieved?

In a generalized approach to problem situations, the hypothesis is
an important intellectual tool. It is a suggested answer or solution to
a problem, a mental model that can help us to organize and interpret
our observations. For example, Darwin's suggestion that natural
selection was the mechanism by which living matter has evolved
into the great variety of life that now exists was a grand hypothesis;
it has helped interpret the multifarious observations that have been
made of organisms that live and have lived. Such a hypothesis helps
us to "make sense of what we see."

It is desirable that a hypothesis be a general one that can be used
in a great variety of systems. It may not necessarily be the only way

of interpreting our observations, but in choosing among possible hypotheses, everything else being equal, there are great advantages to choosing the hypothesis that is most general. The hypothesis that follows has been of value in analyzing physical, biological, and social systems. A hypothesis should also be potentially useful for planning actions to deal with the problems being analyzed. The hypothesis presented here does suggest actions that can be taken to deal with some of the problems related to population.

GENERAL HYPOTHESIS: FEEDBACK CONTROL

The growth and size of populations are regulated by the effects that result from changes within the population.[1] This is essentially a feedback model of population regulation. In feedback systems, a small part of the output of a system is "fed back" into the system to regulate it. In terms of population, some of the effects of population growth and size tend to influence future population growth and size. When children are born, this leads to an increase in the number of potential parents, which in turn results in an increase in both size of population and rate of growth. As the number of children increases, the costs of education, health services, and recreation may rise to a level where families, communities, or nations may try to limit population growth and size. This is an example of feedback, because the increase in population leads to attempts to reduce the rate of growth and limit the size of populations. A simple diagram of the feedback control mechanism is shown in Figure 3-1.

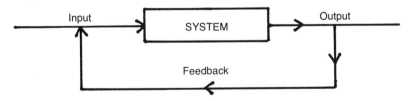

Figure 3-1 Diagram of the feedback control mechanism.

Feedback control is a generalized hypothesis that can be used to interpret, explain, and help plan actions in physical, biological, and social systems.[2] Examples from each of these systems, and observations that can be carried out, may clarify the nature of the feedback hypothesis and suggest some of its power as a tool for interpretation, explanation, and planning.

In Physical Systems An important advantage of some of the examples of feedback control in physical systems is that they can be observed in action. In examining these systems, students can analyze them in terms of such questions as the following: What are the specific change effects that lead to regulation in the system? How are the effects of these changes detected? How is the information about these effects transmitted? What is the mechanism by which the system is regulated?

The float control system in the water tank of a bathroom toilet is a simple example of feedback in a physical system. When the toilet is flushed, the float descends, which opens a valve that controls the inflow of the water. As the water flows in, the level of the water in the tank and the float rise. When the float reaches the appropriate height, the valve is closed and the inflow of water is stopped.

The thermostatic control of heating systems is the usual textbook example of feedback. Many homes have such thermostats; aquarium heaters usually have a thermostatic control that is easy to examine. Commonly, the thermostat contains a bimetallic strip of metal that bends as the temperature lowers. When the temperature descends to a predetermined level, the bimetallic strip closes an electrical circuit and the heating system begins to operate. When the temperature rises to the desired level, the bimetallic strip bends, breaks the electrical circuit, and shuts off the heating system.

In Biological Systems Feedback control is common in many biological systems. Although the actual operation of biological feedback systems is much more difficult to observe than in some physical systems, the effects can be seen, and many of them are obviously of critical importance.

For example, the temperature of the inner body is maintained at a fairly constant 37°C (98.6°F). A fluctuation of more than 3 or 4 degrees can result in death.

Interestingly, there are thermosensors—both in the inner parts of the body and in the skin that control the generation or loss of heat in the body. The sensors in the skin may indicate a sudden change in the temperature of the environment. If these sensors indicate a cooling of the body, more food or fat may be oxidized to generate heat; the flow of blood to the skin may be restricted to reduce heat loss through the skin (causing a cold hand to become grayish-white as less blood flows to the skin), and shivering may take place to generate heat. If the sensors indicate a rise in environmental temperature, less food or fat will be oxidized, more blood will be released into the skin, and the sweat glands will release perspiration, which cools the body as it evaporates. This feedback system maintains an almost constant body temperature.

In Social Systems Feedback control in social systems may be easier to observe than in biological systems, but it is often complicated by factors that may not be evident in physical and biological systems. Since population regulation takes place in the context of social systems, it can be helpful to examine feedback in a social system in terms of such complicating factors as the following:

1. There is often an unavoidable delay between sensing the effect and effecting the response that can regulate the system.
2. The delay between the sensing of an effect and the regulating response makes prediction of future effects more necessary.
3. There are often interlinking feedback loops within social systems, and there may be complicating interactions between these loops.

Boards of education have the responsibility for providing education for the children and young people of a community. To do this they must hire teachers, construct buildings, and provide instructional materials. The number of teachers and buildings and the amount of instructional materials needed will depend upon the number of students they will serve. The number of births in a year will give some indication of the number of children who will enter kindergarten 5 years later. This, along with past experience with dropout rates and the movement of people into and out of the community, will give some indication of how many students there will be in the junior and senior years of high school. However, some change in the community, such as the construction of a new housing development, often brings with it an influx of students, and the buildings that are needed to serve this enlarged student population often take years to plan and build. This is an example of an unavoidable delay in response.

In some cases the loss of a major industry and the outmigration of many people may result in a surplus—the community may have more teachers and educational facilities than it needs.

Because it takes years for a community to construct schools and build a competent staff, it is important to make early predictions of future changes in the school population. However, these predictions are often difficult, and there is considerable risk of error. Certainly, it is often difficult to convince the taxpaying public that they must begin to prepare for the education of children who are not yet in the schools and may not yet even be in the community.

Teachers, administrators, parents, and other members of the community are also interested in the *quality* of the education. They may, for example, monitor the achievements of graduates and use the information they obtain to suggest changes in the educational system—for example, that the size of classes be reduced. But this might be in conflict with other types of feedback, which might suggest that the size of the school staff needs to be reduced. This interlinking of feedback loops makes it more difficult to interpret the feedback, and value judgments have to be made about the relative importance of different kinds of feedback and the relative desirability of various conflicting courses of action.

POPULATION REGULATION IN ANIMAL POPULATIONS

The growth and size of animal populations tend to be self-regulated, and population size tends to stabilize at a level that can be supported by the environment.[3] The human population is growing at a rapid rate, and one of the great predicaments of mankind is how this rapid population growth will be, or can be, regulated. The situation is unprecedented because the population has never been this large before, and it may be growing at a more rapid rate than ever before. We cannot carry out experiments on human populations, but we need to know more about the regulation of population growth and size. We can seek insights from studies of population regulation in animal populations.

Growth Limited by Food Supply A series of experiments has shown how populations of blowflies are affected by food supply.[4] The blowflies were kept in glass containers. The amount of food was carefully controlled. The changes in population that took place under the stress of limited food supply were studied, and an attempt was made to discover the feedback mechanisms.

In this experiment there was direct feedback between food supply and egg production. As long as the blowfly population had a constant food supply, there was a regular oscillation in the number of adults: when the population of adults was small, many more eggs were produced; when the population of adults increased, egg production dropped; when the adult population decreased in size, egg production again increased. Apparently, when adult population size was high, the competition for food was so intense that few adults could obtain enough food to generate eggs. But when population size dropped, there was enough food, and eggs could be produced. Although there were oscillations, the average density remained constant when there was a constant food supply. However, when the food supply was cut in half, the average density was also cut in half. In this population, then, the average density was proportional to the available food supply.

* It has been suggested that shortages of food may be the ultimate limiting factor to human population growth. Certainly, there have been serious famines that have led to many deaths. However, a sensitivity to the possibility of famine can lead to feedback in terms of redistributing available food supplies, improved transportation, and better storage. Possibly, such sensitivity could lead to a slowing of population growth before food resources are exhausted.

Growth Limited by Disease and Accumulated Wastes
If a package of yeast is added to a solution of sugar in water, there is soon evidence of considerable activity. There is a great deal of bubbling, so much so that some of the liquid may actually bubble out of the container. This bubbling is a result of the rapid growth of the yeast population. This process is commonly called fermentation, and two of the products are carbon dioxide, which forms the bubbles, and alcohol.

Eventually, the bubbling ceases, and this indicates that the growth of the yeast population has stopped. It could be hypothesized that the yeast organisms have used up all their food supply. But the addition of more sugar usually does not lead to further activity; the yeast population has been killed by one of the products of fermentation, alcohol. Alcohol is a much sought-after product, but for yeast cells it is a form of pollution that spells death. This ''pollution'' limits the size of the population.

Pollution has affected human populations in the past. When archaeologists excavate down through successive layers of a dig, they frequently find civilizations that have been built on the rubbish and wastes of older civilizations. Sometimes, the wastes have been so overwhelming that cities have had to be built on new sites. More importantly from the standpoint of population, human and animal wastes are fertile breeding grounds for insects, rodents, and other vectors, which have transmitted communicable diseases that have been among the most potent killers of human beings: cholera, typhoid, dysentery, and bubonic plague. It may very well be that one of the most important factors leading to rapid population growth in many regions has been a reduction in the deaths caused by communicable diseases, through improved sanitation, various health measures, and education. Identification of the modes of transmission of many communicable diseases has been accomplished only within the last 100 years: cholera, 1883, typhoid, 1884, and bubonic plague, 1907.

In general, communicable human diseases are transmitted from human to human. When people live close together, the chances are greater that infectious diseases will spread. For example, the common cold, flu, and other diseases to which children are susceptible are among the occupational hazards of teachers and others who work closely with children. More importantly, organisms that cause various human diseases are carried by human wastes and often transmitted by insect and rodent vectors. The development of ways of treating human wastes and of controlling insect and rodent vectors have been tremendously important in controlling communicable diseases.

A number of public health and sanitation measures gradually reduced mortality rates in Western Europe after 1800. Sewage treatment and provisions for sanitary public water supplies virtually eliminated cholera, typhoid, and dysentery as causes of death. The use of DDT and other insecticides has all but eradicated the anopheles mosquito and the body louse, and eliminated malaria and typhus as major causes of death. It has been estimated that the development of aseptic and antiseptic surgical and general medical procedures by Joseph Lister and others may have saved more lives than were lost in all the wars of the nineteenth century.[5] In addition, the development of various immunological procedures has led to the control of such diseases as smallpox, anthrax, diphtheria, tetanus, scarlet fever, and cholera.

The death rates from communicable diseases have also been reduced dramatically in many developing countries. In the period 1940–1964, death rates were reduced by more than half in such countries as Mauritius, Sri Lanka, Venezuela, Thailand, India, Mexico, and Barbados.[6] Such countries have benefited by the fact that public health programs that help control diseases are relatively cheap and are not dependent upon a high level of economic development. It took over 100 years for some of the nations of Western Europe to raise their life expectancy from 41 to 64 years. Some developing countries have achieved the same increase in less than 20 years.[7] The developing countries have been able to use the experiences of other regions and reduce their death rates much faster. Simultaneously, there have been attempts to reduce birth rates, but these usually have been more than compensated for by the decline in death rates. Thus, technical advances, by removing the limits to population growth formerly imposed by communicable diseases, have, in the absence of other regulating factors, been a major factor leading to the population explosion in the developing nations.

Territoriality and Population Regulation[8] Territoriality is a form of competition for food, shelter, nesting space, and other resources of the environment. Territoriality can be viewed as the competition for food and other resources that takes place before these resources reach exhaustion. It is a feedback system for coping with the threat of starvation.

It is probably no mere chance that some of the most striking and most studied examples of territoriality are found among birds. Because of their high metabolism rate and limited capacity for storing food, most birds are in daily need of food. The "early bird" is a creature of necessity. After a night's "starvation," many kinds of birds must have food, and they begin their search with the crack of dawn. While the food supply during some seasons may be much larger than is needed, nonmigratory birds must be assured sufficient food for the entire year. Since birds are so dependent upon the environment for a continuing supply of food, it may be that such behavior as territoriality has evolved to help ensure an adequate supply of food for at least part of the population.

Among birds and many other animals, territories are usually occupied by pairs, and competition is related to reproduction. The territory as a rule contains nesting sites and has sufficient space and resources to make uninterrupted incubation of the eggs possible. The territory is usually defended by the male.

Among many nonmigratory birds the territories are defined and defended not by actual fighting but by various kinds of displays. These displays seem to take the place of actual fighting and provide a way for intruders to be driven out of the territory. It may also be significant that these competitive displays often take place during

defending a territory, animals react to changes in population density before such essentials as food supply and nesting sites are overwhelmed or destroyed. Population size is influenced through various kinds of territoriality behavior. It is interesting to note that, except in extreme cases, defense of territory does not involve actual fighting. The display of outspread feathers of the ruffed grouse, the strutting of the turkey, the individualistic songs of many songbirds, the howls of the howler monkey, the tree shaking of the macaque — each is sufficient to define a territory and warn off intruders. This feedback mechanism has the effect of limiting the number of individuals in the population who can reproduce. Also, individuals who are driven out of the most advantageous environments are much more susceptible to death by predation or disease.

Does man practice territoriality? The often seen "No Trespassing" sign might be considered the equivalent of outspread feathers and ceremonial strutting. Farmers build fences around their fields to keep their cattle in and those of neighbors out. Apartment dwellers in the city and house owners in the suburbs lock their doors and use a variety of devices to protect their property. All these behaviors could be interpreted as territoriality.

States, regions, and nations develop policies that may be interpreted as expressions of territoriality. While nations with small populations, such as Australia and Canada, have until recent years tried to encourage immigration, many more states and nations have erected barriers to immigration. Unusually attractive islands, such as Hawaii and Tahiti, raise barriers to try to ensure that the people who come there will also leave.

The Commission on Population Growth and the American Future expressed its belief that the United States should address itself first to the problems of its own disadvantaged and poor, and recommended civil and criminal sanctions against those who employ illegal border crossers or aliens whose visa status does not authorize their employment.[12] The Commission went on to recommend that immigration levels not be increased and that immigration policy be reviewed periodically to reflect demographic conditions and considerations. More recently, a popular writer on population issues has suggested that the United States should adopt more restrictive immigration policies and that this would provide emotional and moral support for those throughout the world who believe that population growth should be halted.[13]

It may be that, as population densities increase, further attempts will be made to raise barriers to protect living space and precious sources of food supply. An eminent biologist, to the dismay of many, has suggested that countries such as the United States should raise barriers and defend territory.

> In a less than perfect world, the allocation of rights based on territory must be defended if a ruinous breeding race is to be avoided. It is unlikely that civilization and dignity can survive everywhere; but better in a few places than in none. Fortunate minorities must act as the trustees of a civilization that is threatened by uninformed good intentions.[14]

Will we hear more such calls for defining and defending territory in the future?

A distinguished group of British scientists in their "Blueprint for Survival" have suggested that the population of Britain should be reduced by one-half.[15] If population pressures continue to build in various regions, will we see more restrictions imposed against the inflow of population to protect existing food supplies and other resources? And will barricades be erected to safeguard parks, playgrounds, farms, and backyards for communities, families, and individuals? Certainly, it is possible to view some of man's policies and practices with regard to population as manifestations of territoriality behavior. Among some of our fellow primates, territoriality is a way of limiting population growth without serious conflict, before natural resources are stretched to the point where catastrophe for the entire population ensues.

Social Organization and Population Regulation To
consider social structures among animals and population regulation among humans is to court disapprobation both from those who study the behavior of humans and those who study the behavior of other animals because man is different. While some animals apparently have some kind of language, it is very rudimentary compared to ours. (To the best of our knowledge, no animals are writing books about us.) And, while we now believe that some animals do develop a culture that is transmitted from generation to generation, it can in no way compare with the culture transmitted from one human generation to another. (There is a difference between learning that a potato tastes better if it is washed and then transmitting that to the next generation, and accumulating all the knowledge to be found in a

CAMROSE LUTHERAN COLLEGE
LIBRARY

library such as the Library of Congress and leaving that as a legacy for the next generation.) But there is value in studying the behavior of other organisms, in particular to gain a better understanding of ourselves and, perhaps, to observe mechanisms that we may be able to adapt to meet some of our problems.

Among some organisms, notably the social insects, there is a high degree of specialization, even with regard to reproduction. Among the social insects, most individuals have no function in reproduction; reproduction in a swarm is carried out by one female, the queen, and the male drones, whose only function apparently is insemination of the queen. However, this does not seem to limit population growth drastically. Insects as a class are apparently growing in number, and it has been suggested that man and insects are the only two kinds of animals whose populations are growing rapidly at the present time.

Among certain species of birds and mammals, some individuals are apparently excluded from reproduction. In some cases, all males except the dominant one are excluded from the pack or troop. This assertion of dominance is not usually through a fight-to-the-death struggle. It would be fairly easy for a lion or a wolf to rip out the jugular vein of an adversary or for a bird to peck out the eye of a competitor, but this seldom happens. Instead, dominance is achieved through a wide variety of patterns ranging from the feather displays of birds to the violent growling and mock combat of many mammals. As a result, many males, usually the weaker ones, are excluded from reproduction, and, over generations, this is probably an important mechanism of natural selection. It has also been hypothesized that the tensions and strains generated by the competition may reduce the sexual effectiveness of the dominant male and that this may be an additional factor in population regulation.

It could be argued that the exclusion of most males from the reproductive social unit has little effect upon population growth because, after all, it is the female who lays the eggs or bears the young. But in most higher animals there is only a brief period in the estrous cycle, during which a female can conceive. During this brief period there can be intense struggles between females for the attention of a male.[16] These struggles appear to limit the number of conceptions that actually take place.

While aspects of social organization among animals do help to control their population size, these modes of control are more likely to be suggestive of steps that might be taken than descriptive of ways that human populations have been or might be controlled.

Among various religious groups there have been classes of individuals who have practiced sexual abstinence. This has had a very minor effect on total population growth. However, it is conceivable that the number of people who withdraw from the reproductive process could be increased. Voluntary sterilization is one way that individuals forsake reproduction without sexual abstinence. In many cultures it is customary to abstain from sexual activity for an extended period following the birth of a child. In some cultures it is customary to postpone marriage and the having of children until a decade or more after puberty, and this has had a significant impact upon population growth. It is conceivable that these practices could become more widespread.

Large numbers of males are more or less removed from the reproductive process in wartime, and for this and other reasons the rate of population growth often declines during a major war. During World War II, for example, tens of millions of men served in the armed forces. The population pyramid of the United States shows that there were fewer births during the war than in the years preceding it, but that this was followed by a "baby boom" soon after the war. Similar recovery evidently does not take place if the loss of men is more intense and prolonged. In the Soviet Union, for example, severe losses of males in the two world wars and in pogroms between the wars led to a male-female ratio of almost 1 to 2 in many age groups. It will probably be well into the twenty-first century before more normal sex ratios will prevail. This is one of the factors that has led to a relatively low birth rate in the Soviet Union.

Feedback Model of Self-Regulation There appear to be intrinsic self-regulating mechanisms in some animal populations, so that, unless radical changes take place in the environment, a population size will be reached and maintained that is in balance with other populations and with the environment. It has been hypothesized that this self-regulation of populations operates in the form of feedback loops. These feedback loops operate to control the size of populations before such critical limiting factors as food shortages come into play.

Especially in the higher animals, this feedback operates through competition and rivalry. One of the functions of society is to provide a mode and limits to the competition. In fact, a society has been defined as "an organization of individuals that is capable of providing conventional competition among its members."[17] If there are a limited number of rewards, a smaller proportion of the population can win the rewards when the population increases, and the rivalry and competition become greater.

Intense rivalry and competition increase the stress and strain on the individual. In some cases the pressures make it impossible for individuals to take part in the reproductive process. The evidence seems to indicate that there are physiological feedback mechanisms within the bodies of higher animals, particularly such changes as decline in size of the adrenals and thymic involution.[18] This can lead to delayed sexual maturation, reduced body size, and inadequate lactation. In higher animals at least, these feedback mechanisms begin to operate before the resources of the environment are stretched to breaking point. It may be just such feedback mechanisms that result in the sigmoid or "S" curve of population growth.

Exercise: What Factors Regulate the Size of a Population? The factors that limit the size of a population of guppies can be studied in a classroom aquarium. The aquarium should be set up and maintained to support the largest possible population of guppies. This can be done by keeping the temperature of the aquarium set at no lower than 23°C (about 73°F). The aquarium should be aerated, it should contain an abundant supply of plant life in which the newly born guppies can hide, and ample food should be provided.

A number of guppies should be introduced into the aquarium, including some fairly large ones and, if possible, one or more that are pregnant.

Have students record the number of guppies they introduce, and then conduct weekly censuses of the guppy population. Does the population grow? Does the size of the population eventually stabilize? What seem to be the factors that regulate population size?

POPULATION REGULATION IN HUMAN POPULATIONS

Growth and size in human populations have been regulated by effects that result from changes in the population. If the cybernetic feedback model of population regulation is useful in interpreting observations of animal populations, is it also useful in interpreting human population regulation? In many animal populations, population size is regulated so that the environmental limits are not exceeded. As long as there are no radical changes in the environment, checks to animal population growth generally prevent the environment from being destroyed. Have similar kinds of regulatory checks operated on human populations?

Technologically Undeveloped Societies[19] For most of the time that man has existed, the size of the human population has exhibited very slow growth and in many societies probably was relatively stable. How was this stability maintained? If this stability of population size can be explained by the feedback hypothesis, what were the feedback mechanisms by which population growth was regulated?

Unfortunately, we have very little direct information about how population size was regulated in early technologically undeveloped societies. Instead, studies have been made of population regulation among societies that may be somewhat like early human societies. The technologically undeveloped societies that have been studied differ quite considerably from one another, and, of course, we cannot be certain that any of them are like any of the early societies. However, the population regulation mechanisms in these societies are of interest in themselves and may throw light upon the general validity of the feedback hypothesis of population regulation.

Is there significant population regulation among peoples in technologically undeveloped societies? Two students of this question (Benedict and Douglas) answer yes, but they hold that the regulation is not directly related to food supply and other elements of survival, except under the harshest conditions. Instead, the mechanisms of population regulation are associated with prestige in the society. For example, in some societies the prestige of the family is related to the size of the dowry given at the marriage of a daughter, and this can lead parents to limit the size of their families. In societies where control of population growth is seen as desirable, it becomes a matter of prestige to limit the number of children. Among the Tikopians of the South Pacific, for example, there was strong social disapproval and loss of prestige for families that reared more than two or three children.

However, it should be stressed that in most primitive groups prestige is associated with having many children. This is almost invariably under conditions of very high infant and youth mortality, where high birth rate is essential to maintain the population.

Demographic Transition Theory[20]   For most of the 3 million or more years that man has been on earth, the human population has grown very, very slowly. For many regions and periods it may not have grown at all. Population growth was probably regulated by famine, disease, and other mechanisms that have been described as operating among technologically undeveloped societies. It has been hypothesized that in all societies, cultural, social, and economic forces tend to regulate populations. The theory of demographic transition describes conditions that, over considerable periods of time, tend to bring birth rates and death rates into balance. The demographic transition is often delineated into stages, and these stages can be illustrated with the experience of Western Europe.

Stage 1: Upon emergence from the technologically undeveloped stage, death rates begin to drop, largely because of advances in medicine, public health and sanitation, health, and education, and as a result of improved housing and environment. Birth rates tend to increase because more young people survive to the age of reproduction and they live to produce larger numbers of children. However, the birth rates in Western Europe may never have been higher than 35 to 37 per 1,000 population. In Western Europe this stage of the transition probably started about 1800. The decline in death rates was relatively slow and was spread over a period of 75 to 150 years.

Stage 2: Death rates continue to decline. Birth rates begin to decline but remain considerably higher than death rates. Population growth is rapid. Industrialization, urbanization, and other social and economic changes begin to take place. In Western Europe, the population doubling time during this period may have averaged about 70 years. This was also a period of large scale emigration to the New World.

Stage 3: Death rates continue to be low, birth rates decline, and the rate of population growth is reduced. The decline in birth rates during this stage of transition is probably another example of multiple causation. Urbanization makes larger families less advantageous and, perhaps, even a handicap. Improvement in the economic lot of families may suggest that they can improve their economic position even more if they limit family size. Because health conditions improve, more children survive so that parents have to bring fewer children into the world to ensure the family size they want. Men and women may have better access to the knowledge and means of birth control. All these social and economic factors operate over a period of time, sometimes several generations, and they can be slowed or speeded by active societal opposition or support for change, cultural inertia (or dynamism), relative efficiency of communication, and the availability of methods for limiting fertility.

Stage 4: In the final stage, both death rates and birth rates are low and fluctuate very little. In most countries of Western Europe both annual birth rates and annual death rates are below 20 per 1,000 population, and in almost all the Western European countries the population growth rate is less than 1 percent. In all of Asia and Africa in 1978, only two countries, Cyprus and Gabon, had a population growth rate of less than 1 percent. According to the theory of demographic transition, Western Europe should continue to have low, almost balanced birth and death rates.

The United States, the USSR, most countries of Eastern and Southern Europe, Japan, and a few smaller countries may be in or approaching this final stage of demographic transition. Most of these countries have achieved considerable economic development and could be classified as "developed." With the exception of Japan, almost all the major countries that have moved into this stage of transition have a European cultural and ethnic background; and almost all are located in temperate regions — although this may or may not be a factor affecting demography.

Exercise: Stages of Demographic Transition   In simplified form, the four stages are:

Stage 1:   Death rates high. Birth rates high.
Stage 2:   Death rates begin to decline. Birth rates high.
Stage 3:   Death rates decline. Birth rates decline.
Stage 4:   Death rates and birth rates low and approaching equilibrium.

The vital statistics for several countries are shown in Table 3-1. In which stage would you place each of the countries listed? *(Suggested answer: Stage 1—Ethiopia; Stage 2—Algeria, Turkey, Sri Lanka, India, Mexico, Peru; Stage 3—Puerto Rico, Brazil; Stage 4—Japan, Canada, United*

States, Britain, France, USSR) What are some of the characteristics of the countries in each of the stages? Are there reasons for believing that these characteristics are associated with the stage of demographic transition?

Table 3-1
Vital Statistics for Various Countries, 1976

	Annual births per 1,000 Population	Annual deaths per 1,000 Population	Annual deaths of infants under 1 year per 1,000 live births	Percentage of population under 15 years	Percentage of population in cities of 100,000+	Per capita GNP (in U.S. dollars)
Algeria	49	15	126	48	50	650
Ethiopia	49	26	181	44	11	90
Turkey	39	12	115	42	39	690
Sri Lanka	28	8	45	39	22	130
India	35	15	139	40	20	130
Japan	19	6	11	24	72	3,880
Canada	15	7	16	29	76	6,080
United States	15	9	17	27	74	6,640
Mexico	46	8	61	46	61	1,000
Puerto Rico	23	6	23	37	58	2,400
Brazil	37	9	82	42	58	900
Peru	41	12	110	44	60	710
United Kingdom	13	12	16	24	76	3,360
France	15	10	12	24	70	5,190
USSR	18	9	28	28	60	2,300
World	30	12	105	36	38	1,360

SOURCE: Adapted from the *1976 World Population Data Sheet* (Washington, D.C.: Population Reference Bureau, 1976).

There are several variations of the theory of demographic transition, but in its most deterministic form it predicts that all regions and nations will eventually move through the stages of transition to the final stage of stabilized population. A critical question is whether the developing regions of the world, where two-thirds or more of the world's population live, will undergo demographic transition soon enough. Or, to put it another way, will population growth in the developing regions be limited by the socioeconomic forces that have been at work in the demographically advanced regions before population declines are imposed by famine, plague, or other catastrophes?

There are a number of differences between the demographic and socioeconomic conditions prevailing in the developing regions and those of Western Europe — and these differences may be critical. Most of the developing countries have considerably higher birth rates (40 to 50 per 1,000 population) than the Western European countries had at a similar demographic stage. Thus, in these regions, reduction in death rate with no change in birth rate has the potential for a much more rapid population growth.

The reduction in death rates in many developing countries has also been much more rapid than it was in Western Europe, and it has been achieved by relatively low-cost public health and sanitation measures, rather than by general socioeconomic development. The reduction in death rates in Western Europe took place over a period of 150 years. However, the death rates in such countries as India, Mexico, and Thailand declined by 50 percent or more in just 20 years (mid-1940s to mid-1960s). It is difficult for social-cultural feedback mechanisms to take effect in such a short period of time. Moreover, the decline in death rates in Western Europe took place during a period of industrialization and general socioeconomic development. No development on a similar scale has taken place in most develop-ing nations; in fact, economic development has often, even after great effort, been stunted by rapid population growth. And, of course, massive emigration such as that from the countries of Europe to those of the New World can no longer be a significant factor. Although emigration from India in absolute numbers has been considerable, perhaps 250,000 emigrants per year, this figure is put into perspective when we consider that India in the early 1970s was adding about 13 million people to its population each year.

However, there are factors that may help developing nations to move through the demographic transition more rapidly. An impor-tant factor could be the improved technology of birth control. Cer-tainly, the methods of birth control available to people now are much improved over those available in Western Europe in the nineteenth century. Also, there are better communications and educational sys-tems so that people can become aware of problems associated with population and some of the steps that can be taken to deal with these problems. It is noteworthy that some of the most imaginative programs of family planning and population education have been set up in developing nations. Finally, there may be a heightened awareness of population problems and a sense of urgency on the part of governments of developing nations, and this may lead to greater efforts toward population regulation. Many developing nations have evolved population policies and programs, and they are being aided in their efforts by a variety of international agencies. One of the observations that students will be able to make in their lifetime is the extent to which population trends in developing regions conform to the stages predicted by the theory of demographic transition.

The theory of demographic transition is a major paradigm in population studies. It can be considered an application of the feedback model of population regulation to regulation of the growth of the human population.

Theory of Change and Response[21]

The theory of change and response has many similarities with the story of demographic transition, but it attempts to explain the declines in birth rates in countries that undergo economic development by focusing on the family as the basic social unit. As in the case of population regulation in technologically undeveloped societies, it places a great deal of emphasis on threats to social status, prestige, and economic well-being as the motivational forces for family action. It stresses the wide range of demographic responses that families make to protect themselves from loss of status, prestige, and economic well-being.

Japan is used as an illustration of this theory. Japan is the only major Asian country that has approached population stabilization, and it has achieved this in a relatively short period of time. It lowered its gross reproduction rate (GRR) from 2.7 in 1920 to .99 in 1959 — a period of about 40 years. (The gross reproduction rate is an indicator of the number of female children borne by an average mother of the population.) It required 60 years to achieve a similar drop in gross reproduction rate in the United States. The remarkable changes that have taken place in Japan offer some hope that similar changes can take place in other countries in Asia and elsewhere.

The theory suggests that when obstacles to their use are largely removed, families will use a wide range of responses to deal with their demographic situation. The use of abortion may have been a major factor in Japan, which has had probably the sharpest drop in birth rate ever exhibited by a major nation. The annual abortion rate may have risen to about 50 per 1,000 women aged 15–29. (However, it is suggested that the abortion rate as practiced in Europe was probably equally high.[22]) There has been an increased use of contraception and a great deal of sterilization. Marriage has been delayed, and there has also been considerable emigration. Japanese families apparently will use a wide variety of means to limit their families to the size they want, when such means are known and available to them.

Although it is usually assumed that family limitation will be least likely to be practiced in rural areas, studies of the motivations for limiting the desired number of children are illustrated in terms of rural Japan. Technological changes in agriculture make fewer workers necessary. As more capital is needed to purchase larger farms and expensive equipment, it becomes harder for a young man to acquire the real estate and equipment he needs for economic well-being and social status in an agricultural community. When there are many children, there is the problem of inheritance; under conditions of modern agriculture, to receive a small plot of land and a monetary pittance hardly opens the door to either social or economic success. It is suggested that children's experiences as members of a family influence them profoundly when they, in turn, become parents. They make decisions that they consider to be best for them, their children, and other members of the family. And they use a wide range of means to implement their demographic decisions.

The importance of the family unit in limiting population growth has been noted in developing countries.[23] In many cultures, parents want children for a variety of social and economic reasons, such as free labor, and old age insurance; but one of the most important is that they "like to have children." In many parts of the world childhood mortality is still very high. Parents will not practice birth control until they believe that the children they already have are going to survive. Thus, reducing childhood mortality is not only important in itself but also to convince parents that the first child or two they bear will survive to adulthood. In Japan, including rural Japan, this process apparently took little more than a generation.

A major implication of the theory of change and response is that the importance of the family unit should be recognized. Families should be provided with information and, if they wish it, advice, so that they can make demographic decisions that are truly in the best interests of the family. A nation or other political unit that wishes to influence demographic trends will (a) attempt to find out how families try to achieve prestige and improve their social status and economic well-being; (b) improve the nutrition and general health of children, to increase the likelihood that the first children born to a family will survive to adulthood; and (c) through population education, make parents and future parents more aware of the various factors that are involved in the family decisions they may make.

Discussion: How Can Developing Nations Achieve Population Stabilization? There is a continuing controversy over possible approaches to population stabilization in developing countries. The following are some of the points that are made. On a scale of 1 to 5, have students indicate their assessment of each, scoring 5 for "very important," 1 for "not important." In discussion, have students give reasons for their ratings.

1. The most effective way to stabilize population size is by the most direct way, and this is through family planning and birth control. Given the knowledge and the means, people will use them to reduce birth rates and limit the size of their families.
2. Having the ways and means for birth control and family planning is of little avail if people are not motivated to use them. People must feel that birth control and family planning are in their best interests before they will practice them.
3. The most important step toward population stabilization is socioeconomic development. When standards of living in developing countries are improved, birth rates will decline, as they did in Western Europe.
4. Some developed countries have undergone demographic transition, and socioeconomic development may have been an important factor in causing the decline in their birth rates. However, conditions for the developing regions are different. Now, there is no new world to which many people can emigrate, birth rates are higher in developing nations than they ever were in Western Europe, and there is not time for the social and cultural factors that lead to declines in birth rates to operate before we are faced with stupendous calamities associated with very large populations in the developing world.
5. Certainly, socioeconomic development is important and desirable, but rapid population growth is a very serious handicap in development. Some nations have exerted great efforts for development, but these efforts have been largely negated by rapid population growth.

6. The developed nations want to solve urgent problems by preventing the poor from having children. The drive for population stabilization diverts us from the real task of improving standards of living.
7. Population growth is not the real problem. Consumption is the problem, and everyone should try to use resources more wisely so that some are not deprived of what others waste. People throughout the world have a right to be concerned about consumption patterns in nations other than their own.
8. Population policies are a matter for each nation to decide. Outsiders should not set targets of population size or optimum family size for others.
9. A nation's population policies can affect people everywhere. People throughout the world have a right to be concerned about population policies in nations other than their own.
10. Family planning, birth control, and socioeconomic development—all are important factors influencing population. To cope with such complex problems, as those associated with population, it is important to work on several fronts.

Education and Feedback Model In terms of the feedback model, population growth during most of the 3 million years that man has existed was sufficiently slow so that the feedback mechanisms could operate to regulate population size. Now, such measures as improved public health and sanitation, nutrition, medicine, and education have reduced death rates and weakened or broken the feedback loop that served to regulate population growth (see Figure 3-2). There has been a 1,000-fold increase in our population growth rate, and there is a question of whether the social and cultural checks on population that have worked in the past will have time to operate.

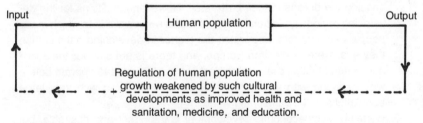

Figure 3-2 Feedback model showing feedback loop weakened by cultural developments.

Undoubtedly, there will ultimately be regulation of human population size. There are a number of factors that could become limits to population growth. However, most would prefer that regulation take place without the catastrophes associated with environmental checks to population growth. In ecological terms, it would be desirable not to have the human population "overshoot" its environmental limits; it would be desirable for population growth to be regulated to follow the "S" curve rather than the "J" curve associated with "overshoot."

In terms of our model, it would be highly desirable to develop a population feedback system that would be more sensitive, one that would start limiting population change before population size becomes too great. There are ways of making feedback systems more sensitive; thermostats that regulate room temperatures, for example, can be made and set so that fluctuations from the desired temperature are very small. Similarly, it would be desirable to have a feedback system that would minimize fluctuations in population size.

Rapid population growth has been due largely to developments in such cultural areas as science and technology, public health and sanitation, nutrition, medicine, and education. It is hypothesized that we can look to these same cultural areas for developments that can lead to more sensitive population regulation. A feedback model based on this hypothesis is shown in Figure 3-3.

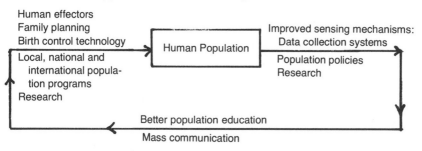

Figure 3-3 A "sensitized" feedback model for population regulation.

Certainly, we need better sensing mechanisms that can tell us what is happening to the human population. There has been no satisfactory census of the population of the world. Many nations do not have effective census systems, and even in developed nations the systems could be improved. In the United States, for example, it is estimated that over 5 million people were missed in the 1970 census. It is also important for social subsystems, such as local communities and families, to be able to get information they can use in their decision making. As we have seen, it is especially important for parents and other members of the family to have the information on which to base sound family decisions.

In this feedback model, population education and mass communication are of critical importance. There seems to be general agreement that population regulation will take place and that it would be desirable that the population be stabilized sooner rather than later. It took perhaps 200 years after death rates began to fall in Western European countries before population began to approach stabilization. But, it might be calamitous if two-thirds of the world's population were to continue to grow at present rates for very long. The populations of the developing nations do not have the escape valve of emigration, and their rapid population growth makes economic development difficult. Thus, it becomes important that population education and mass communication become more effective so that population regulation can be speeded.

If the theory of change and response is correct in suggesting that the family is the most basic social unit relative to population, then it becomes essential that parents and potential parents have opportunities for effective population education in such areas as outlined in this book. Population education should involve developing an understanding of how populations and their environments may be studied and information acquired. It should involve the clarification of values as they relate to population. And it should include explicit information about how families can implement the decisions that they make. Individuals should develop a generalized approach to the analysis of problem areas that will be useful to them as they consider population and other problem areas throughout their lives.

Man's Destiny   Obviously, no one knows what lies ahead for the human race, but our view of what the future may hold in store affects the urgency with which we view population problems and the kinds of steps we are willing to take to deal with these problems.

There are sharply divergent views as to man's destiny. Some believe that the processes of population regulation will almost inevitably regulate population size and that this regulation will take place quite rapidly.

Because of the combined action of these forces, it may be supposed that the efficiency and degree of success with which a population can realize its ideals in practice are much greater today than ever before and will increase even more as further advances are made in contraceptive technology and experience in its use. Within our lifetime we may see fertility control become an integral part of the morals and culture, with highly developed social organizations for maintaining it, in all societies of the world. In other words, the theory of demographic regulation is a positive assertion that nations, when faced with serious overpopulation, will undergo adaptive social change to lower fertility rates and in so doing will invent and adopt a technology of contraception. Moreover, this theory asserts that *modern man is able to foresee demographic catastrophe long before it arrives and takes adaptive action long before it is forced on him by the brute forces of nature.*[24]

Others fear that man, like most other species that have existed, may have evolved into a *cul-de-sac*. With his highly developed brain he has found ways to remove some of the checks to population growth, but he may not be able to regulate the powerful reproductive drives that underlie the intrinsic capacity for growth inherent in all species.

Survival is a rare phenomenon. The vast majority of species that have existed since the dawn of life have become extinct, and those that survive today are but the tip of an iceberg of life, nearly all of which is submerged in the sea of palaentology *(sic)*. Indeed, nearly all forms of life today are similarly doomed. As for individuals, survival is something that sooner or later fails to happen to all.[25]

So, what will be the destiny of Homo sapiens, the "wise one"? He with the opposable thumb, upright walk, minimal body hair, and relatively large cerebrum; he arrived on the scene only 3 or 4 million years ago—a couple of seconds on the planetary clock. He has language and transmits culture from generation to generation. Ironically, he is probably the first to realize that he may have "population problems." Will his population be regulated? Or will he be overwhelmed by his own growth? What is to be the destiny of this "wise one"?

CONCLUSION

Throughout most of our past, the population size of Homo sapiens has been controlled by such natural checks as diseases and famine. In relatively recent times, some of these natural checks on population growth have been reduced or removed. It seems critical that some way be found to reduce the population growth rate and eventually stabilize population size.

For our work in education, a feedback model of population regulation may be useful. The feedback loop has been weakened by cultural developments in such fields as health and sanitation, medicine and education. It may be possible to close this feedback loop again by other cultural developments in such fields as population education, family planning and national and international population programs.

FOOTNOTES

1. For similar cybernetic models of population regulation, see John J. Christian and David E. Davis, "Endocrines, Behavior, and Population," *Science* 146 (18 December 1964): 1550–60; and V. C. Wynne-Edwards, "Self-Regulating Systems in Populations of Animals," *Science* 147 (March 1965): 1543–48.
2. Feedback is one of the central concepts developed in the Engineering Concepts Curriculum Project program for middle and secondary schools. For a discussion of feedback that can be used in schools, see Engineering Concepts Curriculum Project, *The Man-Made World* (New York: McGraw-Hill, 1971), Chapter 7. Also, see Chapter 4 for the Project's discussion of population.
3. One of the basic papers on self-regulating systems in animal populations is Wynne-Edwards, *op. cit.*
4. Adapted from W. J. Nicholson, "An Outline of the Dynamics of Animal Populations," *Australian Journal of Zoology* 2 (1954): 9–65.
5. Ralph Thomlinson, *Population Dynamics: Causes and Consequences of World Demographic Change* (New York: Random House, 1965), 93.
6. Population Reference Bureau, "Spaceship Earth in Peril," *Population Bulletin* 25 (March 1969): 1.
7. Shirley Foster Hartley, *Population: Quantity vs. Quality* (Englewood Cliffs, N.J.: Prentice-Hall, 1972), pp. 57–58.
8. This section is based on sources that include the following: Brian C. Bates, "Territorial Behavior in Primates: A Review of Recent Field Studies," *Primates* 7 (1970): 271–84; David Lack, *The Natural Regulation of Animal Numbers* (London: Oxford University Press, 1954); David Lack, *Population Studies of Birds* (London: Oxford University Press, 1966); and V. C. Wynne-Edwards, "Population Control in Animals," *Scientific American* 211, no. 2 (August 1964): 68–74.
9. Adapted from Lack, "Red Grouse and Ptarmigan in Scotland, in *Population Studies of Birds, op. cit.,* pp. 193–211.
10. Adapted from John R. Krebs, "Territory and Breeding Density in the Great Tit, Parus Major L.," *Ecology* 52, no. 1 (Winter 1971): 2–20.
11. For a review of research on territoriality among primates, see Bates, "Territorial Behavior in Primates," *op. cit.*
12. The Commission on Population Growth and the American Future, *Population and the American Future* (New York: New American Library, 1972), pp. 205–206.

13. Leslie Aldridge Westoff, "Should We Pull Up the Gangplank?" *New York Times Magazine,* (September 16, 1973): 15.
14. Garrett Hardin, "The Survival of Nations and Civilization," *Science* 172, No. 3990 (25 June 1971): 1297.
15. "Blueprint for Survival," *Ecologist* 2, no. 1 (January 1972).
16. Yukimaru Sugiyama has described conflict between the adult females for attention of the one male in a troop of langurs, the male having previously ousted all other males. The struggle among the four adult females led to only one female being impregnated during the estrous period. Yukimaru Sugiyama, "Group Composition, Population Density, and Some Sociological Observations of Hanuman Langurs," *Primates* 5, nos. 3–4 (1964): 33.
17. Wynne-Edwards, "Self-Regulating Systems in Populations of Animals," *op. cit.* p. 1545.
18. Christian and Davis, "Endocrines, Behavior, and Population," *op. cit.* p. 1559.
19. This discussion is based upon sources that include the following: Burton Benedict, "Population Regulation in Primitive Societies," in *Population Control,* ed. Anthony Allison (Baltimore: Penguin, 1970), pp. 165–180; J. B. Birdsell, "Some Environmental and Cultural Factors Influencing the Structuring of Australian Aboriginal Populations," *American Naturalist* 87, no. 834 (1953): 169–207; Mary Douglas, "Population Control in Primitive Groups," *British Journal of Sociology* 17, no. 3 (September 1966): 263–73; and D. H. Stott, "Cultural and Natural Checks on Population Growth," in *Culture and the Evolution of Man,* ed. M. F. Ashley-Montagu (New York: Oxford University Press, 1962), pp. 355–76.
20. This section is based upon sources that include the following: Donald T. Bogue, *Principles of Demography* (New York: John Wiley, 1969); Donald O. Cowgill, "Transition Theory as General Population Theory," *Social Forces* 41:270–74; Dudley Kirk, "A New Demographic Transition:" in *Rapid Population Growth,* Study Committee of the National Academy of Sciences (Baltimore: Johns Hopkins Press, 1971), pp. 103–22; Warren S. Thompson and David T. Lewis, *Population Problems,* 5th ed. (New York: McGraw-Hill, 1965).
21. This section is based upon Kingsley Davis, "The Theory of Change and Response in Modern Demographic History," *Population Index* 29, no. 4 (October 1963): 345–66.
22. See William L. Langer, "Checks on Population Growth: 1750–1850," *Scientific American* 226, no. 2 (February 1972): 93–99 for an account of how not only abortion but infanticide was practised in Europe between 1750 and 1850.
23. Roy E. Brown and Joe D. Wray, "The Starving Roots of Population Growth," *Natural History* 83, no. 1 (January 1974): 47–52.
24. Bogue, *Principles of Demography, op. cit.,* p. 53 (italics in original).
25. W. Lane-Petter, "Population Factors in Survival," in *The Biology of Survival: A Symposia of the Zoological Society of London,* no. 13 (New York: Academic Press, 1964) p. 121.

SELECTED REFERENCES

Allison, Anthony, ed. *Population Control,* Baltimore: Penguin, 1970. 240 pp.
  A collection of papers dealing with population control in plants, animals, and

man. An attempt is made first to put human population problems into general biological perspective and then to deal with human population problems directly.

Behnke, John A., ed. *Challenging Biological Problems.* New York: Oxford University Press, 1972. 502 pp.

Chapter 12, "The Regulation of Human Population," discusses some of the problems involved in population regulation in the years to come.

Bogue, Donald J. *Principles of Demography.* New York: Wiley, 1969. 917 pp.

A basic text in demography. Of special interest in relation to this chapter is Bogue's discussion of population regulation.

Kormondy, Edward J. *Concepts of Ecology.* Englewood Cliffs, N.J.: Prentice-Hall, 1969. 209 pp.

A relatively short basic text in ecology. Chapter 4, "Ecology of Populations," discusses human population growth and regulation.

McLaren, Ian A., ed. *Natural Regulation of Animal Populations.* New York: Atherton Press, 1971. 195 pp.

A technical discussion by a number of experts of the mechanisms of regulation in animal populations. The emphasis is on "single-species populations."

Stanford, Quentin H., ed. *The World's Population.* New York: Oxford University Press, 1972. 346 pp.

A collection of papers written by scholars dealing with various aspects of population. Part I, "The Population Problem: Background," and Part II, "The Population Problem: Causes and Implications," are especially relevant.

Thomlinson, Ralph. *Population Dynamics: Causes and Consequences of World Demographic Change.* New York: Random House, 1965. 576 pp.

A major discussion of population change. Its discussion of factors leading to the decline of death rates and population growth is especially good.

Thompson, Warren S., and Lewis, David T. *Population Problems,* 5th ed. New York: McGraw-Hill, 1965. 595 pp.

A standard text in population studies. It is of special interest because its senior author, Thompson, was one of the first to state a theory of demographic transition.

CHAPTER 4

Families and Population

Couples have a basic human right to decide freely and responsibly on the number and spacing of their children and a right to adequate education and information in this respect.

The Declaration of the 1968 United Nations
International Conference on Human Rights

WHAT IS A FAMILY? How is the family system related to population? What are the biological limits to human reproduction? What are some factors that influence family size? How can conception and birth be controlled? What are some effects of different family sizes? How may the choices we make now affect our future? How do societal policies affect family planning?

When we consider families and population, we touch many of the elements of a "generalized approach" to problem situations. The first need is to *define the problem*. We have listed some of the problems, but each individual and family will have to define its own. Individuals and families have *values*; their meaning may not be clear and precise, but they will nevertheless be the basis for the choices and decisions that are made. Such choices and decisions may be made in the *context* of the family *system*, but the ramifications will touch many other systems. Families may try to see matters from other *frames of reference* than their own to find causes for events that occur. An awareness of *basic laws and principles* will be helpful to them. They will suggest *hypotheses* and try to deduce *possible consequences* of proposed courses of action. Surely, some will ask, *"What can I do?"* Hopefully, the discussions that follow will help achieve a better understanding of some of the factors that affect families and how the actions of families have consequences for national and world populations.

THE FAMILY

The family is the basic human social system for reproduction and nurturing of the young. Although the family may take many forms — it may be a nuclear family, involving only a mother, father and children, or it may be an extended family, involving many other relatives — some kind of family system seems to develop within most societies and cultures. Even in communist societies and communal groups, where there has been a deliberate attempt to emphasize other social systems, family systems still tend to develop. The persistent strength of such primary social groups as the family has been demonstrated at various times.[1] Some aspects of the "youth culture" may appear to weaken the family system. There is well-publicized experimentation with other forms of living, such as delayed marriage and obvious premarital and extramarital sex, but most people do marry. In 1970, 92.4 percent of the males and 95.1 percent of the females in the 45–54 age group in the United States had married. And most children are raised in some kind of family. Even though one of the parents may not be present, there is still usually the insistence that the primary group be called "a family." There are important relationships between family size and the populations of larger social systems such as communities, nations and the world.

The size and rate of growth of a society's population is largely dependent upon family size. Since most children are born and reared in families, a society's population can be considered essentially as the sum of the families that make up that society. Changes in the average family size will have important implications for the size and rate of growth of the population. This is especially true in societies where immigration and emigration are negligible factors and where past medical and health advances make dramatic changes in mortality rates unlikely. Not only is population size and growth a function of the families, but seemingly small changes in family size can have, over a period of several decades, dramatic impact upon the size of a population.

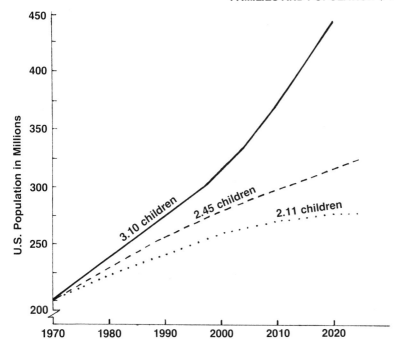

Figure 4-1 The effect of various rates of completed fertility per woman on future U.S. population size. (Based on Table A, "Summary of Projections of Total Population: 1960 to 2020," in U.S. Bureau of the Census, Population Estimates and Projections, Series P-25, no. 470 [November 1971], p. 1.)

Figure 4-1 shows the effects of different levels of completed fertility per woman upon the projected population size of the United States. If the completed fertility rate is 2.11 children per woman (which is approximately the replacement rate), the population of the United States in the year 2020 is projected to be 307,402,000. However, if women were to have on the average one child more (3.10 children per woman) the population for the year 2020 is projected to be 447,003,000. Since this is a difference of about 140 million, we can see the striking impact of seemingly small differences in family size upon the population of a society. Hence, a society that becomes concerned about its population size and wishes to do something about it, will inevitably have to be concerned about family size.

The average family size will also have important bearing on world population. It has been estimated that in 1970 women throughout the world were bearing on the average almost 5 children.[2] If this rate were to continue, world population by the year 2010 would approach 8 billion. However, if the number of children borne had been reduced to replacement level in 1975 (for the world, an average of fewer than 3 children per family) world population in 2010 would be a little over 5 billion. This is a difference of about 3 billion people, which will make a considerable difference to those alive in that year.

Since the family is the basic human social system involved in reproduction, it is important to consider the relationship of the family and reproduction to population. What is the reproductive potential of the family? What are some factors that affect this reproductive potential? What are some of the uniquely human factors involved in reproduction in the family?

HUMAN REPRODUCTION

As with all other species, reproduction is critical for the survival of humankind, but, unlike other species, man can exert some control over reproduction. Reproduction is the process by which species survive. Perhaps as an expression of the general struggle for species survival, the drive to reproduce among humans is very strong. After sheer survival, it may be for the individual among the strongest of human drives.

Reproductive Capacity It has been suggested that one of the basic laws of life is the "law of mass production": all species have a capacity to reproduce at a rate much greater than that necessary to maintain a population at a given size. We can question, however, whether the "law of mass production" holds for the human species. Does man have the capacity to reproduce at a rate much greater than that necessary to maintain the population? It is easy to answer yes, but it is much more difficult to determine what the human capacity for reproduction is. It is even more complicated and difficult to analyze the various factors that can and do lead humans to reproduce at a rate that is usually far less than their capacity.

In studying human reproductive capacity, the focus is inevitably on the female. While both the sperm of the male and the egg of the female are necessary for reproduction, sperm is produced in such abundance, truly mass production, that the supply of sperm is seldom a serious limit to the human capacity to reproduce. However, there are limits to the number of children that a woman can have.

The term *fecundity* refers to a woman's capacity to have children. We will try to determine the human capacity for reproduction by analyzing the nature of the reproductive process in women and by studying reproduction in a society where there appear to be very few limits placed on reproduction.

One way to analyze human reproductive capacity is to consider the nature of human reproduction. The human female can begin to conceive soon after menarche and continue until menopause. The age at which females can begin to conceive, *menarche*, has been declining in the American population, so that the median age of the beginning of puberty is now about 13. The age of *menopause*, when conception no longer can take place, has been rising, and the median age at which menopause occurs is now about 50. The human gestation period is about 9 months, and it would, in theory, be possible for a human female to give birth to offspring about once a year. So, theoretically, a woman might have about 37 births during the period of life when she can bear children. (There might be some multiple births, but also some fetuses and offspring would not survive birth.) Although there are reports of women bearing up to 32 children, most women have far fewer. Obviously, humans reproduce at a rate far below that which is theoretically possible.

Because humans are very social and greatly influenced by the society in which they live, another important way to gain some understanding of the human capacity for reproduction is to study it in a social system in which very few limits are placed upon reproduction. The Hutterites of North America have a social system in which there has been little social restriction of reproduction. In fact, reproduction is socially encouraged. Additional advantages to the study of reproduction among the Hutterites are that the vital statistics seem to be unusually reliable and the subjects of the study have been very cooperative.[3]

The Hutterites are a small religious sect; they live in colonies, mostly in the states of Montana and South Dakota and in the Canadian provinces of Alberta and Manitoba. In 1874, 440 Hutterites emigrated to North America to escape religious persecution. By 1968 their population had grown to over 15,000. Thus, there are now over 34 times as many Hutterites as there were when they arrived in North America. Their population is doubling every 18 years, and it is believed that they are reproducing at a rate that is close to man's capacity.

The Hutterites value children and follow the biblical charge to "be fruitful and multiply." There is practically no premarital conception among them. Almost all adults marry. The median age of marriage for Hutterite women is about 22 years. This is considerably beyond the age of menarche and may be one of the few limits on the reproductive rate. There are strong social and cultural pressures against birth control, and it is believed to be seldom practiced. The entire community assumes responsibility for the support of everyone, including newborns, so that there are none of the economic pressures that limit family size in many societies. There is excellent medical care. There is practically no divorce. Husband and wife are seldom separated during the fertile period, and married women almost always have the chance to reproduce throughout their reproductive years.

How many children do the Hutterites have? The average completed family size of women between the ages of 45 and 54 was 10.6 live births, but women who married at the age of 18 had nearly 12 live births per woman. However, no Hutterite woman was found to have had more than 16 children. The peak of fertility was between the ages of 25 and 29, when the women averaged one birth every 2 years. It has been estimated that, if the Hutterite women were exposed to pregnancy throughout their entire reproductive period from menarche to menopause, they would average between 12 and 14 live births. This may very well be close to the reproductive capacity of the human population.

The Hutterite population continues to grow. Population growth approximates the steep slope of the logistic "S" curve. But the Hutterites have been able to increase the number of their colonies, and there have been no apparent checks on population growth that would lead to a flattening of the curve. Can this continue? The Hutterite population is growing at a rate of about 4 percent per year and doubling every 18 years. In contrast, the population of the United States is doubling every 117 years (1977). Will we see among the rapidly increasing Hutterites in their social-cultural isolation and with their high standards of medical and health care, some of the checks to population growth that we may eventually see in other populations? There are reports of growing hostility from neighboring groups as the Hutterites buy more farmland and expand their colonies. Whatever the future holds, the Hutterites have given us some insights into the human capacity for reproduction.

Probably, no group of humans, even the Hutterites, is reproducing at full reproductive capacity. While it is important to gain some appreciation of fecundity, *fertility,* the number of children a woman actually bears, is even more important. Fertility is probably the most important factor affecting population growth or decline, and to reduce population growth rates, it is essential to reduce fertility.

Process of Human Reproduction[4]   New individuals in populations are the products of reproduction. Among humans, this reproduction is sexual, that is, both male and female are essential to the process. The male produces sperm and the female eggs. For reproduction, a sperm must penetrate an egg. This fertilized egg is nourished and develops within the body of the female, and about 9 months after the egg was fertilized, a baby is born. In this process of reproduction there are a number of essential stages that we have called *critical stages of reproduction.*[5] *Accidents, or deliberate intervention, at one or more of these critical stages can prevent conception and birth.* Contraception and birth control practices involve intervention at one or more of these critical stages.

In this section we will discuss both the critical stages and the contraceptive and birth control practices by which we can intervene at these critical stages (see Figure 4-2). We suggest that the concept of critical stages is a useful approach to analysis, explanation, and teaching in this area.

The male is born with a large supply of the cells that produce sperm. From the time of puberty on throughout the lifetime of the male, large numbers of sperm cells continuously mature. A critical stage in the male is that the sperm must pass through some thin tubes called the *vasa diferentia* (singular, *vas deferens*) before they can enter the urethra and then leave the body. Another critical stage where intervention can take place is at injection of the sperm into the reproductive tract of the female. If this is prevented, reproduction cannot take place.

Once injected into the lower regions of the female reproductive tract, the sperm will usually remain viable for 48 to 72 hours within the female, and it is during this period that a sperm may fertilize an egg, if an egg is available to be fertilized.

For one male sperm to survive to fertilize a female egg, each of the following conditions must hold — and each represents a critical stage for intervention to prevent fertilization:

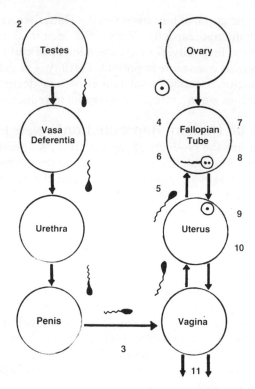

Figure 4-2 *Critical stages of reproduction and corresponding methods of birth control:*

Critical Stage	Method of Birth Control
1. *Ovaries must produce egg cells*	*Contraceptive pill*
2. *Testes must produce sperm cells*	
3. *The sperm must be injected into the vagina of the female*	*Vasectomy, condom, coitus interruptus*
4. *A ripe egg must be present in a Fallopian tube at the time sperm are introduced into the vagina*	*Contraceptive pill, rhythm*
5. *The sperm must remain alive until one cell can reach an egg and fertilize it*	*Contraceptive pill, rhythm, possibly IUD*
6. *At least one of the sperm must swim up the vagina and the uterus to the Fallopian tube to fertilize the ripe egg*	*IUD (?), chemicals, diaphragm*
7. *A sperm must pass through the cell membrane of the egg*	*Contraceptive pill (?)*
8. *One sperm must enter the egg cell and the two nuclei unite there to form a fertilized egg*	*Contraceptive pill (?)*

9. *The embryo must become fixed to the   Contraceptive pill*
   wall of the uterus
10. *As a fetus, it must grow in the uterus for   Induced abortion*
    the next 281 days
11. *The matured fetus must emerge and*
    begin independent life

1. The conditions within the female reproductive tract must be such
   as to allow sperm to remain alive and viable. The presence of a
   chemical, such as a weak acid, or a foreign substance, such as a
   plastic or copper IUD, will adversely affect or kill the sperm.
2. The sperm must be able to move through the lower opening of the
   uterus, up the uterus, and into the Fallopian tubes. If the opening
   to the uterus is blocked, the sperm will not be able to enter.
3. A viable sperm must make contact with a viable egg in the upper
   reaches of the Fallopian tube, and the head of the sperm must
   penetrate the wall of the viable egg.

The female is born with many thousands of undeveloped egg cells
in her ovaries. At the age of menarche, some of these cells begin to
mature and are released into the Fallopian tubes (see Figure 4-3).

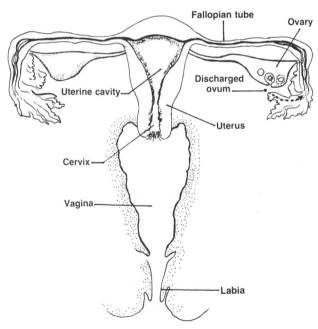

Figure 4-3 Female reproductive organs

Usually, one egg is released about every 28 days. During a female's lifetime, up to 400 eggs may ripen and be released from the surface of the ovaries. Between the maturation and release of an egg and the birth of a baby there are a number of critical stages of reproduction.

The development and release of an egg from one of the two ovaries is stimulated and triggered by hormones from the pituitary gland. Without these hormones, an egg will not mature and be released. Secretion of the essential pituitary hormones is stimulated by a decline in the level in the blood of the hormone *estrogen*. If there is no decline in the estrogen level in the blood, the essential hormones will not be secreted by the pituitary, and no egg will mature and be released from an ovary.

If an egg is released from an ovary, it is swept into one of the Fallopian tubes. For about 40 hours, while it is in the upper reaches of the Fallopian tube, it can be fertilized. If no sperm enters it during this period, the egg will disintegrate and pass out of the body.

If the egg is not fertilized, the lining of the uterus, which had been made ready for the implantation of the fertilized egg, is shed by the uterus and passes out of the body as menstrual flow. *Menstruation* goes on for about 4 days, and it is a natural, healthy action that takes place each 28 or so days when an egg has not been fertilized.

If an egg is fertilized, it moves down the Fallopian tube, and in 3 or 4 days it reaches the uterus. For the fertilized egg to develop as a fetus, it must be implanted on the wall of the uterus. If it is not implanted, it will disintegrate and be aborted.

For a fetus to develop, it must receive adequate nourishment from the mother and remain in the uterus until the time of birth—about 9 months after fertilization has taken place.

If adequately cared for and nourished, 13 to 15 years after birth this child will, in turn, have the potential for reproduction, to create more of its kind.

Exercise: What Are the Critical Stages of Reproduction in Other Organisms? Other organisms are also involved in reproductive cycles, and many of them are involved in sexual reproduction that has many similarities to the human reproductive cycle. Students can gain a better understanding of the critical stages in human reproduction by analyzing the critical stages in the reproductive cycles of other organisms.

Figure 4-4 shows the reproductive cycle of a flowering plant. On this diagram have students indicate those places where accidental or deliberate

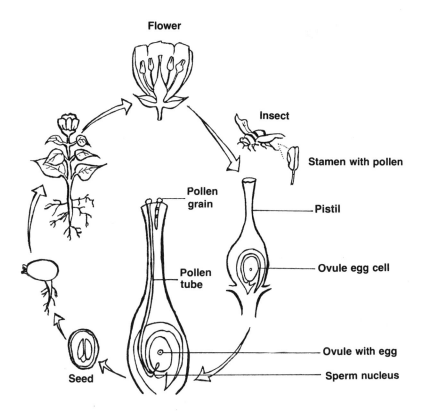

Figure 4-4 Diagram of the reproductive cycle of a flowering plant.

intervention would prevent reproduction. Have students examine a relatively simple flower, such as a lily, to see what would be involved in an intervention at any of these critical stages.

Birth Control and Contraceptive Methods

MENSTRUAL CYCLE AND CONCEPTION There is a period of about 40 hours in the menstrual cycle when an egg is available for fertilization. One approach to birth control is to abstain from sexual activity during the time that an egg is present in the reproductive tract. This is the so-called *rhythm method* of birth control.

To practice the rhythm method, the time when the egg is released from the ovary needs to be determined. The egg is released from the ovary about 14 days before the beginning of the next menstruation. For many women, this is also 14 days after the onset of the previous menstruation. However, the critical period is not just the 2 days during which an egg is available for fertilization, because sperm cells may remain active in the female for up to 72 hours. Also, many women have irregular menstrual cycles, so that it is difficult to pinpoint the time of ovulation. For example, some women have a menstrual cycle of up to 35 days. Maintaining a record of body temperature can help determine the time of ovulation: There is often a drop in body temperature about 2 days before ovulation begins and then a slight rise in body temperature, of up to 1°C, when ovulation takes place. If the temperature is taken every morning, and if no slight illness upsets the temperature pattern, this can help determine the time of ovulation. When all factors are taken into consideration, for women with a 28-day menstrual cycle it is usually recommended that no sexual activity be undertaken between the tenth and eighteenth day of the menstrual cycle if conception is to be prevented.

PREVENTING THE UNION OF SPERM AND EGG For conception to take place, the sperm must enter the vagina, move up into the uterus and beyond that to a Fallopian tube, and one sperm must penetrate the egg. Some of the oldest and most widely used methods of birth control involve procedures or devices that prevent the sperm from reaching and entering the egg.

Withdrawal, or *coitus interruptus,* is one of the oldest and most widely used birth control practices: The male withdraws from the female just before ejaculation of the sperm, so that the sperm will not enter the reproductive tract of the female. This method requires control by the male and to a certain extent by the female, and it may sometimes be physically and psychologically difficult.

The *condom* is a thin sheath that fits over the penis and prevents the sperm from entering the female reproductive tract. It is put on immediately prior to intercourse and, used properly, is a very effective contraceptive device. The condom also can help prevent the transmission of venereal disease. The condom and *coitus interruptus* are two contraceptive practices that are largely under the control of the male; both are immediately associated with the sex act.

The *diaphragm* is a thin sheath that fits over the opening into the female uterus; it prevents sperm from entering the uterus and making contact with the egg. The appropriate size of the diaphragm is usually determined and prescribed by a physician. It can be inserted before intercourse and should be left in place at least 8 hours after intercourse. Contraceptive jellies or creams are used in conjunction with the diaphragm. The use of the diaphragm is under the control of the female.

INHIBITING RELEASE OF THE EGG Oral contraceptives ("the pill") intervene in the reproductive process in several ways. In general, these interventions are much the same as those that occur during a pregnancy. Some oral contraceptives, in a sense, simulate pregnancy, and they are sometimes said to create a "pseudo-pregnancy." Fertilization cannot take place as long as a condition of "pseudo-pregnancy" is maintained.

Ordinarily, an egg is released from a female ovary once every 28 days. The release of this egg is stimulated by the secretion of a hormone by the pituitary gland in the brain. In turn, the pituitary gland is stimulated to release this hormone by a decline in the estrogen level in the blood. Oral contraceptives contain synthetic estrogen, and, when ingested regularly, inhibit the release of the pituitary hormone. Without this hormone, an ovary will not be stimulated to release an egg. With no egg present in a Fallopian tube, fertilization cannot take place.

During pregnancy, another hormone, *progesterone,* stimulates the uterus opening to thicken, and this prevents sperm from entering the uterus. Some oral contraceptives also contain synthetic progesterone, which stimulates the thickening of the opening to the uterus. Even if an egg were released and entered a Fallopian tube, the action of the progesterone in the oral contraceptive would prevent a sperm from entering the uterus, reaching an egg and fertilizing it.

During pregnancy, progesterone also inhibits the growth of new lining of the uterus. If fertilization were to take place, the fertilized egg would have to be implanted on the uterine lining and receive nourishment for development to take place. The quantity of the synthetic hormone progesterone in "the pill" interferes with the development of this lining. Even if there were a fertilized egg, the lining of the uterus would not be receptive to its implantation.

In a sequence of using birth control pills, a pill is taken each day for 21 days starting with the fifth day after the start of menstrual flow. Sometimes, "placebos," pills that contain no hormones, are taken for the following 7 days, when no hormones are necessary, so that the daily habit of taking a pill is not broken. During the 7 days that no hormones are taken, the estrogen level in the blood drops. This allows the lining of the uterus to be shed in the monthly menstrual flow. Then, the sequence of pills for 21 days is begun again to raise the estrogen level in the blood which will inhibit the pituitary from secreting the hormone that would stimulate the release of an egg from an ovary.

"The pill," when used as directed, is almost 100 percent effective. The "safety" of oral contraceptives is due, in part, to their intervention at several critical stages in the reproductive cycle. Oral contraceptives inhibit the release of an egg, prevent sperm from entering the uterus, and make the uterus wall unreceptive to the implantation of a fertilized egg. Usually, oral contraceptives must be taken daily for at least 21 days of the menstrual cycle, and this requires some care and discipline on the part of the woman. Most reported failures of "the pill" have probably been due to some break in the sequence of taking the pills as prescribed.

Oral contraceptives are under the control of the female, and their use is not associated with the sex act. Their use is reversible, and a woman can become pregnant when she stops taking the pill. In the United States, more married couples use oral contraceptives than any other form of contraception. There seems little doubt that the pill has been a major factor in the decline of the birth rate in the Western world.

For some women, there are side effects to the use of oral contraceptives. A connection between thromboembolism (blood clots) and the use of the pill has been shown for some women. They are usually advised to use some other contraceptive method. Interestingly, there is some evidence that use of the pill may also have beneficial side effects, such as somewhat more acute hearing and, among women over 40, a lowered concentration of cholesterol in the blood.

CREATING AN ENVIRONMENT UNFAVORABLE TO CONCEPTION
Conception takes place within the reproductive tract of the female, and a variety of devices have been developed that are believed to create an environment within the reproductive tract that inhibits conception. In addition to oral contraceptives, these include use of chemical spermicides and the insertion of an *intrauterine device* (IUD). Many modern IUDs are made of plastic or copper and are well tolerated by the uterus. A variety of shapes for IUDs have been developed (see Figure 4-5).

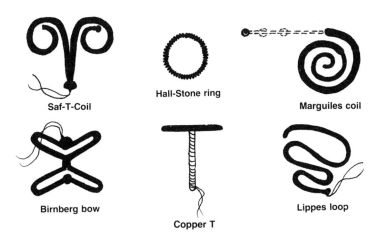

Figure 4-5 Some Intrauterine Devices (IUDs)

Although widely used and very effective, we do not know (1978) how the IUD works. One theory is that it serves as a mild irritant, which causes the body to generate mucous and other defense materials that may destroy the sperm cells. These defense materials may also destroy the egg cell or greatly speed up the passage of the egg cell through the reproductive tract. Another theory is that the defense materials that are generated by the body prevent the implantation of fertilized eggs on the wall of the uterus. Even though we do not know how they work, IUDs are quite effective, with a pregnancy rate among users of only about 2 per 100 woman years of use.

The IUD has been used primarily by women who have already borne one child. New designs in IUDs may prove to be effective for women who have not had a child. The IUD is a widely used contraceptive method in developing countries. Since it does not require continual decision making, women who are not strongly motivated toward birth control and family planning have found it a very suitable approach to contraception.

The use of an IUD is under the control of the female. The decision to use an IUD is not related to the sex act. There is some chance of expulsion of an IUD, and most of these devices have some attachment, such as a string, so that a woman can check to see that the device is in place. The action of the IUD is completely reversible; once the IUD has been removed, normal conception can occur.

Some women are uncomfortable with an IUD in place. In some

cases it leads to menstrual disturbances, bleeding between periods, and pelvic irritation. If these symptoms persist, it is usually recommended that a shift be made to some other birth control method.

VOLUNTARY STERILIZATION   Sterilization is a surgical procedure for preventing conception. It is a way of ensuring complete protection from conception and is most popular with older people who have achieved the size of family they want.

Sterilization of the male, which is simpler than sterilization of the female, can be performed in a few minutes with only a local anesthetic. Essentially, male sterilization involves closing or plugging the *vasa deferentia* which are the two thin tubes through which the sperm move (see Figure 4-6). Because the operation is on the vas deferens, it is called a *vasectomy*. After a vasectomy, sperm cannot move up the tubes to join the semen. Instead, the sperm are absorbed by the body like many other secretions. A vasectomy has no effect upon physical sexuality; it is a way in which a couple can achieve complete protection from unwanted conception.

Sterilization of the female involves cutting and blocking the Fallopian tubes and is called *tubal ligation*. Tubal ligation makes it impossible for egg and sperm to meet. It has no effect upon physical sexuality, and there are no known physical side effects.

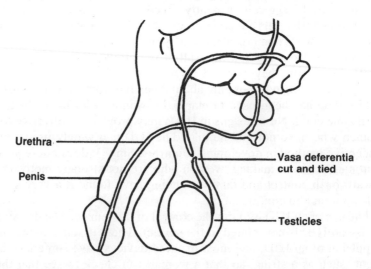

Figure 4-6 In male sterilization, the tubes that carry the sperm are closed.

While sterilization of the male, and in some cases of the female, can under certain conditions be reversed, the procedure is usually recommended only for men and women who are quite certain that they do not want any more children.

TERMINATION OF FETAL DEVELOPMENT After conception takes place, the fertilized egg develops over a period of about 9 months into the baby that emerges from the mother's womb. The fertilized egg and the subsequent fetus can be stopped from further development and/or removed from the uterus. An *abortion* is the ending of a pregnancy before the fetus is sufficiently developed to survive outside the mother's body. There are spontaneous abortions, which are unintentional, and induced abortions, which are deliberate.

Worldwide, abortion may be one of the most widely practiced methods of birth control. Abortion is believed to be the birth control method largely responsible for the sharp reduction of birth rates in countries such as Japan. In Hungary, where abortions have been legally sanctioned and very inexpensive, the number of abortions has exceeded the number of live births. In New York State, which in 1971 passed one of the most liberal abortion laws in the United States, there were an estimated 262,000 abortions in the first year following enactment of the law. About 61 percent of these were performed on out-of-state residents.

A major deterrent to abortion has been its illegality in many states and countries. However, the United States Supreme Court, in a momentous 1973 decision, ruled that many of the state laws prohibiting abortion were unconstitutional. The Supreme Court ruled that states cannot prohibit voluntary abortions during the first 3 months of pregnancy and that during this period the decision should be left to the woman and her doctor. States may regulate abortion procedures during the remaining 6 months of pregnancy in ways reasonably related to maternal health. During the final 10 weeks of pregnancy, states may prohibit abortion except in cases where doctors find the life of the mother endangered.

The implications of the Court's decision have been profound and far-reaching. Certainly, it will henceforth be much easier for a woman in the United States to terminate a pregnancy by abortion.

Discussion: Abortion The abortion issue involves profound moral questions that young and old should be aware of and give careful consideration to. The following are some of these questions and issues:[6]

When does the life of an individual human being begin? Is it when the sperm and egg join and conception takes place? Is the life actually in the sperm and the egg before conception takes place? Is it after the fertilized egg is implanted on the wall of the uterus? Is it after the fetus has attained a human shape? Is it after the fetus has developed to the point where it might survive outside the body of the mother? Is it when the child is born?

Who should have the right to decide whether a pregnancy should be terminated? Should a woman have that right, which some argue involves the right to decide what happens to her own body? Should it be a joint decision by the wife and her husband? Should a doctor be involved and make the judgment in terms of the health of the pregnant woman? If health is a consideration, should mental health be one of the factors considered? Should a pregnant, unmarried girl have the right to an abortion without having to consult her parents? Does the state, nation, and broader society have the right to determine the conditions under which abortions can take place? Are abortions largely a religious matter to be decided in terms of religious and ethical doctrine?

Should abortions be permissible sometimes and not other times? For example, even if abortion is generally considered to be wrong, should an unmarried girl who becomes pregnant through ignorance or bad judgment have a right to terminate the pregnancy? Should a woman who becomes pregnant late in her fertile years and long after completion of a family that has been planned have a right to terminate the pregnancy? (Actually, many abortions are had by older women who become pregnant relatively late in life.) Should an abortion be permitted if a woman's health and possibly her life are threatened if the pregnancy is carried to completion? Should an abortion be permitted if the conditions into which a child will be born are so bad that it would have little chance of leading a decent life? Should abortion be permitted if pregnancy is the result of rape or incest?

Physically, mentally, and morally, abortion is almost invariably a more profound and traumatic experience than contraception. In many cases, the need or desire for an abortion is the result of a failure—often because of ignorance or carelessness—of contraceptive practices.

The Search for Better Methods of Birth Control

Table 4-1 shows the percentage of married couples in the United States who, in the period 1965-1970, used the various kinds of interventions discussed earlier. The pill was used by more couples than any other approach. Its popularity is especially striking since it was not made available to the American public until 1960. Its rapid growth in popularity may be indicative that married couples are receptive to new and more reliable ways to ensure that they have only the number of children they want, when they want them.

However, the search continues for still more effective ways to intervene in the reproductive cycle.[7] It would be desirable to have a contraceptive pill that did not require women to remember to take a pill every day for at least 21 days out of the reproductive cycle. Certain pill regimens are even more complicated, in that different kinds of pills have to be taken at different times in the menstrual cycle. One possibility is a small pill that could be implanted under the skin; it would slowly release the contraceptive substances and would last for a long time. A similar pill to suppress the generation of sperm in the male would be useful. A "morning-after pill" has been developed and is especially useful for those who do not engage in regular sexual activity, but, since it involves large dosages, there are often undesirable side effects that a better contraceptive might avoid. And, of course, it would be highly desirable to develop a contraceptive pill that had no detrimental side effects.

The search also continues for better IUDs. It would be desirable to have IUDs that did not cause internal irritation and that could not be accidentally expelled. Fully reversible male and female sterilization would be especially useful to those who cannot be absolutely certain that they will never want another child.

Table 4-1
Percentage of U.S. Couples Using Various Types of Interventions, 1965–1970

Type of intervention	Percentage
Avoiding the fertile period (rhythm)	6
Preventing the union of egg and sperm (condom, diaphragm, withdrawal)	22
Inhibiting release of eggs (pill)	34
Creating an environment unfavorable to conception (IUD, chemicals)	17
Sterilization (wife, 8.5; husband, 7.8)	16
Other	5

SOURCE: Adapted from Charles F. Westoff, "The Modernization of U.S. Contraceptive Practices," *Family Planning Perspectives* 4, no. 3 (July 1972): 11.

It is obviously of great importance for us to gain a better understanding of human reproduction. We probably know more about reproduction in some animals than we do of the process in humans. Following are some of the questions to which we do not have satisfactory answers (1978):

1. We know that a female egg is available for fertilization for only a short period during the menstrual cycle; how can this fertile period be more accurately detected, and why does its timing vary from woman to woman and even from period to period in the same woman?

2. For fertilization, a sperm must enter an egg; how long can a sperm cell continue to "live" within the reproductive tract of the female, and what are factors that inhibit or prolong the effective life of sperm?

3. All IUDs have been developed only on the empirical basis that "they work," with very little understanding of how and why they work; what are the mechanisms by which the intrauterine device prevents pregnancies?

4. Some fertilized eggs develop into females, others into males; what are the factors determining the sex of the fetus that develops from the fertilized eggs?

5. There are men and women who are sterile and cannot have children, and others who are subfecund and have difficulty in conceiving children. What factors are involved in sterility and subfecundity, and what are the underlying causes of these conditions?

Experience in many sciences indicates that some of the most important advances are achieved as we struggle to find out, to understand, to know more about a phenomenon. The path to better contraceptives and more effective birth control may come through a better understanding of human reproduction.

SOCIAL FACTORS THAT INFLUENCE FAMILY SIZE

Family size is influenced by social, psychological, and technological factors that operate within the biological limits. No human population is reproducing at as high a rate as is theoretically possible. In addition to the biological limits, reproduction rates are influenced by a number of social factors associated with families.

Age of Marriage and of Bearing First Child[8] The period of reproduction for a woman may be considered to be the 37 years between the ages of 13 and 50. Generally, a woman is more fecund during the first half of this period than the second. Also, some individuals who have not married by their late twenties may not marry at all. For reasons such as these, any tendency in a society toward postponement of marriage and waiting until the middle or late twenties to have a first child will generally lead to smaller families and to a lower rate of population growth.

Ireland provides a dramatic example of the effect of the postponement of marriage upon population. The introduction of a new potato from South America, which became known as the "Irish Potato," provided the food that made it possible for the population of Ireland to double in the 50 years between 1795 and 1845. Then, a potato blight struck. In 15 years, over one million people died of starvation and diseases related to starvation, and 1.5 million Irish emigrated to the New World. Since then Ireland has had the highest average age of marriage, and the largest proportion of men and women who never marry, of any area of Europe. Largely because of these two factors, Ireland is one of the areas that has approached population stabilization. The combined populations of the Republic of Ireland and North Ireland are only slightly larger now than they were in 1795.

The United States has the lowest median age of first marriage of any developed nation. In 1970 the median age of first marriage was 20.8 years. Couples that marry at this age usually can have all the children they want, and usually the earlier they marry the more children they will have. A woman who marries between the ages of 14 and 17 will, on the average, bear slightly more than 2.5 times as many children as a woman who marries between the ages of 30 and 34. If all women were to postpone marriage until 20 and had the same fertility rates as those who were married after 20, it has been estimated that there would be approximately 16 percent fewer births.[9]

Many children are born to mothers in their teens; if these births were postponed or eliminated, population growth rate would be reduced considerably. If three-quarters of the births to teen-age mothers were postponed until the 20–24 age bracket and the remainder to 25–29, the U.S. population would be 6.6 percent smaller. If teen-age births were completely eliminated, the reproduction rate would approximate that of a stabilized population.[10]

Intervals Between Births The gestation period between conception and birth for humans is about 9 months. Allowing some time for recovery after childbirth, it is possible for women to give birth once a year. However, there is evidence that this is physically harmful to women and possibly to the offspring. There is a higher rate of prematurity of birth when the interval between births is low. The chance that children will survive after birth also increases as the interval between births increases. Because the mother of a newborn child cannot give as much attention to the children she already has, and possibly because of the economic effect of a newborn child upon the family, the health of the other children in the family may suffer. For example, a young child may be nutritionally deprived when a new baby is born into the family. In fact, the literal meaning of the protein deficiency disease named *kwashiorkor* is "the disease of the deposed baby when the next one is born." In general the health of a newborn child, its siblings, and the mother are affected if the interval between births is short. The effects are especially serious if the interval is 13 months or less.[11]

The spacing of children has been found to be associated with educational level and economic status. The college educated tend not only to start their families later but also to have longer intervals between children; this pattern probably ensures that the careers and aspirations of husband and wife are least adversely affected by children. We find longer intervals between births also in families of higher economic status. However, families that deliberately plan to have their children at short intervals tend to improve their economic status rapidly after what is often a "poor start." Many of these parents want to have their children over a relatively short period of time and are willing to pay the economic price for it.

The evidence tends to indicate that couples whose first child is conceived premaritally continue to be unable to control their fertility.[12] These couples will tend to have more children than those who conceive their first child after marriage.

Number of Children The number of children that a family may desire is influenced by a variety of social factors:[13]

1. The desire to have offspring to carry on the family name and inherit the family property: There is a desire in many cultures to "have one's line continue," to know that "I am not the last of the – – – – s."

2. The desire to have a son/daughter: In some cases this is closely connected to the desire to have the family name carried on. If the family name is carried on only by sons, then a family may continue to have children until they have one or more sons. Families may also want both sons and daughters and may continue to have children until they have as many of each as they want.

3. To strengthen the family's social and political status and its economic position through the ties of marriage of the offspring: In many political, social, and economic systems, kinship ties are extremely important. A family's status can be advanced through a "good" marriage; its economic future can be made more secure through a relationship with other families.

4. To demonstrate a man's virility and a woman's productivity: In many cultures a large number of children is considered to be a clear demonstration of a man's virility. A woman's status in the family and society may be dependent upon having children or upon bearing a son. In well-publicized instances, royal wives have been repudiated because of failure to bear an heir to the throne.

5. Religious doctrines: The Muslim and Hindu religions and some branches of the Christian religion place high value on having children. For example, the Hutterites and the Algerian Muslims have very high fertility rates, and these rates are influenced by religious factors.

6. Economic factors: In many rural, self-contained agricultural systems, children are an economic asset. In families where all children are expected to get at least a college education, and preferably at a prestigious college, children can be a considerable economic burden upon the family.

7. Urbanization: The birth rate dropped 50 percent in a community in central Italy when it changed from a rural community to a dormitory suburb of a nearby city.

8. The desire for upward mobility: In some societies large families are not a prestige factor, and nepotism (favoring members of one's family) is frowned upon or considered illegal. In such societies, large families may be a handicap to social and economic advancement.

9. Family allowances: Payments to families based on the number of children they have—as in Britain and some other countries—may encourage families to have more children.

10. Tax credits: Many nations, states, and municipalities allow tax-payers to claim tax exemptions for dependents, which may also encourage large families.
11. Social welfare services: Such social welfare services as subsidized food, free or inexpensive health care, free education, and day care for young children make it easier for parents to support large families. Obviously, not all of these factors are operative in all societies.

Discussion: What Factors Influence Family Size? Students might consider (a) What factors seem to influence the number of children that their friends and neighbors have? and (b) How might they themselves be influenced by some of the factors listed, when planning the size of their families?

Changing Normative Roles of Women[14]   At some times, in some cultures, in some societies, the major role that has been seen for women and the major role that they have seen for themselves has been that of the childbearer, homemaker, and mother. There are probably limited opportunities for self fulfillment in the ancient prescription for women, "Kinder, Küche und Kirche." If one of the few avenues toward self-fulfillment is to have as many children as possible, then many women are likely to choose to have many children and the woman who chooses not to have many children will be considered somewhat deviant. This has been the prescribed role of women in many societies and cultures, and it has had an impact upon the percentage of women who marry, average family size, and population growth. It is quite conceivable that the relatively recent struggles for alternative roles for women might have the effect of reducing family size and population.

Developments in contraceptive technology have given the female more control over what happens to her body. Unlike some of the earlier contraceptive practices, the use of the pill and the IUD are controlled by the female. The woman can decide whether or not to take the pill or to have an IUD inserted. Hence, women can decide not to become pregnant. While they still do not have complete control over whether or not they will have a child, they do have the power to *decide* not to have one. While most American women marry and have children, they usually complete their childbearing by the age of 30. The increased control over what happens to her own body gives the female a greater choice of normative roles.

Child rearing in a self-contained agricultural community is often a cooperative venture, in which wife and husband and other members of the family take active parts. But in the modern suburb, the responsibilities for child care often devolve almost entirely upon the mother. Father rushes to catch the 7:16 to the city and returns home tired and frazzled on the 6:58. Mother's day, on the other hand, might include caring for the infant, getting the other children ready for the school bus, preparing meals, cleaning the house, shopping for the entire family, chauffeuring offspring to social engagements (ranging from Little League baseball to "seeing my best friend on the other side of town"), and then being the attractive, loving wife when her husband returns home in the evening. It has been said that the modern suburban housewife has to be mother, cook, seamstress, maid, plumber, carpenter, contractor, buyer, chauffeur, public relations expert, community citizen, and loving mistress. The termination of childbearing can make it possible for the wife to shed some of these responsibilities and assume new ones. Now, in most American homes, all the children are attending school by the time the mother is in her mid-30s and most of the children will have left the home by the time she is 50.

The changing sociocultural view of the role of women may have a marked impact upon family size and population growth. If the ideal is for women to have as many children as possible, then the woman who has many children tends to be looked upon with great favor and the one who has no children or does not even marry tends to encounter social disfavor—ranging from the silence of a displeased parent and the snide remarks of friends to increasing isolation within a community. However, as alternative roles for women emerge, the social pressure upon females to have children decreases, and some women find other avenues toward self-fulfillment. It has been suggested that, in the future, women who bear more than the two or three children needed for population replacement may be socially reproached for "exacerbating the population problem." Young people in some youth subcultures are already showing this kind of social bias.

In many societies it has been difficult for women to enter such professions as medicine, law, and engineering, and it has been very difficult to achieve success in business and in other vocations. If these alternative normative roles become more readily available to them, some women may choose not to have families; others may choose to have smaller families so that they can continue their careers. And, as we have seen, the numbers of families formed and their average size ultimately have a critical influence upon population size.

Widowhood, Separation, Divorce, and Abstinence[15]

Social factors that tend to separate male and female can affect fertility. The extent to which these factors are influenced varies from culture to culture.

In some cultures, when a woman's husband dies, she is forbidden to remarry and usually will have no more children. In other cultures, the mores dictate that she must wait at least a year or two before remarrying, and the number of children that she is likely to bear in her lifetime is reduced.

Women who are involved in separation or divorce tend to have fewer children, and this in turn has an impact upon population growth. In the United States, for example, the separation and divorce rate is gradually increasing; in some states, over 50 percent of marriages end in divorce. Although some of the women who become separated and divorced remarry and have more children, the total number of children they will have in a lifetime tends to be reduced.

In many cultures some members of the society abstain from sexual activity and thus do not contribute to the overall fertility. More commonly, there is a period of sexual abstinence on the part of husband and wife after the birth of a child. The length of this postpartum abstinence ranges from a few weeks to 2 or more years. In some cultures there is sexual abstinence during the period that the mother is breast feeding a child. In some societies there is sexual abstinence on certain ceremonial days. Because many other factors are almost always involved, it is difficult to ascertain the effect of sexual abstinence upon fertility in a population. However, it does reduce the total number of times that conception can take place and hence would tend to reduce fertility.

YOUNG PEOPLE AND THEIR FUTURES

Events that occur early in life may affect an individual's entire future. The young people of today and the generations to come will have to live with the choices made now.[16]

Jacqueline sits at her desk—seems to be dreaming but is really thinking. She is a very modern young girl, but she thinks of the past and the history she has been reading. For Jacqueline is living in the year 2020, and she has been reading about the 1970s and the quaint and seemingly unreal discussions that people had "way back then" about population and population problems.

"Way back then! Let's see, I am 15, and I was born in 2005. My mother was born in 1980 and my grandmother in 1960. My grandmother was in school when they were discussing the 'population problem'!"

"When my grandmother was in school, the world's population was only about 3.9 billion. The population of the United States was only about 210 million. My grandmother can remember those days! I must ask her what it was like.

"Here it says that in 1970 the world population had an annual growth rate of 2 percent, so that world population was expected to double in about 35 years. And the annual growth rate of the U.S. population was 1 percent, so U.S. population was expected to double in 70 years. It's 50 years since 1970! I wonder if the people back then really had an idea of what would happen?"

It is very difficult for young people, or anyone, to make deeply personal decisions on the basis of the possible effect of those decisions upon people who will live 50 years from now. The sexual drive is one of the strongest natural urges, and the longing to have children can be one of the most compelling of human desires. Actions in this area are not always the result of careful deliberation. The consequences, even for the individual, are not always considered, much less the consequences for future generations and the broader society. However, one of the important functions of education is to develop a concern for long-term consequences and some ability to consider them.

One of the actions of youth that has important consequences for the individual, for society, and for future generations is teen-age childbearing. In 1968 in the United States, one-quarter of 20-year-old girls had borne at least one baby in their teens.[17] In fact, one-sixth of all the births in that year were to girls in their teens, and one-third of those teen-age births were to girls 17 or younger. Almost 60 percent of the babies born to mothers 15–19 years old were conceived out of wedlock, and 27 percent were also born out of wedlock. Thus, teen-age childbearing is not a small-scale phenomenon — something that happens to the young people in someone else's classroom. On average, 1 out of 4 girls that a teacher teaches will have a baby while in her teens and 2 out of 5 babies borne by mothers 17 or younger will be born out of wedlock. Certainly, young people should become aware of some of the possible consequences of having a child in one's teens.

The drives and emotions associated with love are universal. Certainly, the literature of some Eastern cultures is at least as romantic as our own, but in some Eastern cultures there are practically no illegitimate births. There are practically no divorces either. The price paid in loss of freedom may be great, but the example set by other cultures indicates that it is possible to channel drives and emotions in different ways with different consequences. One of the strengths of a relatively free society is the opportunity it offers to consider other possibilities, rather than to proceed blindly down whatever genetic-cultural road the society has chanced upon.

"Love conquers all." "Much the greatest thing is love, love, love." In the American culture, who wants to be against love? Certainly, the word *love* connotes some of the strongest drives and most deeply felt emotions of humankind. It is perhaps the single most important theme in literature, and without it most music would have no meaning. Certainly it is unromantic to mention "consequences" and "love" in the same breath. But . . .

Some Consequences of Teen-age Childbearing One of the very disturbing consequences of teen-age childbearing, and particularly of bearing an illegitimate child, is that probably no other event in a girl's entire life will so limit the range of future possibilities and restrict the number of future choices that can be made.

> The problems posed by births to unmarried women are especially serious. The girl who has an illegitimate child at the age of 16 suddenly has 90 percent of her life's script written for her. She will probably drop out of school, even if someone else in her family helps to take care of the baby; she will probably not be able to find a steady job that pays enough to provide for herself and her child; she may feel impelled to marry someone she might not otherwise have chosen. Her life choices are few, and most of them are bad.[18]

Every girl deserves to be made aware of some of the possible consequences before beginning to act the script.

Very young mothers run greater risks of fetal mortality, premature birth, or death of the child during the first year than do mothers in their 20s. (Older mothers, over 30, also run some of these risks.) A child born of a mother aged 15 or younger is more than twice as likely to die before the end of the first year than a child born of a mother in her 20s. The differences are most pronounced in the prenatal period and during the first month of life, when the biological factors related to pregnancy are critical for survival.

The most critical risk involved in teen-age pregnancy is probably that of premature birth. Prematurity is usually judged by weight of the baby at birth. It has been estimated that a child that weighs less than 2,500 grams at birth is 17 times more likely to die before the end of the first year than a baby that weighs more than 2,500 grams. The risk of premature birth and of infant mortality is especially great when young mothers already have had one or more births.

Although the evidence is inconclusive, children of very young mothers, particularly second and third children, may run greater risks of being born with congenital defects and other handicaps. Some of these children, especially the second and third children who are born prematurely, may be born with considerably smaller heads. This is especially important because the head is the one part of a baby that grows very little after birth, and there may be a relationship between unusually small head size at birth and eventual intelligence of a child.

The problems associated with teen-age childbirth have been explained in terms of adolescent development. Adolescence, particularly early adolescence, is a period of very rapid growth and development, but the fetus within the young mother's body makes demands upon the same nutrients as does the mother's body. Sometimes they both suffer. Sometimes there is enough for the first child, but the demands of the mother's development shortchange a second or third child. Certainly, the case for carefully planned, adequate nutrition for the pregnant teen-ager is very strong. There are two bodies that are developing, and both must be nourished.

Childbearing is a momentous event. The teen-ager may be hardly more that a child herself, but she brings another child into this world. If the child was conceived out of wedlock — and 60 percent of babies born to teen-agers are — or born out of wedlock — and 40 percent of those born to mothers 17 or younger are — the social and psychological pressures upon the girl and those near her may be very great. Adequate nutrition, prenatal care, and care of the infant during the first year of life may suffer through ignorance, or lack of means, or be neglected in view of the overwhelming concerns that face the young mother and those who care for her.

Almost all teen-age mothers have their formal education disrupted. Some large school systems, such as that of New York City, provide special facilities and schools for pregnant girls and teen-age mothers. The mother, however, must find some way of having her child cared for while she is in school. On the other hand, many school systems still require a girl to leave school as soon as it is known that she is pregnant. This is the end of formal education for many girls. To what extent is their social and intellectual growth stunted? To what extent is their effectiveness as mothers limited?

If all teen-age births were prevented, U.S. population in 50 years would be about 15 percent smaller than is now projected. The reproduction rate would be reduced to about that required for a stabilized population. The postponement of the teen-age birth to later in life would probably also increase the spacing between subsequent children and reduce the period of time between the birth of the last "wanted" child and the time of menopause. Both of these factors would reduce the number of children that women on the average would have and would help to achieve a reproduction rate approximating that of a stabilized population.

Discussion: Family Size, Population Growth, and Quality of Life It is hazardous to make population projections and to forecast the possible effects of population changes. But it may be even more hazardous not to explore the collective effects of people's actions in the years ahead. What they do—or do not do—will influence the future.

Figure 4-1 may help students understand the consequences of various patterns of childbearing.

What might happen to the U.S. population if today's young people had in their lifetime

1. One child per family
2. Two children per family
3. Three children per family
4. Four children per family

How might the population projections in Figure 4-1 be affected by the following:

1. Increase or decrease in death rate
2. Increase or decrease in immigration
3. Economic depression
4. Global war

How might the following be affected by the various rates of childbearing shown in Figure 4-1.

1. Education
2. Health and health services
3. Material standard of living
4. Living space
5. Such dimensions of culture as theater, music, and literature

FAMILY PLANNING AND PUBLIC POLICIES[19]

Families can be greatly affected by a society's policies, or lack of them, with regard to population and family planning. Without adequate educational and information services, parents may not know how to plan the number and spacing of their children, and it will certainly be difficult for them to carry out their plans. If, instead of having laws that prohibit the sale and use of birth control devices, the society provides family planning clinics and makes birth control devices readily available at little or no cost, it will be much easier for a couple to have the kind of family they want. The society may permit or prohibit abortions; subsidize or penalize the having of children; support research into problems of human reproduction or ignore such problems; have carefully developed policies with regard to family planning and population or a laissez faire approach, with no clearly defined policy to guide or help anyone. Whatever the role and attitude of society, families will be affected in making their choices for the future and in their ability to carry out those choices.

But the broader society also has a stake in how families do or do not plan. An opportunity to be educated may be considered the birthright of every child, but education can be expensive, and it may be difficult to provide the teachers and schools needed to educate large numbers of the young. In many societies there is a deeply felt moral obligation to provide medical and health facilities, to provide everyone with at least the minimum food, shelter, and clothing needed for survival, and to make it possible for all to lead decent lives. However, if many families have many children, it becomes difficult for a society to ensure that everyone has the basics for life. In developing nations with limited resources, a rapidly growing population may tax those resources to the breaking point and frustrate the best laid plans of conscientious developers.

While societies at times have decided that it was important to increase the rate of population growth, today most societies are trying to achieve the opposite result. There is concern that populations may grow too rapidly — exacerbating already complex social and economic problems, and making it more difficult to achieve some kind of eventual control over population growth. One of the profound issues that we may face more starkly in the future is the extent of the stake that the broader society has in the number of children that families have and what policies and actions should be taken to implement societal population policies.

The issues and problems that involve possible conflict between public policies and family plans can be extremely complex. If there are to be public policies with regard to population and family planning, who is to decide these policies? The population experts? Religious leaders? Are these policies to be developed through public discussion and legislative action in the same ways that other policies are decided upon in democracies? Or, are they to "grow like Topsy" and develop in a laissez faire manner without deliberate action?

Then, there are problems of implementation. Logically organized, carefully developed, and eloquently enunciated plans and policies are of little avail if they are not actually implemented, and to be implemented, they must become a part of the lives of people. If all life is a play and we are the players, these policies must become acts in the play, and it may be that the players should help write the drama.

Education is critically important in the development and implementation of public population and family planning policies. The decisions and actions that lead to having or not having children are those of individuals — usually individuals living in families. Public policies reflect the concern of the broader society with the implications and impact of these decisions and actions. If public policies are to be developed through democratic discussion, debate, and legislative action, then it is essential that those who participate in this process know how to ask the right questions, realize what the issues are, and be aware of various possible courses of action. To ensure informed public action, then, it is important for future citizens to have had the experience of investigating some of the issues and problems associated with population and family planning.

Kinds of Public Population Policies
Among the different kinds of possible population policies are some that have been tried at various times in various societies:

To increase population: Some nations have had a need for a larger population to develop natural resources and to populate large, relatively uninhabited areas. Australia and some South American countries have in the past had a policy of encouraging immigration and have taken other steps to increase their populations. Some nations view an increase in population as contributing to military power and national prestige. Both Germany and Italy prior to and during World War II had a policy of encouraging fertility. Other nations, while having no official policy, have viewed growth, including population growth, as "natural" and highly desirable. Some critics have argued that the United States has followed an unofficial policy that encouraged population growth.

To reduce the size, or at least the rate of growth, of population: Few states and nations have had a policy of actually reducing the size of their populations, but many have had policies to reduce the rate of growth. States such as Colorado and Oregon have had policies to limit immigration and reduce the rate of population growth. Many nations support family planning and have taken actions to reduce birth rates in attempts to reduce population growth.

To achieve population stabilization: (A population can be considered stabilized when the number of births approximates the number of deaths, and population size remains relatively constant.) It has been suggested that it is to the advantage of present and future citizens to aim for population stabilization. For example, "Recognizing that our population cannot grow indefinitely, and appreciating the advantages of moving now toward the stabilization of population, the Commission [on Population Growth and the American Future] recommends that the nation welcome and plan for a stabilized population." There is obviously a limit to the size to which a population can grow, and it is wise and humane to stabilize population size before inhumane ecological factors begin to limit population growth.

No articulated comprehensive population policy: A majority of societies in the world have policies that affect population size and population growth but are not articulated as public population policy. Sometimes various policies are inconsistent and contradictory. The United States, for example, has restricted family planning counseling and services and has had tax laws that many have considered to be pronatalist. However, the United States Supreme Court has now interpreted the Constitution in such a way that the decision to have or not have an abortion in the first 3 months of pregnancy is left to the judgment of the woman and her attending physician, and this could be viewed as antinatalist.

Of course, it is not necessarily public policies that determine people's family plans. Often, these plans are made simply on the basis of what is considered best for the family. For example, birth rates in Western and Northern Europe began to decline in the last quarter of the nineteenth century and in Eastern and Southern Europe in the early years of the twentieth century. This was after decreased death rates and continued high fertility rates had led to a sharp increase in population. The decrease in birth rates was not due to official policy or any dictum from above. Instead, it was largely the result of many families deciding it was in their best interests to limit family size, and finding some way to do it.

The most effective public policies are those that are in harmony with the plans and desires of the majority of individuals and families, because there is then a better chance that the policies will be implemented. One of the strong arguments for broad participation in the development of public population policies is that there will then be general congruence between those policies and individuals and family goals. A major function of education is to help individuals to be informed about issues that will affect their lives and those of future generations and to participate intelligently in policy making.

An instructive example of an attempt to achieve congruence is relating a proposed policy of population stabilization to the prevention of unwanted births.

Many children are born whose birth is not planned and who are in a sense "unwanted." In the period 1960-1965, an estimated one-fifth of all births in the United States were unwanted.[20] The number of unwanted births for the period 1965-1970 is estimated to have been 36 percent less than for 1960-1965. This probably was a major factor in the decline of the population growth rate in the United States. Although many of the children may have come to be wanted after birth, they were not planned for and would not have been born if the parents had had complete control. A series of studies has shown that about 90 percent of American couples, regardless of income, class, or color, want four children or fewer.[21] In this respect, the goals of most American families and the proposed policy of population stabilization are congruent.

The elimination of unwanted births would be an important step toward population stabilization. The elimination of unwanted births in 1965 would have reduced the fertility of women who were near the end of their childbearing years from 3 to 2.5 births per woman.[22] Since a zero rate of population growth requires a cohort fertility of about 2.14 births per woman, the elimination of unwanted births would not be sufficient to achieve population stabilization, but it would be a major step toward it.

When a proposed public policy is in accord with family goals, there is a better chance for it to be enacted and a far better chance that, once enacted, it will be implemented. An official policy aiming at population stabilization can be implemented by providing the information, education, and services that make it possible for families to have only the children they want. Although there is a convergence of values with regard to family size among various groups in the American population, the poor and the poorly educated have more unwanted births than those with better incomes and education. Making information and birth control services available at little or no cost would make it more likely that even the poorest and the least educated would have only the children they want.

The Commission on Population Growth and the American Future, in recommending that the nation welcome and plan for a stabilized population, recognized that a population cannot grow indefinitely. There are limits to the natural resources that are available to support a population, limits to the space available for living. The social and economic costs of a very large population living under conditions of high density might become overwhelming. Although there are many factors that lead to pollution and environmental degradation, a growing population is certainly one of them. While population growth is not the source of all our social and environmental problems, solving those problems becomes more difficult as population grows.

Some societies have proposed and tried to implement policies that differ from or go beyond widely held family goals. Efforts have been made to motivate, propagandize, cajole, force, or make it easier for couples to have more children or fewer children—whichever was consistent with public policy. Such efforts may be partially successful, but they usually encounter serious difficulties and obstacles. Let us consider some of these approaches.

There is some evidence that the number of children people want is above the level necessary for population stabilization. Following are some proposals of additional steps toward population stabilization:[23]

Changing the concept of desirable family size: In a sense, this is an extension of family planning. Through population education, advertising, and counseling it may be possible to influence families about the number of children they want. Population education—

in which students explore the implications, for themselves and for society, of family size — may also lead to an eventual reduction in the size of family people want.

Changing the conditions of parenthood: In many societies, children, particularly male children, have been seen as a way of providing for the social and economic welfare of parents and for their security in old age. The development of effective social security systems reduces the need to have children for this reason. (The development of ways to determine the sex of the fetus early in pregnancy might be a corollary way of reducing the number of children couples have.)

One way of reducing the number of children is to raise the minimum age of marriage. In countries such as Ireland, the birth rate has been reduced by a voluntary postponement of marriage. However, it may be much more difficult to legislate a rise in the age at which marriage may take place. Unless there were almost universal agreement, how could such legislation be enforced? Would such legislation only lead to more children born out of wedlock?

It has been suggested that there might be two kinds of marriages: One type would enable couples to have the companionship benefits of marriage but would be childless and easily dissolved. The second type would lead to childbearing and child raising, and it should be stable, lasting, and difficult to dissolve. It has been argued that, with such arrangements possible, couples would be more likely to postpone childbearing until they were ready to assume the responsibilities associated with it.

Changing the conditions of childhood: In some societies children are an important source of labor or income for families. For example, in some agricultural systems (including U.S. farming communities in earlier years) children provide extra hands to help with the many tasks on the farms. School schedules may be planned so that children can be available for the extra work of the harvest seasons. Children have also been an important source of labor in factories and shops. Child labor laws that establish a minimum age for obtaining a work permit and that regulate the conditions under which children may work tend to reduce the economic benefits of having children and, hence, may be considered antinatalist policies.

Compulsory education also tends to remove children from the labor force. Moreover, the need for more extended and sophisticated education before young people can make their optimum contribution to the economy makes education more expensive than it was in the past. If the education has to be paid for by the parents or by the local community, the cost of such education becomes vividly apparent to parents and local taxpayers.

Economic incentives: Most tax systems involve some kind of policy with regard to children. In the United States there are tax exemptions for each dependent. The size of these exemptions is a factor that influences the extent to which children are an economic burden. It has been suggested that if exemptions were given only for the first two children in a family, this might become a factor in family planning. A tax on births after a family has had a certain number of children has also been suggested, as well as a reduction of maternity, medical, educational, and housing benefits after a certain number of births. One of the dangers associated with some such proposals is that often it is the children who will suffer the penalty, rather than the parents.

Incentives are sometimes given for participating in various kinds of birth control programs. Payments have been made to individuals who participate in sterilization programs and to couples who refrain from having children for specified periods of time.

Involuntary controls: Some of those who are deeply concerned with the population problem, and pessimistic about the success of voluntary programs, have suggested that sooner or later there may be a need for involuntary controls imposed by society. They propose *population control* — the attempt to control various characteristics of a population, particularly its size and growth rate. (Birth control, the attempt to control the number of children that are born, is only one aspect of population control.) All such proposals involve not only difficult scientific and technological problems but sensitive political actions and profound moral issues.[24]

It has been suggested that chemical contraception agents be developed that would control births in entire populations. Such agents could be administered through a community's drinking water. Then, everyone would be sterile. Or, viruses that might inhibit the development of fertilized eggs might be spread through the atmosphere. To have a child a positive decision would have to be made and an appropriate antidote to the sterilant or virus would have to be administered. No such birth control chemical or virus has been developed (1978), but one or both may become available in the future. However, the biological, political, and moral issues associated with the use of such an agent are awesome.

Compulsory sterilization programs have been suggested. For example, all men who have had three or more children might be compelled to undergo a vasectomy. The immensity of such a program would tax the surgical and health facilities of any country. The storm of protest and political upheaval that ensued when an attempt was made to implement compulsory controls in India is indicative of the difficulties such proposals are likely to encounter anywhere.

Discussion: Effects of Population Policies   One of the goals of education, and certainly of population education, is to increase sensitivity to how various proposed policies might affect various groups. Students might consider how each of the following groups might be affected by (as well as their own feelings about) each of the proposed population policies that follow:

Children	Middle-income people
Parents	Minority groups
Poor people	The broad society
Rich people	Future generations

1. Programs to persuade parents to have fewer children
2. Measures to provide women with more satisfactory opportunities outside the home for work and self-realization
3. Raising the minimum age of marriage
4. Instituting two kinds of marriage: childless and easily dissolved, childbearing and lasting
5. Separating child raising from marriage by developing means for unmarried persons who want children to adopt them
6. Raising the age at which children can be employed
7. Raising the age of compulsory education
8. Making abortion free and easily obtainable
9. Providing economic incentives for sterilization and birth control
10. Making available contraceptive capsules that can be removed following the decision to have a child
11. Infusing chemical contraceptive agents into drinking water, with antidotes to be given to a predetermined number of people to enable them to have children
12. Compulsory sterilization after having had three children

CONCLUSION

The family is probably the most basic and enduring of all social systems. To the best of our knowledge, families have existed as long as humankind has existed; although there have been and may yet be many changes in their nature, families are so basically human that the system will probably persist into the future. Apparently, most people find some of their deepest needs and desires best fulfilled in families. However, what happens in families will profoundly affect the broader society. If many families have many children, populations may grow to a size that cannot be supported. Conversely, what happens in the broader society will affect families. There may be a level of population size beyond which high-quality family life cannot be maintained. Thus, the goals and interests of families and the goals and interests of the broader society are ultimately congruent, but they will only be perceived as congruent when there is deliberate consideration of goals. Through population education young people can consider life in families, become aware of relationships between families and the broader society, and prepare themselves for responsible participation in both family and society.

FOOTNOTES

1. Kingsley Davis has demonstrated that, in the United States, "The net effect of social change seems to have been, if anything, to strengthen family motivation." See his "American Family in Relation to Demographic Change" in *Demographic and Social Aspects of Population Growth,* ed. Charles F. Westoff and Robert Parke, Jr. (Washington, D.C.: U.S. Government Printing Office, 1972), pp. 237–265.
2. This discussion is based on projections by Tomas Frejka, *Future of Population Growth* (New York: Wiley, 1973), p. 220.
3. This short discussion of human fertility among the Hutterites is based upon Joseph W. Eaton and Albert J. Mayer, *Man's Capacity to Reproduce: The Demography of a Unique Population* (Glencoe, Ill.: Free Press, 1954).
4. There are many excellent discussions of reproduction, fetal development, and birth control. One of the best is Lawrence D. Crawley, James L. Malfetti, Ernest I. Stewart, and Nini Van Dias, *Reproduction, Sex, and Preparation for Marriage* (Englewood Cliffs, N.J.: Prentice-Hall, 1973).
5. I am indebted to my former colleague Lucille Spence for help in developing the concept of "critical stages." For further elaboration see her "Critical Stages in Reproduction," mimeographed. (New York: Teachers College Population Instructional Materials Project, 1966).
6. One of the best discussions of such questions and issues is in Daniel Callahan, *Abortion: Law, Choice, and Morality* (New York: Macmillan, 1970).
7. For a discussion of some directions of research into more effective birth control practices, see Sheldon J. Segal and Olivia Schieffelin Nordberg, "Fertility Regu-

lation Technology: Status and Prospects," *Population Bulletin* 31, no. 6 (Washington, D.C.: Population Reference Bureau, 1977).

8. For a discussion of changes in society that are conducive to early marriage, see Davis. *op. cit.*, pp. 242–48.

9. Ibid, p. 248.

10. Jane Menken, "The Health and Social Consequences of Teenage Childbearing," *Family Planning Perspectives* 4, no. 3 (July 1972): 52.

11. For a summary of the health consequences of birth interval, see Joe D. Wray, "Population Pressure on Families: Family Size and Child Spacing," in *Rapid Population Growth,* Study Committee of the National Academy of Sciences (Baltimore: Johns Hopkins Press, 1971), pp. 434–45.

12. L. C. Coombs and R. Freedman, "Pre-marital Pregnancy, Childspacing, and Later Economic Achievement," *Population Studies* 24, no. 3 (1970): 392.

13. For a discussion of social factors that can influence human fertility, see Burton Benedict, "Social Regulation of Fertility," in *The Structure of Human Population,* ed. C. A. Harrison and A. J. Boyce (Oxford: Clarendon Press, 1972), pp. 73–89.

14. There is a voluminous literature on the changing normative roles of women. For a short, succinct discussion of the relationship between these roles and population, see Commission on Population Growth and the American Future, *Population and the American Future* (New York: New American Library, 1972), pp. 150–56.

15. For a further discussion of such factors, see Benedict, *op. cit.*

16. For a further discussion of some of the issues raised in this section, see Jane A. Menken, "Teenage Childbearing: Its Medical Aspects and Implications for the United States Population," in *Demographic and Social Aspects of Population Growth,* ed. Charles F. Westoff and Robert Parke, Jr. (Washington, D.C.: U.S. Government Printing Office, 1972), pp. 331–53.

17. The data for teen-age childbearing are adapted from Menken, *op. cit.*, pp. 45–53.

18. Arthur Campbell, "The Role of Family Planning in the Reduction of Poverty," *Journal of Marriage and the Family* 30, no. 236 (May 1968): 238.

19. Three helpful discussions of family planning and public policies are: "Population and Public Policy," in *Population and the American Future,* Commission on Population Growth and the American Future (New York: New American Library, 1972), Chapter 8; "Population Policy," in *Rapid Population Growth,* Study Committee of the National Academy of Sciences (Baltimore: Johns Hopkins Press, 1971), Chapter 6; and Bernard Berelson, "Beyond Family Planning," *Studies in Family Planning,* no. 38 (February 1969).

20. Larry Bumpass and Charles F. Westoff, "The 'Perfect Contraceptive' Population," *Science* 169, (18 September 1970): 1179.

21. Frederick S. Jaffe, "Toward the Reduction of Unwanted Pregnancy," *Science.* 174, (8 October 1971): 121.

22. Bumpass and Westoff, *op. cit.*, p. 1180.

23. These proposals have been adapted from Berelson, *op. cit.*, and from *Rapid Population Growth, op. cit.*, pp. 83–89.

24. For a discussion of some of the moral issues, see Chapter 8 of this book and Arthur J. Dyck, "Population Policies and Ethical Acceptability," in *The American Population Debate,* ed. Daniel Callahan (Garden City, N.Y.: Doubleday, 1971) pp. 351–77.

SELECTED REFERENCES

Baldwin, Wendy H. "Adolescent Pregnancy and Childbearing—Growing Concerns for Americans." *Population Bulletin* 31, no. 2. Washington, D.C.: Population Reference Bureau, 1976. 36 pp.
An extended discussion of the extent and ramifications of pregnancy and childbearing among American teen-agers.

Behrman, S. J.; Corso, Leslie Jr.; and Freedman, Ronald, eds. *Fertility and Family Planning: A World View*. Ann Arbor: University of Michigan Press, 1969. 503 pp.
A collection of technical papers dealing with fertility trends, biological aspects of fertility control, and public policy.

Commission on Population Growth and the American Future. *Population and the American Future*. New York: New American Library, 1972. 362 pp.
The report of a commission established by the President and the Congress of the United States to examine the growth of population and its impact upon the American future. A key recommendation is that a national policy and voluntary program aim to reduce unwanted fertility, improve the outcome of pregnancy, and improve the health of children.

Crawley, Lawrence O.; Malfetti, James L.; Steward, Ernest I. Jr.; and Vas Dias, Nini. *Reproduction, Sex, and Preparation for Marriage*. Englewood Cliffs, N.J.: Prentice-Hall, 1973. 254 pp.
An excellent discussion of human reproduction, sex, and family planning.

Espenshade, Thomas J. "The Value and Cost of Children." *Population Bulletin* 32, no. 1. Washington, D.C.: Population Reference Bureau, 1977. 48 pp.
A discussion of the value and the cost of children in developed and less developed countries.

Family Planning Perspectives. New York: Center for Family Planning, Program Development.
A quarterly published by Planned Parenthood Federation of America, Inc., that usually contains a variety of articles related to family planning.

Study Committee of the National Academy of Sciences. *Rapid Population Growth*. Baltimore: Johns Hopkins Press, 1971. 696 pp.
The research papers are of special value. Especially appropriate for further study of this topic are "Population Pressure on Families: Family Size and Child Spacing" and "Population Policies and Ethical Acceptability."

Westoff, Charles F., and Parke, Robert, Jr., eds. *Demographic and Social Aspects of Population Growth*. Washington, D.C.: U.S. Government Printing Office, 1972. 674 pp.
A collection of research reports prepared for the Commission on Population Growth and the American Future. Part III, "Family and Women," and Part IV, "Unwanted Fertility," discuss in detail many of the topics raised in this chapter.

Westoff, Leslie Aldridge, and Westoff, Charles F. *From Now to Zero*. Boston: Little, Brown, 1971. 358 pp.
Deals with such subjects as reproduction, contraception, the pill, abortion, fertility trends and differences, and zero population growth. The 1965 National Fertility Study, which one of the authors helped direct, is the most important source of data.

CHAPTER 5

Population and Space to Live

I just love the hustle, bustle, and excitement of the city. Most of all I love all the people.

A lady emerging, with thousands of others, from a theater on Broadway

It's hard to keep an eye on your children from the fifteenth floor.

A mother in St. Louis

WHAT IS "CROWDING"? How may crowding affect people's lives? What relationship is there between population density and crowding? How are population size and population density related? How may they affect the lives of people? Do population size and population density affect human fertility? If so, how? What relationships are there between population density and such social pathologies as crime and juvenile delinquency?

What is open space? What is its importance? What factors affect people's choices of where to live?

The consideration of population and space to live embraces many of the processes involved in studying social phenomena, and it is well to bring these processes to the level of cognition. It may lead not only to a better understanding of the particular relationships between population and space but to a more general understanding of how complex problems can be approached, studied, discussed — and possibly resolved.

Multiple causation is an especially important feature of many of the phenomena and problems associated with space to live. Intuitively, it might be generally believed that crowded conditions are linked to a social pathology such as mental illness. After all, isn't there usually a great deal of mental illness in an area where many people are crowded together? But the link may be spurious. There may be more mental illness simply because there are more people; the number of mentally ill may be no more than a function of the number of people in the area. The rates may be proportionately just as high in areas where there are fewer people. Even if the rates are higher, it may be because in areas where there are many people there are also more clinics and trained personnel to detect mental illness and better institutional resources for treatment. Even if this factor is controlled for, there are a number of other factors that may be associated with a high rate of mental illness, such as the age structure of the population, the nature of people's employment or unemployment, divorce rates, and the availability of religious and other social institutions. All of these may be causative factors, and it is often difficult, and perhaps unwise, to try to isolate one factor to the exclusion of others.

WHAT IS CROWDING?

The way we approach and deal with problems can be affected by the way we define terms.[1] Many terms related to population can be defined in several ways. Slight nuances in definition can be important because they illuminate differences in ideas. "Crowding" can mean that there are many individuals in a small area. However, "crowding" can also mean a messy, disorganized condition with very little open space available. These two definitions are different, and in some analyses the different definitions embody important differences in meaning. Differences in definition tend to make communication and teaching more difficult.

Crowding is sometimes defined in psychological terms; Daniel Boone is supposed to have felt crowded if he could see the smoke from a neighbor's chimney. It can also be defined in terms of services; a city may be considered crowded if its transportation system cannot handle the movement of people and freight, or its sanitation services cannot cope with the volume of sewage or garbage. However, in population studies the term *crowding* is usually defined in terms of *population density,* that is, the number of people per unit of area:

$$\text{population density} = \frac{\text{number of people}}{\text{unit of area}}$$

The area may be stated in terms of a square mile, square kilometer, hectare, or acre. As an example, in 1970 the state of New Jersey had a population density of 953 persons per square mile. The more usual scientific definition of density is mass per unit of volume. It has been argued that in cities where there are very tall buildings and where even "air rights" over roads and railroads are valuable, volume would be the appropriate denominator for the calculation of population density. However, almost everyone who has studied and written about population density has defined it in terms of area.

The way we define a term can affect the way we see a problem. With too narrow a definition, we may fail to consider some critical factors, but too broad a definition may obscure a real issue and be of little value in dealing with critical problems. Terms related to population can be defined in differing ways.

What is the area of a unit such as New York City? Is it the geographical area encompassed by the city? If so, the population density of some parts of Manhattan is about 75,000 people per square mile. (The population changes during the course of the day. On a working day there are parts of Manhattan that may have a population density of more than 100,000 people per square mile.) However, the inhabitants of New York City get their water from the Catskill mountains, their food from such places as California, Iowa, Florida, and Guatemala, their oil from Texas and Venezuela, their automobiles from Detroit, and some of their electronics hardware from Japan. Since the people who live in New York City probably depend to some extent upon much of the world for what they need and use, should that be the area considered in calculating the city's population density?

If the surface of the earth is the appropriate area, then, of course, to the people who live in New York City, and in many other communities, must be added all the other people on Planet Earth, and the population density of the world becomes about 70 persons per square mile. (The area of Antarctica, where practically no one lives is excluded from this calculation.) But world population density is of little relevance to the city planner concerned that there be enough housing units for families in his or her city, or for the child living in a fourth-floor walk-up whose only playground is a narrow street filled with double-parked cars.

What people should be included when population density is being calculated? Most cities have many more people in the daytime than at night. Many people commute into a city in the morning, use many of its facilities during the day, and return to their homes in the suburbs in the evening. Should the population density of a community be calculated in terms of the daytime or nighttime population? Similarly, the population of many communities differs seasonally; a resort town may have ten times as many people in the summer as in the winter.

For some purposes, it is useful to bring other factors into the consideration of population density. For example, 50,000 people can sit comfortably around a football field without any feeling of "interpersonal press." But if 50,000 people were in a park each trying to do her or his own thing—from flying a kite or playing basketball to playing chess or reading a newspaper—there would be considerable "interpersonal press." A large number of people may live comfortably and with considerable living space in a high-rise apartment building covering a given ground area. A much smaller number of people might feel quite crowded in a smaller structure covering the same ground area.

The following are factors sometimes considered in dealing with population density:

Number of persons per room
Number of rooms per housing unit
Number of housing units per structure
Number of residential structures per unit area

Other factors can also be considered, such as the number of persons per acre of park or playground space, the number of persons per school or library, and the number of persons per hospital or clinic. Population density, population size, and population movement are some of the factors to be considered in planning transportation systems, water supply systems, sewage and garbage disposal, and electrical generation and distribution systems. It may be of interest to have students explore the extent to which population density is a factor to be considered when communities are planning to meet their needs and desires.

Exercise: Population Density of Your Community A useful exercise is to have students inquire into the population density of their community. How does it vary during the course of the day? With the seasons?

The population of a community may be obtained from such sources as the U.S. Census Bureau, almanacs and guidebooks, and the local Chamber of Commerce. The area covered by the community may be obtained from local planning boards or governmental agencies. The areas of states and nations are given in atlases. When the population and area have been determined, divide the area into the population to find the population density.

Population densities may vary during the course of the day and with the seasons. Students should try to obtain estimates of the daytime and nighttime populations of their community and the winter and summer populations, and then calculate the population density in each case. How much variation is there? Which population density should one use in determining the need for housing? Parks and recreational facilities? Sewage disposal facilities? Fire and police protection? Schools? Transportation systems? Electrical generating systems?

POPULATION DENSITY VERSUS POPULATION SIZE

Framing the question is an important aspect of problem solving. Sometimes, the questions we ask are of crucial importance. A beclouded issue or a knotty problem may be made clearer and a way opened to solution by changing the nature of the question. For example, for many years investigators asked, "Which is the most effective approach to teaching—lecture-demonstration or laboratory experience?" and the results of their investigations were inconclusive. But when the nature of the question was changed to, "Under what conditions and for what purposes are lecture-demonstration and laboratory experience effective approaches to teaching?" a great deal was learned about both approaches.

Similarly, in the study of population it is important to consider the nature of the questions asked. Many questions raised about the effects of human population density have been suggested by studies of the effects of various levels of population density on other animals.

Although the effects seem to be different for different species, the results of high population density on many animals are striking and thought provoking. However, in studies of human populations and their environments, the total size of the population may in many cases be more critical than the population density. In other cases both population density and population size may be significant factors.

Exercise: Density or Size—Which Is More Important? For this discussion, let us accept the definition of *population density* as the number of individuals per unit of area, and of *population size* as the total number of individuals living in an area.

Listed below are some of the factors that are important to many communities. Have students examine the evidence, discuss other elements that should be considered, and try to determine in each case whether population density, population size, or a combination of the two should be considered the most important influence. (There is often a tendency to "play it safe" and say it is a combination of the two. But we have a less definitive understanding with this finding than when a clear relationship is established between either population density or population size and the factor being considered.)

Transportation: Consider both public and private transportation. Is a certain population size/density needed in order to have a public bus or subway system? How is private automobile transportation affected by population size and density? How is parking affected? If the population size, density, or overall area of your community has increased (or decreased) in the last few decades, how has transportation been affected? What plans are needed for improving transportation to serve the changing population? In some parts of the world, the bicycle is an important mode of transportation. Could this be a major means of transportation in your community? What would be the effects of the widespread adoption of such a mode of transportation?

Pollution: Consider such forms of pollution as air, water, solid waste, and noise. Which are affected primarily by population density, which by population size? If possible, try to compare the pollution, in its various forms, in very large communities, in very densely populated communities, and in very sparsely populated communities. What are some of the population factors that seem to affect the amount of pollution in an area? How do different forms of pollution affect people under various conditions of population size and density?

Cultural resources: Consider such cultural resources as museums, theaters, orchestras, botanical and zoological gardens, colleges and universities, and football, basketball and baseball teams. Is there a certain minimum population density needed to support these activities? Is there a minimum population size needed?

Education: How is the quality of education affected by population size? By population density? It may be desirable to consider how various aspects of the education available to students are affected by population density and population size. In rural areas, the sometimes controversial issue of school consolidation may be related to population factors. In urban and

Table 5-1
Aspects of School Life Affected by Population Density and/or Size

Aspect of School Life	Population density	Population size	Population density and size	Ways that effects can be utilized or overcome
Quality of classroom discussion				
Quality of teachers and teaching				
Opportunities to meet a variety of people and make friends				
Opportunity to take part in school gov. and interscholastic activities				
Use of libraries and other school resources				
Opportunities for phys. ed. and recreation				
Other				

suburban areas, the sometimes controversial issue of school busing may be linked to population factors.

Hospitals and health services: Is a certain level of population size/density required to support certain kinds of health facilities and services, such as a high degree of specialization by physicians and surgeons, laboratory facilities, and research and development activities? Are certain sizes or densities in any way detrimental?

When working with young people, it is desirable to translate large and abstract problems into terms that are immediate and familiar. Thus, the problems we have been discussing might be viewed in terms of their own school, their own classroom.

Exercise: Effects of Population Density and Population Size The effects of population density and population size are not always on someone else some place else; they may affect students as they live and learn.

The density and size of the population might affect such aspects of school life as the following: quality of classroom discussion, quality of teachers and teaching, opportunities to meet a variety of people and form varied friendships, opportunities to take part in such school activities as school government and interscholastic activities, use of libraries and other school resources, discipline problems, and opportunities for physical education and recreation. For each of the aspects of school life listed in Table 5-1, have students check which of the two population factors would affect it, note how it would be affected, and suggest ways that these effects of population might be utilized or overcome.

POPULATION DENSITY AND SOCIAL STRESS

Effects of Population Density on Animal Populations

Among such animals as mice and rats, which apparently interact with one another socially, social disturbance can be a population regulating factor. These social disturbances may take the form of fighting or, more often, threats to fight and competition to establish dominance. The following is a description of a famous experiment showing how social pressures build up.[2] (The study has been replicated several times with similar results.)

To study the effects of high population density, the behavior of rats was observed when the population was artificially stabilized at twice the level normal for the given space. Four interconnecting pens were provided, somewhat as in Figure 5-1.

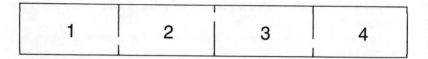

Figure 5-1 Diagram of interconnecting rat pens. (From John B. Calhoun, "Population Density and Social Pathology," Scientific American 206 [February 1962], pp. 139–48.)

Note that there is no interconnection between pens 1 and 4. The only way to get to pens 1 and 4 is from pens 2 and 3. In each of the pens, water, food, burrows, and paper for nesting were provided.

Thirty-two rats were introduced into this cage complex of four pens. After 12 months there were 80 adults. Thereafter, infants that survived birth and weaning were removed, to maintain a steady, high-density population.

The population within the cage complex distributed itself unevenly. Soon after the male rats reached maturity (after about 6 months), fighting between males took place to establish dominance. Dominant males took over control in pens 1 and 4. They maintained dominance by keeping other males out. Small sleeping groups, usually composed of 8 adults, established themselves in the end pens. There were seldom more than 2 males in these groups. The sleeping groups in the middle pens were larger, and there were many more males than females. The female population was about evenly distributed among the four pens. The male population was overwhelmingly concentrated in the middle pens.

A *behavioral sink* is a situation in which all forms of pathology that can be found within a group are aggravated. Such a behavioral sink developed in the middle pens. Females eventually stopped building nests out of the strips of paper provided; females in pens 1 and 4 continued to build nests in the burrows. These nests provide essential protection and warmth to litters of young.

The rats tended to eat at the hoppers where other rats ate at and to avoid those at which there were no other rats. After 16 months, over half the rats were sleeping as well as eating in the pens where the favored food hoppers were. Even rats sleeping in the end pens would go to eat from a hopper in a middle pen several times a day. This meant that almost every rat made some kind of adjustment to almost every other rat in the population at least once a day.

In the middle pens, when a female came into heat, she would be pursued relentlessly by packs of males. Although she might try to burrow, there was no escape. Nearly half these females died of disorders during pregnancy or while giving birth. However, one-fourth of the females in the outer pens, who were sheltered from these stresses, also died.

Among the males, the dominant individuals usually behaved in ways that are characteristic of male rats, although they had more of a tendency to bite the tails of other rats than is normal. However, among the males lower down on the social scale some were apparently quite sexually undiscriminating. They made sexual advances to other males, juveniles, and females not in heat. Another group of males apparently resigned completely from the struggle for dominance; they ignored rats of both sexes, including females in heat, and moved through the pens ignoring others and being ignored. A third group of male rats, called "probers," were very active. They always lived in the middle pens. They took no part in the status struggles but made sexual advances to both males and females and pursued females in heat relentlessly, abandoning the courtship rituals that are common among rats. The "probers" followed females into their burrows. If they found dead young, they devoured them. Eventually, they were among the rats that became cannibalistic.

The pregnancy rates in the four pens were about the same. In the end pens (1 and 4) the mortality rates among infants and females were low. The mothers built nests and, if danger threatened, the mother carried the young to a safer place, allowing nothing to distract her. Half the infants in these pens survived. In the middle pens (2 and 3) a smaller percentage of the pregnancies resulted in live births. The mothers ceased to build nests, nor did they carry their young to safer places. The young were abandoned or seldom nursed; 96 percent died before the time of weaning. The dead young were eaten by adults. However, during the time of the experiment enough young survived to increase the population.

At the end of the experiment the four healthiest males and the four healthiest females were kept. They were in their reproductive prime. However, they produced fewer litters than might have been expected, and none of the offspring survived to maturity. "The evidence indicates . . . that in time failures of reproductive function would have caused the colonies to die out."

What are the physiological mechanisms whereby individual animals and the population are affected by social disturbance? In the physiological studies made of mice and rats who have lived under high population pressure, the animals apparently were affected by social disturbances.[3] As might be expected, enlargements of the outer parts of the adrenal glands — the glands probably involved in fear and aggression — were found. Body growth was suppressed, and sexual maturation delayed or totally inhibited. Under very dense conditions, no females reached sexual maturity. The weight of sex organs declined, fewer eggs were fertilized, and more fetuses died within the body of the female. Among the major factors affecting population size apparently were the failure of the young to mature and the decline in the mature animals' ability to reproduce.

Does social stress under high population density conditions affect human population growth and size? We really do not have very good answers to this question.[4] There is evidence to indicate that family size tends to be smaller in urban conditions and in some urban areas the age at which couples have their first child may be later than in rural areas. There is some evidence to indicate that human fertility is inversely related to the size of the urban area.[5]

But man is a very adaptable animal, and he can apparently learn to live under rather high population density. It may be a sudden change in condition, such as a rapid increase in population density or the immigration of strangers, that results in social stress. (The same situation holds for rats). Man has apparently been able to live under conditions of high population density in Holland, Belgium, and Hong Kong without a buildup of social stresses. Perhaps the populations have learned over time to make the social adjustments necessary to live under these high-density conditions. But in cities like New York — which have experienced rapid growth, had a succession of influxes of new peoples, and had to struggle with "the problem of the stranger" without periods of stability when social adjustments can be made to ameliorate social tensions — the stresses associated with high population do tend to develop. "Men are not rats, yet the most unpleasant thing about overcrowded rats is that they behave so much like human beings in some crowded communities."[6]

How Relevant to Man Are Animal Population Studies?
One of the questions raised in many studies of other organisms is, How relevant is that study to the human problem being investigated? Population density studies provide an opportunity for stu-

dents to gain experience in dealing with the important question of *relevance*.

Following are some of the reasons that support the relevance to human population of studies of the effects of population density on other animals:

1. Humans are a part of the universe, and it is useful to consider that general physical, biological, and social principles that hold for other populations also hold for them. Much of the remarkable success in such fields as medicine, nutrition, physiology, anatomy, biology, and psychology is, at least in part, due to the application of this "principle of universality."
2. With animals we can carry out studies — such as testing the effects of very high population density — that we would hesitate to do with humans. From such studies we may obtain some insights into what might happen to humans under similar conditions.
3. By means of animal studies we can see the effects of certain conditions, such as high population density, over many generations. To do similar studies with humans would take hundreds of years.
4. Studies of animal populations can be suggestive of factors to investigate in human populations. For example, studies of the effects of high population density on animals suggest that we should, in particular, study the effects of high human population density upon children and young people.

Following are some of the reasons for questioning the relevance of studies of the effects of population density on other animals:

1. Humans are more intelligent than other animals. They have developed more sophisticated ways of solving problems. These ways of dealing with problems may be so different from those of other organisms that the results of studies of other animals are really not relevant to humans.
2. Humans have culture. They can learn and transmit what they learn from one generation to the next. For example, they have learned how to plan for family size and are able to transmit this knowledge to future generations.
3. Humans are very adaptable and have greater control over their environment than any other animal. For example, they are one of the few animals who have adapted to practically every type of environment to be found on earth.

4. To learn about humans and how they are affected by different conditions, it is preferable to study them directly. "The proper study of mankind is man."

Discussion: Relevance of Animal Population Studies Have students consider and discuss each of the reasons given for supporting or questioning the relevance of animal population studies to the population problems of humans. Then let the students themselves examine the various findings from animal studies, which are summarized in the list that follows,[7] and decide to what extent they consider them relevant to human populations.

1. Among some animals there is a breakdown of normal behavior patterns under high population density conditions. Some males tend to become more aggressive. There is an increase in fighting, indiscriminate sexual behavior, attacks on pregnant females, and invasion of nests. There is a lack of adequate nest building, a sharp rise in unsuccessful pregnancies and a breakdown in care of the newborn among females. There is the development of a "behavioral sink."
2. Under population pressure, different individuals in the population are affected in different ways. Some tend to withdraw, others huddle together, a few dominate. Apparently, it is those who happen to be born when the population density is at its lowest who tend to dominate.
3. High population density results in a high infant mortality.
4. High population density leads to a decrease in litter size and fertility.
5. In the struggle for food and the other necessities of life, young animals tend to suffer most.
6. Apparently there is a decrease in emotionality as population density increases.
7. Under conditions of high population density, there appear to be such physiological effects as enlargement of adrenal glands in some animals and a decrease in the weight of testes and seminal vesicles in males.

Effects of Population Density on Human Populations

Theory may be helpful in explaining discrepant observations. There is a discrepancy between observations of the effects of population density on fertility in various animal populations and in humans. However, this is a situation in which students can examine some of the relevant studies and suggest theoretical explanations that could account for the discrepant observations.

A study of possible relationships for human populations between population density and pathology was carried out in Chicago using data for the year 1960.[8] A definition of population density involving the following components of density was used: number of persons per room, number of rooms per housing unit, number of housing units per structure, and number of residential structures per acre.

Seventy-five community areas in Chicago were studied. Their populations and land areas were used to calculate population densities. Rates of fertility, mortality, public assistance, juvenile delinquency, and admission to mental hospitals were obtained for each of the areas. An attempt was made to find out if there were relationships between population density and these rates. Since there are reasons for believing that social class and ethnicity may be variables that are associated with population density, an attempt was made to control for these factors.

In this study it was found that *the greater the population density, the greater the fertility.* As with mortality rate, public assistance rate, and juvenile delinquency rate, it was found that the *number of persons per room* was the most important determining component of density. (For mental illness, rooms per housing unit was the most important component.)

Discussion: Explaining Results That Seem Contradictory In studies of animal populations, such as the one on rat populations that has been described, an increase in population density seems to lead to a decline in fertility. But in the study of a human population in Chicago, higher levels of population density seem to lead to an increase in human fertility. What may account for these differences?

Several explanations have been suggested. Students might think about them and decide which seem to be the most plausible.

1. There is a very important physiological difference between humans and the other animals that have been studied. The human female can conceive throughout the year; in most other populations, the female can conceive only for a very specific and limited period of time. Among animals, crowding often leads to increased sexual activity, but, since the female cannot conceive most of the time and in fact may be harmed by this activity, this hypersexuality will not lead to greater fertility. Among humans, increased sexual activity can lead to greater fertility.
2. It may be that factors that limit fertility among many animals, such as food

supply and shelter, are not operative with humans under the conditions of population density that have been studied.

3. Perhaps severe crowding makes it difficult for individuals to step back and gain a perspective on life, plan for the future, and carry through on those plans. For example, under overcrowded conditions it may be very difficult to carry out family planning.

What are the implications for human population growth of this increased fertility under conditions of high population density? There are no studies that have explored this potentially critical question. Students might wish to speculate.

It is often difficult to assess various factors that may be insepara-ble. The National Commission on the Causes and Prevention of Violence stated that violent crime is primarily a phenomenon of large cities. The National Advisory Commission on Civil Disorders, discussing conditions of life in the racial ghetto, noted that crime rates in cities over 1 million were more than double the national average. Such observations would lead one to suspect that there is some relationship between population density and crime rates. But the attempt to find out whether there is such a relationship can illuminate the difficulty of ascertaining the influence of any one factor—*the problem of multiple causation.*

Although there seems to be no doubt that areas of high population density tend to be areas of high crime and juvenile delinquency, the question remains: Are these high rates due to the high population density or to other factors that also seem to be often associated with these pathologies? Hoch, for example, on the basis of crime studies in 56 cities with populations over 250,000 and 99 California cities of different population sizes, stated:

> It can be concluded that population size and density are associated with increasing levels of crime even after accounting for other explanatory variables. However, the degree of association is greatly overstated when the effect of the other explanatories is neglected.[9]

Low educational and economic levels, racial and ethnic segregation, and lack of a sense of community among recent migrants into central cities may be other factors associated with urban crime and juvenile delinquency.

Discussion: What Factors Might Lead to Crime and Juvenile Delin-quency? Have students list the various conditions in their community that might lead to crime and juvenile delinquency. How many of these conditions would be aggravated by many people living in a small area? What are some things that might be done about these conditions in the community?

Early in the study of this section you may wish to have students try to think through how they could find out which of the conditions they have listed actually contribute to crime and juvenile delinquency. Even more difficult, they might try to determine the relative importance of the factors that may lead to juvenile delinquency. Or are these factors so interconnected that it is useless to try to separate them?

There are statistical procedures (such as multiple-partial correlations) that can be used to try to ascertain the influence of various variables upon the factor being studied. In a study of relationships between population density and five different social pathologies, an attempt was made to find the appropriate weight to give measures of social class and ethnicity.[10] A rather complicated interrelationship was found. Social class and ethnicity appeared to affect the pathologies through population density. Density seemed to be an "intervening" variable somewhat as in the diagram:

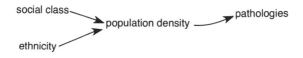

An additional interpretation is that such factors as social class and ethnicity are factors associated with population density and hence are factors associated with such pathologies as juvenile delinquency.

In this study by Galle and his associates, four components of population density were defined: number of persons per room, number of rooms per housing unit, number of housing units per structure, and number of residential structures per acre. Population density was found to be related to juvenile delinquency and to each of the other pathologies. Of the four components of population density, number of persons per room had the highest correlation with juvenile delinquency. However, it is also interesting to note that housing units per structure had more effect on juvenile delinquency than on any of the other pathologies.

In discussing their results, Galle and his associates suggest that, "In an overcrowded environment parents are likely to be irritable, weary, harassed, inefficient. Children, in turn, are apt to find the home a relatively unattractive place full of constant noise and irritation, with no privacy, no place to study, and so on."[11] They suggest that the factor of a large number of housing units per structure may give the young people who live there a sense of autonomy, and a high degree of autonomy seems to be an important factor in the development of delinquent gangs.

Similar attempts have been made to study the impact of population density upon crime, juvenile delinquency, and other measures of health and social disorganization in Honolulu.[12] As in some other studies, the meanings of population density and overcrowding were defined in terms of persons per room, population per residential area, household with four or more members, married couples without own households, and dwelling units in structures. The census tracts in the Honolulu Standard Metropolitan Statistical Area (SMSA) were categorized on the basis of each of the measures of density and overcrowding. The studies were made with data centering on 1950.

In Honolulu a close association was found between population density and juvenile delinquency. Of the various measures of density, population per residential acre and persons per room were the two measures most consistently related to juvenile delinquency and adult crime. Schmitt concludes:

> There is a close association between population density and juvenile delinquency and adult crime in Honolulu. Disproportionate numbers of juvenile offenders and prison inmates come from neighborhoods characterized by overcrowding of dwellings, multiunit construction, doubling up of families, large households, and high ratios of population to residential land.[13]

However, other factors, such as lack of education and low income, are also suspected of being associated with juvenile delinquency and adult crime. In a second study, Schmitt tried to control for the education factor in terms of the percentage of the population 25 years of age or more with 12 years or more of schooling, and for income in terms of the percentage of families and unrelated individuals with annual incomes of $3,000 or more. When education and income were thus controlled for, population per residential acre continued to have a close association with juvenile delinquency and crime. However, when education, income, and all other density variables were controlled for, the persons per room factor continued to have fairly high relationships with juvenile delinquency and crime, although lower correlations were found between the persons per room factor and other elements of health and social disorganization.

To illustrate how difficult it is to separate the influence of individual factors when each of the factors probably has some influence, Jonathan L. Freedman, in his comprehensive survey of most of the studies, criticizes the way that Schmitt controlled for both education and income.[14] Freedman suggests that to use the percentage of persons 25 years or older with 12 or more years of schooling simply divides the population into the well educated and less well educated. This gives no indication of how many had very little schooling. Similarly, to use $3,000 annual income as a dividing line does not provide sufficient distinction among incomes. (It should be noted that $3,000 in 1950 would be the equivalent of at least twice as large an income today.)

Reviewing previous research in an article reporting his own study, Freedman stated, "There is little doubt that crime, mental illness, suicide, and even some physical illnesses occur more in areas of high than low population density.[15] However, he continued to stress the difficulty of interpreting findings, and this was substantiated by his study carried out in New York City. In this study it was found that income and ethnic factors had higher correlations with juvenile delinquency and mental illness than did population density. However, Freedman again cautioned that correlational studies, "do not ordinarily allow one to draw definitive conclusions about causation."[16] He recommended that everyone try to keep an open mind about population density until more results are available.

Another possible way to try to control for various factors would be to compare communities that are alike in every respect except in population density. Pressman and Carol[17] compared metropolitan areas in the United States that seemed to be equivalent in terms of poverty and other characteristics and found no appreciable relationship between population density and crime rate. But the critic will be quick to ask, "How can you know that these areas *are* equivalent with regard to all possibly critical factors?" More importantly, the crucial differences in population density are probably within a single metropolitan area rather than among different metropolitan areas.

It may be that many factors in social situations are inseparable and cannot be isolated. For example, it may be that both population density and lack of education are related to juvenile delinquency and adult crime. But, population density and quality of education are probably also related. Many educators, for instance, would hold that strong physical education programs, a wide variety of athletics and other types of extracurricular activities, outdoor education programs, and a challenging assortment of after-school and summer programs are essential elements of modern education if education is to be attractive and useful for children and young people. But it is difficult to provide many elements of this kind of education where the population density is high and land values are so great that it becomes almost impossible to provide the playgrounds, athletic fields, and outdoor facilities that are needed. So, education becomes unattractive, absentee rates soar, and many young people drop out as soon as possible. In a similar way there may be interrelations between many of the other factors that are in turn related to juvenile delinquency, crime, and other social pathologies.

How can we study and deal with social situations in which there are many interrelated and perhaps inseparable factors? An easy response is to say that we do not know for certain whether there is a relationship between population density and crime. But as individuals we usually have a certain amount of freedom to decide where we wish to live; communities plan for the location of new housing; regions decide on the location of new industries and transportation routes; and nations can control, in part, the regions in which industrial or economic activity is to take place. If these decisions are to be intelligent ones, they should be based on the best possible information. Unfortunately, the best possible information is often very limited and fraught with weaknesses. Yet the young people of today will have to draw upon whatever information is available as they deal with important problems, and some of these problems may be associated in confusing ways with population density.

Exercise: Multiple Causation To gain an understanding of some of the difficulties involved in studying phenomena associated with several possibly interrelated factors, students can gather data about their own behavior and the behavior of other students in their school and try to determine what factors influence it. One phenomenon that can be studied is absenteeism.

Have the students obtain the daily numbers of absentees from their school for a period of time of at least a month. (They may also find it of interest to gather the data for absenteeism among their particular classroom group.) Have them consider the form in which those data would be most useful. The daily absentee rate, for example, can be obtained by dividing the number of absentees by the total number of school days. It might also be useful to graph either the raw data or the rates.

They may wish to explore further the nature of the absentees. For example, are younger students absent more than older students? Boys more than girls? They probably can suggest other questions which, when answered, might help to clarify the nature of the absenteeism.

Then, ask them to try to suggest direct causes for the absences. Is it sickness? Is it a dislike for school or some part of the school program? They will probably be able to suggest other possible causes.

How can the required information be obtained? How can causal relationships be shown? As they struggle to find out which of the proposed factors are actually associated with school absenteeism, they will be dealing with some of the same knotty problems that students of population density have to struggle with.

PROBLEMS FOR RESEARCH

What more do we need to learn about the effects of population density on humans?[18] It has been suggested that one of the most important results of scientific research is the identification and clarification of new questions and problems for investigation and further research. Science has been compared to a balloon, with the thin rubber of the balloon symbolizing the interface between what is known and what is not known. As the balloon expands, the area of contact with the unknown also increases. The more we learn, the more there is to be learned.

Framing questions and problems for further investigation and research is one of the most important facets of science and one with which young students have too little experience. However, students can begin by suggesting questions and problems related to the effects of population density, about which we have an inadequate understanding. The questions and problems should be framed in such a way that it might be possible to investigate them. For example, "global" questions sometimes have to be redefined into a series of questions that can be more manageable. In some cases, students may be able to explore and begin to investigate some of the questions and problems they identify. This is particularly true of questions related to local community conditions.

Three problems of which we have inadequate understanding are suggested as examples of needed research:

1. *What are the effects of very high population densities upon humans?* There has been little study of the effects of population density on humans in cities where the densities are very high. Some of the most important density studies have been carried out in Chicago and Honolulu. However, little research has been done in such cities as Calcutta, Tokyo, and New York, where the densities are very high. In parts of New York City the population density may be as high as 75,000 people per square mile. Densities within cities vary greatly; there is a need for studies of the density effects in sections of cities where the densities are highest. Such indicators of social and personal disorganization as narcotics addiction suggest that very high population densities might have some effect on humans. (It has been estimated that more than half of the narcotics addicts in the United States are concentrated in Harlem.)

2. *Is there a critical level of population density?* In many natural phenomena there is a critical level, or threshold level, beyond which an effect appears. For example, in some studies of the effects of population density among animals, population density seems to have very little effect until a certain critical level is reached. Then, very pronounced effects are noted. One study reported that there may be a critical limit of home living space needed per person.[19] The critical level in the culture studied was 8 to 10 square meters of room space per person. When the available room space was less than this, the incidence of social and physical pathologies doubled. Further study of the possible effects of very high population densities might also help determine whether there is a general critical level of population density at which social and personal pathologies rapidly increase.

3. *What are the effects of high population density on children and adolescents?* A cursory analysis of the way in which many families live suggests that high population density might have its greatest impact on children and adolescents. A modern apartment on the twenty-third floor with a dazzling view of the skyline may be quite attractive to adults, but where are the children to play? How are adolescents to respond to all the admonitions from adults about minor indiscretions, such as running and jumping in hallways, that in other living conditions might go unnoticed? In each of the sophisticated studies of the effects of population density on humans, some relationship between population density

and juvenile delinquency was noted. But there is a paucity of studies exploring the possible adverse effects of high population density on nondelinquent children and adolescents.

Discussion: Research into Population Problems After students have devoted some time and attention to population studies, it may be desirable to have them suggest questions and problems that they think are in need of further study. (These might include problems that already have been studied.) Research in this area is complicated and difficult, but, they might be able to explore some dimensions of our ignorance and identify some of the things we do not know. This in itself can be a valuable experience.

Students might be able to identify problems related to the population of their school or community. Some of the information needed may be available, some may be unobtainable; much of it may be difficult to interpret. However, as they begin to explore questions and problems related to population in their school or community, they will gain a better understanding of some of the difficulties and perplexities that other investigators of problems related to population have encountered.

CONCEPT OF "OPEN SPACE"[20]

In *Walden* and other writings, Henry Thoreau wrote of some of the pleasures and satisfactions of living close to nature and distant from people. His descriptions of the peacefulness of solitude and the richness of a communion with nature have aroused nostalgia in many for a past they never experienced. But other writers — Jane Jacobs in *The Death and Life Of Great American Cities,* for example — have described values associated with cities. They have described the cultural resources, the ethnic diversities, the rich variety of personal associations, and possibilities for self-fulfillment when people live close together in cities. Are these competing views? Will we have to decide between them?

By the year 2000, the world population will probably be 6 to 7 billion. The population of the United States will probably be at least 270 million. How much living space will there be? How much open space will there be? Is it important to have open space? Are there possibilities that can provide us with both individual living space and open space? These are questions that will probably be of continuing concern to us in the future, and they are questions that are inextricably intertwined with our values. There are probably several possible responses, and we will not make wise choices among them if we do not even know what they are. This is a section of population study in which students can begin to consider what it is they value and to explore the possible options that lie before them. It can only be a beginning; our students will probably be dealing with such questions for the rest of their lives.

Questions of Values and Possibilities

Values may be considered to be one's idea of what is of worth, what is important; they are the criteria by which we decide what we should or should not do. For example, we value the life of the individual, meaning the life of each individual is of worth and importance. One of the major contributions of education, certainly of population education, is to lead each of us to become aware of and examine our values.

There are systematic ways in which to analyze our values. One approach is to analyze them in terms of a more general and comprehensive set of values and ultimately in terms of a generalized and abstract statement of value—on which almost everyone can agree, but which, admittedly, may have different meanings to different people. This can be illustrated with a situation of conflicting values related to living space: For a variety of reasons that he is quite willing to expand upon, one individual values the ability to handle firearms safely and with accuracy, and for this he needs a place to practice. As the population density increases, there are neighbors who complain about his firearms practice in a densely populated area. These neighbors value the safety of their children and the option to sleep late on a Sunday morning without the peace and quiet being shattered by a bang. Such conflicts of value can be analyzed and possibly resolved, although usually not to the satisfaction of all, by relating the conflicting values to a broad, generally accepted value, such as, "The greatest good for the greatest number" or "Survival is of the greatest importance because all other values depend on it." However, there may still be the concern for the "inalienable rights of the individual." (Some philosophers will argue that these rights also can be analyzed and evaluated in terms of broad, abstract, and generally accepted values.) Students can begin to analyze statements of value in terms of broader and more generally accepted values.[21]

Fortunately, in many social situations, including most issues related to population and open space, there are a variety of possibilities. The conflict between the individual who believes in the importance of knowing how to handle firearms safely and accurately and those in the community who value safety and peace and quiet has been resolved in many communities by providing special firing ranges, with better facilities than most individuals could afford, that are safe and located either indoors or at a sufficient distance from populated areas where no one is bothered by the noise. In most situations of value conflict, certainly in those related to population density, it is probably wise to explore various possibilities before making final judgments. Some possibilities change the nature of the problem; others cause the problem to disappear. Students should begin to explore imaginatively the various possibilities (What are the different things we could do?) related to planning for our future population.

What is Open Space?　From the perspective of the traveler in the stratosphere, there would seem to be a great deal of space available to man on Planet Earth. Human habitations seem few and far between in many parts of the American West. If the 200+ million people in the United States were evenly distributed, there would be only about 58 people per square mile (1970). Even in the most densely populated state, New Jersey, with a density of about 953 people per square mile, there are still farms, forests, and thinly populated areas. If we wished, we could probably build floating cities over the more than 800,000 square miles of the continental shelf; and we have not begun to realize the possibilities for cities under the ocean's waters and in layers underground. Viewed abstractly, it would seem possible for everyone to have plenty of living space.

But our populations, for multifarious reasons, are not evenly distributed. In the United States 75 percent or more of the people live most of the time on about 2 percent of the land. In the most densely populated parts of Manhattan in New York City, the population density may be more than 75,000 people per square mile. To the child living in the crowded ghetto, the thousands of square miles of the Rocky Mountains and hundreds of thousands of acres of national forest are not really available as open space.

What is open space? There seems to be no widely accepted definition. Thoreau implied that it was a place where a person could be by himself, close to nature, but with limited contacts with other people. But, a somewhat perplexed group of teen-agers in a large city park finally decided, "Guess it's a place where we could play baseball if we wanted to." Open space may be characterized as:

1. A place where a person can, at least in a psychological sense, be by himself or herself.
2. A place that provides some opportunity for contact with plants and animals, and possibly a variety of geographical features.
3. A place where one may engage in various types of play and recreation that require some space.

Exercise: Open Space—How Much? How Accessible? Students might undertake to investigate the open space in their community. Large-scale maps and aerial photographs may sometimes be obtained from such governmental agencies as the local planning commission or the soil conservation service, or from such commercial firms as Fairchild Aerial Surveys. Have students examine the maps, trace and measure the areas used for different purposes, and calculate the percentage of the total land area that is used for different purposes. What percentage of the land could be classified as being open space? Where are the open spaces located? How accessible are they to people in different parts of the community? How much open space is there for each 1,000 people in the community? Are there ways that the amount of open space available to people in the community could be increased?

The following are some of the most common functions of open space:

Recreation. Recreation can take many forms, such as hiking, camping, swimming, boating, nature study, bird watching, playing various sports, or just sitting quietly under a tree. Polls of recreation area users indicate that the availability of water for swimming, boating, and fishing is of special importance.

Conservation. Open spaces, such as marshes, swamps, and lakes, are probably essential for some wildlife and for maintaining groundwater levels and, in some cases, for flood control.

Preservation of unique natural areas. One of the arguments for wilderness areas is that we should preserve, free from human interference, some areas where various natural processes can be observed and studied. We should also try to preserve unusual natural formations.

Attractive landscapes. Many people consider open spaces to be a necessary part of an attractive landscape.

Exercise: Open Space—How Is It Used? Have students identify the parks, recreation areas, nature preserves, and other areas of open space in their community (possibly using large scale maps or aerial photographs of the community used in the preceding exercise). What functions do each of these areas serve? How could the areas be made more useful to more people in the community? Would there be drawbacks to increased usage?

How are open spaces used? Ask each member of the group to enumerate the different ways in which she or he has used a park or other open space. How many different ways have they been used?

Another way of finding out how open space is used is by an on-the-spot census: How many people are in a particular park or other open space at some specific time of day, say 4 P.M.? What kinds of activities are they engaged in?

How Much Open Space Do We Need or Want?

The answer to this question is greatly dependent upon the values that we hold. The outdoors person sitting by a campfire beside a bubbling brook will plead for more open space where people can be alone with nature. The sophisticated cosmopolite will enthuse about concerts, theater, and other cultural resources of the city that make life worth living and be less concerned about open space. Too often forgotten or neglected in discussions of such questions, children and adolescents should also make their voices heard — for they have more to gain and much more to lose. You may wish your students to begin to consider and discuss how much open space they think they need and want.

Groups and associations that are concerned about open space have studied the question and made recommendations. A national association in this field has suggested as a standard a minimum of 10 acres of park and recreation land for every 1,000 population. Such a standard relates open space requirements directly to population; as an area's population grows, the amount of open space should also be expanded. In heavily populated New York City, the Regional Plan Association has recommended that 25 percent of the region's land area should be open space. This would mean tripling the current amount of open space.

Early planning has made open space available in some cities. In 1859 the great community planner Frederick Law Olmsted developed the design for Manhattan Island's priceless Central Park.

Early planning maps for Manhattan Island show that many of the other parks of this densely populated island were laid out long before the city expanded to the boundaries of Central Park. Land that formerly belonged to royalty constitutes much of the park area in old cities such as London and Paris. In Brazil, two "new" cities provide a striking contrast and demonstrate what planning for open space can mean. Booming, bustling, industrial Belo Horizonte, with a population of more than 1 million, has only one park, and streets are marked out for further expansion with no evident provision for open space. Brasilia, on the other hand, a meticulously planned city, has generous expanses of open space designed for a wide variety of recreational uses, from special areas for flying model airplanes to small lagoons for sailing; it is acclaimed by many as one of the most beautiful cities in the world.

Some groups in densely populated cities apparently confine themselves to relatively limited areas that they seldom leave. Informal studies of some Puerto Rican communities in New York City, for example, indicate that they seldom use resources outside of a three-block radius of their homes. These considerations have been used as an argument for small neighborhood parks. Space for such parks is difficult to find, but proponents argue, "It always seems to be possible to find space for expressways."

There are special problems associated with providing open space in very densely populated areas. Urban planners point to high-rise apartment building complexes, such as Marina City in Chicago, which is almost completely self-contained, having everything from a liquor store to a boat basin within its confines. Usually, however, it is adult needs that are met, and there is very little space for the play and caprice of children and young people. Where there is play space, some parents hesitate to have their children use it. As one mother in a relatively new St. Louis high-rise apartment building that has now been abandoned put it, "It's hard to keep an eye on your children from the fifteenth floor."

It has been suggested that the people of some cultures have less need for open space than others. The study of other cultures provides interesting and suggestive alternatives to what is generally considered open space. There is some evidence, for example, that in the Arab world crowds are enjoyed more than in some other cultures, and this may help to explain the crowded bazaars of the Middle East, even though there may be ample room for spatial expansion. The Japanese, on the other hand, provide a feeling of space through the miniaturization of everything from gardens to interior ornamentation. Many visitors have commented on the striking contrast between the careful attention to order and detail in the inner space of the Japanese home and the apparent disorder and sprawl of Japanese cities.

As populations grow there is increasing possibility of conflict regarding matters that some people value deeply but which can only be planned and provided for by all. For example, some people believe wilderness areas are precious and should be protected even at the cost of reducing the amount of open space available to the public. It is argued that wilderness areas provide watershed protection, natural wildlife habitats, and the only remaining opportunity to study interrelationships and balances in natural ecosystems where man has not intervened; they offer what many consider to be the supreme human experience. But wilderness areas can only be planned and provided for by all. The Wilderness Act, which has served as a model for other nations, protects about 10 million acres, but less than 1 percent of these wilderness areas are east of the Mississippi River. Many nations no longer have such virgin lands to protect. Other nations, notably in Africa and South America, still have a chance to protect unique wilderness areas that, once lost, are irretrievable. Defenders of wilderness areas fear that booming population growth will lead to unremitting pressure for *lebensraum* and threaten the existence of the relatively few remaining natural areas.

Discussion: Questions about Open Space The study of population, and of open space in particular, is replete with unspoken assumptions, unexplored alternatives, and questions of value. It is not too early for students to begin exploring, thinking about, and discussing many of these matters. Following are a few of many questions that can be raised and discussed:

• How important is open space to us? What would we be willing to sacrifice to gain more open space?

• To what extent should we respect the concern of a few individuals for certain kinds of open space, such as wilderness areas? If a wilderness area that presently can be used by only a few, could be made into a park that could be used by many, which choice should we opt for?

• Should we limit the number of buildings in an area so that we can have neighborhood parks?

• Should we have small neighborhood parks or larger parks with a greater variety of facilities?

WHERE DO PEOPLE WANT TO LIVE?

There are many factors involved in people's choice of a place to live. Sometimes, people have a choice as to the community or region in which they will live, and this is certainly a very important choice. However, when making such a choice, the relative importance of many factors has to be weighed: location of friends, climate, cultural resources, opportunities for work, taxes, recreational facilities, and the quality of the natural environment. Weighing the relative importance of various factors is a characteristic feature of many of the choices that individuals make.

In social situations, the whole is often greater than the sum of the parts and the parts are very much interrelated. In much research, an attempt is made to find whether there is a relationship between one factor and some other factor. For example, we try to find out whether there is a relationship between population size and air pollution. In almost all situations several factors are influential; if we try to eliminate some of these factors, we change the nature of the situation to a point where the results may be practically meaningless. For example, the quality of teaching and the ability of students influence the effectiveness of an educational program. Yet, when trying to assess the value of a new program, the study would be practically meaningless if the program were tested only in schools where the teaching was excellent and the students above average. We can learn something about the relative importance of various factors by studying the choices people make and to what extent they would choose differently if they had complete freedom of choice.

In 1900, 60 percent of the people in the United States lived on farms or in villages. In 1970, only 26 percent of the U.S. population were classified as rural. In the 15 years from the late 1950s through the 1960s, 10 million Americans moved from rural areas into urban areas. It could be argued that these people voted with their futures when they left families, friends, and communities to seek a new life in cities. However, many of them did not have complete freedom of choice. The mechanization of agriculture made for fewer jobs on farms, and many of those who were displaced migrated to the cities in search of employment—"I moved to the city to look for a job when there were no longer any jobs around home." When all factors are considered, do people choose where they want to live primarily on the basis of where they believe they can make a living?

In the United States in the 1960s 15 of the 21 large central cities lost population. In fact, the central cities lost more population in this decade than did the rural areas. Where did the people go? Most of them went to the suburbs. What did they seek? Better schools? Fresh air? A plot of grass to call their own? Or did they want to escape the people who were migrating into the central cities from the rural areas? "We moved to the suburbs to get better schools for our children." Do families primarily make their choice of where they want to live on the basis of the quality of the education that is available?

There have also been great regional redistributions of population. In the 1960s states such as North Dakota, South Dakota, and West Virginia lost population, and others, particularly northern and central states, grew at a slower rate than the nation as a whole. On the other hand, states such as California, Arizona, New Mexico, and Florida grew at a much more rapid rate than the rest of the nation. New electronics and space technology factories, which can be located almost anywhere, were built in these regions because this is where the people that were to be employed wanted to live. Perhaps people moved to these regions because of the climate—"We moved to California because I got tired of shoveling snow every winter." What weight do people give to climate and environmental quality when they choose a place to live?

Of course, where people choose to live may not be where they would choose if they had complete freedom of choice. Table 5-2 shows the results of a Commission on Population Growth and the American Future survey of where people live and where they would prefer to live. The largest proportion (34 percent) would prefer to live in the open country. It has been suggested that this expressed preference may be due to a nostalgia for the "good old days," an anguish over the conditions of modern life; or it may be that American people actually want what they say they want. In a survey of Wisconsin residents it was found that 70 percent would prefer to live in a rural area within commuting distance of a metropolitan central city. Perhaps respondents saw this as a way of having the best of both—rural and urban.

It may also be significant that 20 percent of the American population, about 40 million people, change homes each year. One in 15

Americans, about 13 million people, move across a county line. Does this mean that the American people have a hard time deciding where they want to live?

Table 5-2
Where Americans Live and Where They Would Prefer to Live (in percentages)

	Where do you live now?	Where would you prefer to live?
Open country	12	34
Small town or city	33	30
Medium-sized city or suburb	28	22
Larger city or suburb	27	14

SOURCE: Commission on Population Growth and the American Future, *Population the American Future* (New York: New American Library, 1972), p. 36.

Exercise: Choosing a Place to Live There are various ways that students can be led to consider the multiple factors involved in choosing a place to live. One is to have each student make her or his own list and then develop a composite list for the group.

Obviously, all factors are not of equal importance, so students might want to rate the factors according to the weight they are likely to be given.

Also, we do not always have a completely free choice. What factors often restrict our freedom to choose where we wish to live?

CONCLUSION

Population density is the number of people living in a unit of area. The effects of high population densities upon animals have been studied with results that are suggestive. For example, these and other studies suggest that the effects of high population density may have the greatest impacts upon children and adolescents. The extent to which results from studies of animal behavior can be applied to humans is often questioned.

It may be that some social pathologies are exacerbated by population density. Pollution, delinquency, and crime are among the pathologies that may be affected by high population densities.

Optimum land use is an important issue in many communities. There may be differences of opinion as to the value of "open space" and community growth. Usually, it is important to become aware of the values we hold as we consider these community issues.

FOOTNOTES

1. For a further discussion of the definition and the desirability of reaching some general agreement, see Jonathan Freedman, "Conceptualization of Crowding," in *Population, Distribution, and Policy,* ed. Sara Mills Mazie (Washington, D.C.: U.S. Government Printing Office, 1972), pp. 499–509.
2. Adapted from John B. Calhoun, "Population Density and Social Pathology," *Scientific American* 206 (February 1962): 139–48.
3. John J. Christian and David E. Davis, "Endocrines, Behavior, and Population," *Science* 146 (18 December 1968): 1550–60.
4. For the comments of a distinguished scientist-philosopher on this question, see René Dubos, *Reason Awake: Science for Man* (New York: Columbia University Press, 1970), pp. 188–92.
5. John I. Clarke, *Population Geography* (New York: Pergamon Press, 1965), pp. 108–11.
6. Dubos, *op. cit.,* pp. 188–89.
7. Two of the best reviews of these studies are Jonathan L. Freedman, "The Effects of Population Density on Humans," mimeograph (1972) and Robert L. Snyder, "Reproduction and Population Pressures," in *Progress in Physiological Psychology,* ed. Eliot Stellar and James M. Sprague (New York: Academic Press, 1968), pp. 119–60.
8. Omer R. Galle, Walter R. Gove, and J. Miller McPherson, "Population Density and Pathology: What Are the Relations for Man," *Science* 176 (7 April 1972): 23–30.
9. Irving Hoch, "Urban Scale and Environmental Quality," in *Population, Resources, and the Environment,* ed. Ronald G. Ridker (Washington, D.C.: U.S. Government Printing Office, 1972), p. 272.
10. Galle et al., *op. cit.*
11. Ibid, p. 29.
12. Robert C. Schmitt, "Density, Delinquency, and Crime in Honolulu," *Sociology and Social Research* 41 (1957): 274–76; and Robert C. Schmitt, "Density, Health, and Social Disorganization," *Journal of American Institute of Planners* 32 (1966): 38–40.
13. Ibid., p. 274.
14. Freedman, *op. cit.*
15. Jonathan L. Freedman, "Population Density, Juvenile Delinquency and Mental Illness in New York City," in *Population, Distribution, and Policy, op. cit.,* p. 515.
16. Ibid., p. 523.
17. Unpublished study mentioned by Freedman in "The Effects of Population Density on Humans," *op. cit.,* p. 17.
18. Probably the best summary and analysis of research studies on the effects of population density on humans is Jonathan L. Freedman, *Crowding and Behavior* (San Francisco: Freeman, 1975).
19. Paul Chombart de Lauwe, *Famille et Habitation* (Paris: Editions du Centre National de la Recherche Scientific, 1959) reported in Edward T. Hall, *The Hidden Dimension* (Garden City, N.Y.: Doubleday, 1969), p. 172.
20. Other sources for discussions of open space are: Hall, *op. cit.;* William K. Reilly,

ed., *The Use of Land: A Citizens' Policy Guide to Urban Growth* (New York: Crowell, 1973); Stewart L. Udall, *The Quiet Crisis* (New York: Avon Books, 1963); U.S. Department of Agriculture, *A Good Life for More People: 1971 Yearbook of Agriculture,* (Washington, D.C.: U.S. Government Printing Office, 1971); and U.S. Department of the Interior, *The Population Challenge: Conservation Yearbook No. 2,* (Washington, D.C.: U.S. Government Printing Office, 1966).

21. For a more detailed discussion of values, see Chapter 8.

SELECTED REFERENCES

Clark, Colin. *Population Growth and Land Use.* New York: St. Martin's Press, 1968. 406 pp.
Especially valuable for its historical analysis of population growth and land use on a worldwide basis. The discussion of land use in urban areas has special relevance to this section.

Freedman, Jonathan L. *Crowding and Behavior.* San Francisco: Freeman, 1975. 177 p.
An analysis of how crowding affects people, particularly in urban settings. In general, an optimistic view of the issue is presented.

Griffin, Paul F., ed. *Geography of Population.* Palo Alto, Calif.: Fearon, 1969. 370 pp.
A yearbook of the National Council for Geographic Education; sections include "The World's Population," "Giant Population Aggregates," "Lands of High Population Density," "Lands of Low Population Density," and "Future of World Population."

Hall, Edward T. *The Hidden Dimension.* Garden City, N.Y.: Doubleday, 1969 217 pp.
Particularly good for its discussion of social and personal space and of man's perception of space and how it varies with cultures.

Mazie, Sara Mills, ed. *Population, Distribution, and Policy.* Washington, D.C.: U.S. Government Printing Office, 1972. 719 pp.
A collection of research reports prepared for the Commission on Population Growth and the American Future. Chapter 6, "Conceptualization of Crowding," and Chapter 7, "Population Density, Juvenile Delinquency, and Mental Illness in New York City," are of special interest.

Reilly, William K., ed. *The Use of Land: A Citizens' Policy Guide to Urban Growth.* New York: Thomas Y. Crowell, 1973. 318 pp.
Report of a task force sponsored by the Rockefeller Brothers Fund.

Ridker, Ronald G., ed. *Population, Resources, and Environment.* Washington, D.C.: U.S. Government Printing Office, 1972. 377 pp.
A collection of research reports for the Commission on Population Growth and the American Future. Chapter 6, "Outdoor Recreation and Congestion in the United States," and Chapter 9, "Urban Scale and Environmental Quality," are of special interest.

Singer, S. Fred, ed. *Is There an Optimum Level of Population?* New York: McGraw-Hill, 1971. 426 pp.

A collection of papers and comments of participants in a symposium on optimum population. Of special interest are the papers dealing with population and the quality of life.

U.S. Department of Agriculture. *A Good Life for More People: 1971 Yearbook of Agriculture.* Washington, D.C.: U.S. Government Printing Office, 1971. 391 pp.
A collection of short articles some of which suggest imaginative ideas for the better use of space for living.

CHAPTER 6

Populations and Their Environments

Population education is the study of populations in their environments.

Willard J. Jacobson

UNDER WHAT CONDITIONS do various populations live? How does a population depend upon its environment? What density of population can various systems support? Is there an optimum population size? Is migration from the earth a possibility? How do human populations affect their environments? How can we deal with problems that arise as populations and environments interact?

Human beings cannot live in a vacuum. They are utterly dependent upon the environment for the food and fiber that they need to survive, and for the great variety of materials that make survival "human." But, man also affects the environment in which he lives; sometimes man's impact upon his environs may be so great that the ability of the environment to support a population may be threatened. The study of populations leads us to consider the natural-social environments in which populations live. In this study, in keeping with our generalized approach to major problem areas, the focus is on a *system* approach to delimiting and analyzing problems.

CONCEPT OF "SYSTEM"

A system is composed of all the elements that should be considered when we study a phenomenon or deal with a problem. When we study how the human body processes food, we study the mouth, stomach, small intestines, and all other parts of the digestive system. These are among the relevant parts to be considered if we are to gain an understanding of how the food we eat is processed. In the study of population, it is also important to consider which elements are relevant and which are not. The systems that may be considered in the study of population range from small local systems, involving few people, to the global system, involving all the people on earth. The family is one of the most important systems. But, the family itself lives in some kind of environmental system from which it derives all of its necessities for life. It also is a part of some larger social systems, such as the community and the nation, through which it can take action to deal with problems. And all individuals and families are part of a global system. Although we have not yet developed very effective means for dealing with problems on a global scale, the lives of the young people in our classrooms will probably be increasingly affected by global conditions and by actions or inaction in various parts of the world. An important dimension of population education is to consider the various systems in which individuals live and to view problems from the perspective of those various systems.

Exercise: Example of a System To clarify the concept of a system, it can be useful to consider a fairly clearly delineated system, such as a space capsule. Here, the system exists within a shell that protects it from outside environmental conditions.

What are the elements of such a relatively self-contained system? First, there is the human population that inhabits it. Members of the population live under conditions that simulate those on earth. Their environment has oxygen, water, food, and other essentials brought from the earth. (It might be useful to have students consider what items it would be feasible to have in the capsule.) There are containers into which the population expels its wastes. Over a prolonged period, it might be possible to recycle many of the wastes and use them to grow food. The green plants that are a potential source of food can use the carbon dioxide resulting from respiration and liberate oxygen for use by all living organisms in the capsule. The individuals communicate with one another, make decisions, and take the actions necessary to maintain themselves and their system. Such a system is relatively self-contained, in that it could remain viable in space for quite a long period of time.

But even a space capsule is not a completely self-contained system. It is still only a part of other, larger systems. First, there is the earth–earth satellite system; if it were not for the gravitational attraction of the earth, the space capsule would speed out into the solar system or beyond. Then there are the communications links between the space capsule and stations on earth. Thus, even though a self-contained system out in space, the capsule and its population are still a part of the system earth. (Students might be intrigued to ponder how long the capsule and its inhabitants could remain viable—psychologically and emotionally as well as physically—if all contact with the earth were severed.

Then, too, the space capsule must be viewed as a product of the research and inventiveness of thousands of people over many years; the result of the painstaking work of additional thousands, ranging from workers in factories to very highly trained technicians; the fruit of taxes paid by many millions; an instrument for research investigation; and, perhaps, vicarious adventure for many. Thus, even when considering a space capsule, it is necessary to consider more than one system.

For different purposes, all individuals are members of several different systems. We need to view populations and environments from these different perspectives.

Discussion: Aspects of Systems *What are the various systems in which we live?* To answer this we can think about the various systems on which we depend and what the limits of each are.

- Where do the foods we regularly eat come from? Where were they processed?
- Where have the materials used in our clothing come from? Where were the clothes manufactured?
- Where have the main materials used in building our homes come from? Where were they manufactured?
- Where and how are our wastes disposed of? Who does the job of disposal?
- What systems assume responsibility for education?
- What systems collect information about populations?
- Who is really concerned about your future and the quality of life that you will lead?

In what system is it most useful to view population problems? Many are concerned about the size of the world's population and the rate at which it is growing.

- Who collects information about world population and its rate of growth? How is it done?
- What factors, beyond the size of the population, lead some people to be concerned about the world population? In which systems should such factors be considered and studied?
- Who could take action to deal with such a situation?

In what system is it useful to view problems of migration? Many are concerned that most of the young people they know will not remain in the communities in which they were born and reared.

- Who collects information about such movements of population?
- What are the factors that lead some people to be concerned about this migration? In which systems should such factors be considered and studied?
- Who could take action to deal with problems of migration?

It is possible to consider population and environment in a variety of ways. Often, it is done in terms of political units, such as city, state, or nation. These are the systems that collect information about populations and their environments, and they are among the agencies most likely to be able to take action to deal with problems. Another possible approach is to focus on the types of systems in which individuals live — the systems that provide what is needed for survival and for quality of living. The five systems we will consider are natural ecosystems, self-contained agrarian systems, modern farming systems, industrialized urban systems, and the global system.[1] There are various kinds of social organizations operating within all of these systems.

NATURAL ECOSYSTEMS[2]

A natural ecosystem can support a small human population; man as part of the natural ecosystem usually has little impact upon the environment. An ecosystem consists of the living organisms and their nonliving environment in a given area. Ecosystems pass through a succession of stages that lead to a climax ecosystem. In the climax ecosystem there is a balanced interrelationship between populations of different organisms and the environment, and no organism (such as man) dominates. The nature of a climax ecosystem depends upon such factors as rainfall, temperature, and type and condition of the soil. Under warm, moist conditions, the climax condition may be a tropical rain forest. Under cold, Arctic conditions, it may be the tundra. Because of the balanced interrelationships under the climax condition, a climax ecosystem tends to persist indefinitely. If changes take place through fire or other catastrophes, the ecosystem will pass through stages of succession and return to the climax condition. Any outside intrusion, whether it be a plowed field or a city street, is an artificial change in the environment. If left untended, it will eventually be absorbed, and the system will revert back to climax. For example, a small field that has been laboriously cleared in the rain forest, will soon be covered with vines and other vegetation if left untended. The interrelationships within a climax ecosystem are intricate and tend to be self-regulating. As we shall see, some proposals for human population stabilization can be viewed as attempts to approximate and maintain a climax ecosystem.

Exercise: What is a Natural Ecosystem Like?   If possible, have the student locate an area in the community that shows little evidence of having been changed by man. There still are examples of natural ecosystems extant in some areas; if you have access to such an area, it is ideal for this study. Have students study the natural ecosystem and answer such questions as the following:

• What different kinds of plants and animals are there?
• What seems to happen to the wastes of the organisms? (If there are trees, have them dig into the soil with their hands to see what happens to the fallen leaves. Have them search for dead animals and the excrement of animals and see what seems to be happening to the animal remains.)
• Is there any evidence of changes in the natural ecosystem that have been wrought by man or any other organism?
• Is there any evidence of pollution—on the ground, in the atmosphere, or in the streams, ponds, or lakes?
• Does there seem to be any one organism that dominates the ecosystem?

In the climax ecosystem, no one organism dominates. For example, in the hardwood forest that covered much of eastern North America, there were trees, moss, ferns, and grass, there were bacteria in the soil and water; and there were insects, rodents, mammals, and birds.

There was a balance between the various kinds of plants, with the hardwood deciduous trees most conspicuous because there was enough water in the soil for their needs and they had access to the needed sunlight. Man was part of this natural ecosystem, but he did not dominate it. He derived his food and other raw materials from the environment.

Hunting, fishing, food-gathering man makes few demands upon the ecosystem. He competes with other organisms for fruits and berries but does not get more than his share. He hunts but does not kill enough of any one species to endanger that population. He may clear a small plot of land, but when he abandons it, natural succession soon begins to operate. Man makes few and minor alterations in the system. As he moves throughout the ecosystem, his wastes are dispersed and biodegraded like those of other organisms.

The natural ecosystem supports a relatively small human population. It is estimated that the population density of pygmies in the Central African rain forest is about one person per square mile.[3] The pre-Columbian American Indian probably had a similar population density. It may be that the slow early growth of the human population was due to the checks and balances in the natural ecosystems of which man was a part; even under the best of conditions, no more than about one human per square mile could be supported.

The size of human populations in natural ecosystems is regulated largely by a high death rate in childhood and partially by a variety of cultural practices. Although life in the natural ecosystem has often been romanticized, it usually is very harsh. The mortality rate among children is often very high, and in some cultures a child is not given a name until he or she has survived for a certain length of time. This high death rate among the young reduces the number of individuals that reach the age of reproduction and serves as a severe check on population growth. There are also various cultural practices that tend to limit population growth, ranging from obligatory sexual abstinence over relatively long periods of time to restrictions on who may or may not marry and have children. But such cultural practices usually can also be found among other groups and seem not to be essentially a function of environment.

There are human populations that still live as integral parts of natural ecosystems, and through a study of these populations we have been able to gain a better understanding of man's life under such conditions.[4] Apparently, there is often a very intimate relationship between man and his environment. Perhaps because the environment is so important to him for survival, and he feels so much a part of his environment, plants, animals, and objects become important elements in his rituals and beliefs and in the hunting, food gathering, and other activities by which he supports himself.

Man in the natural ecosystem tends to live as a part of the environment. His techniques for hunting and food gathering may be clever, but they make no great impact upon the environment. Among the Tasadays in the rain forests of the Philippines, the food and fiber needed to supply the relatively small population are easily obtained, and the people continue to live in the same caves for extended periods of time. When the food supply in one particular area of the Central African rain forest is depleted, a pygmy band will move to a new site, and, since population density is low, there is usually plenty of room for this kind of mobility. In the harsh desert environment of the Australian aborigines, there is evidence of a correlation between rainfall and population density.

Man in the natural ecosystem does have wastes, and these have an impact upon the environment. It has been suggested that one of the reasons for nomadism is the need periodically to leave the accumulation of wastes in the immediate environment. In the tropical rain forest, these wastes are soon degraded and absorbed by the ecosystem. In the desert or in the Arctic tundra, the process of degradation may be slower. However, in all such ecosystems there are the scavengers, ranging from worms to vultures, that help to process the wastes.

Although human populations have existed in natural ecosystems for long periods of time, many of these societies are now threatened from the outside. Agriculturists clear away the natural vegetation to plant cultivated crops. Visitors bring in diseases to which there often is little resistance. Alcohol, tobacco, drugs, and the other accoutrements of "civilization" also take their toll. The number of people living under the conditions of the natural ecosystem is probably declining worldwide.

While the culture and way of life of humans living in relatively unchanged natural ecosystems should not be denigrated, they differ greatly from that of more complex societies. Few great works of art, literature, or science have come out of hunting and food-gathering cultures. The natural ecosystems provide stability and continuity, but they can support only a sparse human population. The support of larger populations, and, in particular, of dense urban concentrations, entails far greater demands upon the environment, and this brings with it increased environmental problems and risks.

Many ecologists and other students of natural ecosystems are so impressed by the complexity of the checks and balances of natural, ecosystems and the resulting stability, that they are convinced we run great risks when we make radical changes in such systems. For example, in a natural ecosystem, man can utilize many different kinds of plants and animals for food; if one of these food sources should for some reason disappear, it would be of little moment because there would still be many others. But if a large population is almost completely dependent on a single staple such as rice or wheat, a crop failure can be disastrous. A logical correlate of this view is that we should try to reduce the size of the human population to one that can be supported with less tampering with natural systems, and this has been suggested by at least one group of ecologically oriented scientists. They have argued that in many regions the size of the human population must eventually be reduced.[5]

VILLAGES AND SELF-CONTAINED AGRARIAN SYSTEMS

In self-contained agrarian systems, most of the necessities of the population are produced within the system and much of the waste is cycled back into the system. To grow more food and fiber, which, in turn, can support a larger population and offer hope of a higher standard of living, man has tried to control the growth of plants and animals on the land and to a smaller extent in the waters.[6] Where grass grew on the plains, the soil was scratched or turned over to grow wheat, oats, and other cereals that are of special value to man. In the desert, where only cacti and other hardy plants grow, irrigation makes possible the cultivation of cotton and sugar beets, wheat and corn. By slashing and burning the trees and undergrowth of the tropical rain forest, it is possible to grow a crop or two of maize. Agriculture can be considered an attempt to control the growth of plants and animals in an ecosystem to provide more food and fiber—usually to support a larger population. However, the process of control is usually reversible; the abandoned farm eventually reverts to a natural ecosystem.

It has been estimated that three-fourths of the world's population, including most of the people in South and Southeast Asia, Latin

America, and parts of Africa, live in self-contained agrarian systems. To understand population and population growth in the most populous regions, it is essential to consider and understand some of the factors related to population in such systems.[7]

The people live in villages. Many spend their days tilling the soil but return to their villages at night with their cattle and draft animals if they have any. While many of the villagers are engaged in agriculture or in processing the products of the land, the agrarian economy is usually also able to support students, teachers, religious leaders, government officials, tradesmen, and others who do not work the land.

In many self-contained agricultural systems there are social and economic incentives to have children. In addition to being wanted for their own sake, children are often a distinct economic asset. Agriculture in such systems involves a tremendous amount of work, particularly at times of planting and harvesting, and children are an essential labor pool. In addition, when children grow up, they are usually expected to care for their elders; they provide a form of social security for old age in societies where there is as a rule no other support for the aged. Thus, the desire for children is not only biological; it is also an essential element of the society's needs and cultural mores. Probably much of the population pressure on a worldwide basis stems from the high reproductive rates in self-contained agrarian systems.

It has been estimated that at one time about 90 percent of the people in the United States lived in such systems.[8] Like their counterparts in other areas of the world, these systems were relatively self-contained. Children were seen as an asset, and there was a relatively high reproductive rate. The demographic picture in the United States has been greatly complicated by continuing immigration from other continents and the migration westward. However, as we shall see, one of the most profound changes in North American life may have been the almost complete shift from self-contained agrarian systems to modern farming systems.

In many self-contained agrarian systems there has been relatively little movement away from the home village and little contact with the outside world. In a study conducted in such a village, the question was asked, "If you could not live in your own village, where in the world would you like best to live?" The interviewers were astonished that many of the respondents could not, or would not, conceive of living anywhere else. This absence of contact with the outside has made it difficult to bring to the attention of villagers the possibilities (or need) for family planning and the opportunities afforded by new technology. But radio and other forms of mass communication are now making contact possible. Some population education programs have made substantial use of radio, newspapers, and even television to reach agricultural villages.

Some agrarian societies are nomadic. The people and their animals range over a considerable distance. Sometimes, this travel takes advantage of seasonal changes — for example, north for the summer to plant and tend crops and graze their animals on fresh grasslands, and south for the winter for better grazing, less severe cold, and perhaps a second crop. Animals, a share of the crop, tents, cooking utensils, and the family valuables are carried with the nomads as they travel. The life is usually harsh, and poor health and primitive sanitary conditions often lead to high death rates. While children can contribute a great deal to productivity of the society, provisions for child care and education are minimal. In most parts of the world, the number of nomads, in the usual sense the term is used, is declining.

We tend to think of nomadic agriculturists as always existing "somewhere else," but the migrant farm workers in the United States might be considered nomads. Many of them move as families to find agricultural work where it is available, to plant, tend, and harvest crops. As with most nomads, housing and public health conditions often leave much to be desired. Their children usually have limited opportunities for education. Unlike many nomads throughout the world, migrant farm workers are usually not organized into social units such as tribes with well recognized leadership. But certainly they are an important element in the American population. In 1975, there were 188,000 American migrant farm workers 14 years and older. An additional 25,434 migrant farm workers were officially admitted from other countries. However, since many migrant workers are known to come in illegally from Mexico and other countries, it is generally accepted that there are many more migrants in any given year than is shown by the official count.

Exercise: Migrant Workers in the Community Students may not be aware of the presence of migrant workers and their families in their communities. The following questions may alert them to their presence and promote a better understanding of the conditions under which migrants live:

- Are there agricultural crops being produced in your community?
- If so, who does the work in planting and harvesting these crops?
- Where do these farm laborers come from?
- Where do they live? What is the condition of their housing?
- How do the laborers and their families fit into the community?
- What is life like for the children of the laborers? Do they work? Do they go to school?

One of the key ecological characteristics of self-contained agrarian systems is that very little matter or energy is brought into the system and very little leaves it. The major portion of the produce of the system is used within the system, although a small fraction may be exchanged for products from the outside. The main sources of energy are the sun, which is utilized by plants to produce organic matter; draft animals such as horses, mules, and bullocks; and man himself. Animal wastes are spread over the land; they decompose and release nutrients for future crops. In some societies, animal dung is used as fuel for cooking and heating homes, but even then the ashes can be returned to the soil.

Many self-contained agrarian societies have existed for several thousands of years, supporting populations at subsistence or a little above subsistence levels. Therefore, this type of system can be considered quite stable. While radical changes are made in the natural climax ecosystem, the plants and animals are usually adapted to local conditions. Catastrophe can and does strike some self-contained agrarian societies, but many more continue to survive.

It has been estimated that most self-contained agrarian systems will support about one person per acre of agricultural land in regions where there is ample water either directly from rainfall or through irrigation. This is 600 to 700 times as many people as can be supported in a natural ecosystem such as the tropical rain forest. When there is ample water, good soil, periodic replenishment of soil nutrients, and not too harsh a climate, and where population pressure is not too great, the self-contained agrarian system can supply its population with all the essentials for life. Where one or more of these conditions do not hold, the human population suffers; thus, some of the poorest people live in self-contained agrarian societies. In some systems of this type, the pressures are very great. Distribution of goods among regions is generally poorly developed, so that in the event of a drought or other calamity, there may be a failure to get food to those who are without it. Some of the most tragic famines have occurred among people dependent on this kind of agricultural system.

A characteristic feature of the self-contained agrarian system is the high proportion of produce consumed by the system's draft animals. One of the ways the amount of food available for human consumption has been increased has been through substituting the internal combustion engine and the electric motor for animals as a source of power. For example, in 1918, when the horse and mule population of the United States was at its highest, one-fourth of the harvested crop acreage was used as food for these animals. By 1960, horses and mules had been largely replaced by tractors, and much of the agricultural produce formerly consumed by them became available as food for humans.

It seems very doubtful that the self-contained agrarian system, with its low yields per acre and high proportion of produce consumed by draft animals, could support populations of the size projected for the future.

MODERN FARMING SYSTEMS

Through the use of great amounts of energy, new strains of plants and animals, chemical fertilizers, pesticides, and the support of a broader industrial system, relatively few people can produce a great deal of food and fiber, but with considerable environmental risk and impact upon the society. Modern farming systems make even more radical interventions in natural ecosystems than do self-contained systems.[9] The former are characterized by the introduction of large amounts of matter and energy from outside the system, high productivity, the use of sophisticated technology, research and development (R&D) for the continuing improvement of agricultural practices, a substantial reduction in the percentage of the population engaged in agriculture, and a comparatively high economic standard of living for many of the people in the system. Matter is introduced as fertilizer, pesticides, equipment, building material, and seeds. Energy in the form of fossil fuels, sometimes converted to electricity, is used to do much of the work, and there is no longer a need to devote part of the produce of the land to the feeding of draft animals. Hybrid seeds, pesticides and herbicides, and new plant and animal care and feeding practices are innovations wrought by R&D. The tractor, electric motor, and many kinds of ingenious machinery are artifacts of modern farm technology which are used to achieve dramatic increases in agricultural productivity.

Among the most profound and consequential questions related to population and agriculture is whether or not modern farming systems can provide the food and fiber needed by populations of the size projected for the next century. Certainly, such systems are very productive, but will they be productive enough? It may very well be that the only hope of feeding a world population that may grow to 7 billion by the year 2000 is through the further extension of modern farming systems. It has been estimated that the present world population might be supported by the products from one-tenth of the acreage now under cultivation in the world if it were farmed as much of the land now under cultivation in Iowa is farmed. If such modern farming practices were universally used, it has been estimated that enough food could probably be grown to support a population of 40 to 50 billion.[10]

But what would be the consequences of extending the modern farming system? Would its environmental impact be critically deleterious? And what would be the social impact of the modern farming system on the developing regions of the world?

The development of modern farming systems has made agriculture much more dependent upon outside support. In the self-contained agrarian system, the farmer saves part of his crop to use as seed for the next crop. But the modern farmer is dependent upon seed suppliers for the hybrid seeds that are so much more productive. The suppliers, in turn, are dependent upon research and experiment stations for the new varieties. Experimenters scour the world for new varieties that might be used to develop a hybrid seed corn or a new strain of wheat or rice. Similarly, for energy, the modern farmer uses a tractor that is manufactured from materials from many places in the world, and he uses gasoline or diesel fuel that has been pumped out of the ground in Saudi Arabia, Venezuela, Canada, or Texas and been refined in Louisiana or New Jersey. The millions of people who work in manufacturing, well drilling, oil refining, and other industries are, in turn, dependent upon modern farming systems for their food and fiber. The modern farming system is an integral part of a broader industrial system. When it works as intended, and so far it usually has, it is wonderfully productive. But there is the nagging concern that, as it assumes more and more of the responsibility for feeding a rapidly growing population, a shortage of some essential element or a breakdown in one of the critical industrial segments that support the system might lead to very serious consequences.

The introduction into self-contained agrarian systems of new and more productive strains of wheat and rice, the so-called Green Revolution, illustrates both the promise of modern farming and its risks. Rice yields in the Philippines are five times higher with the new rice than with the old. Similar increases in wheat yields have made important contributions to the support of Mexico's rapidly growing population. However, much of the effectiveness of these new strains is dependent upon the use of more water and fertilizer. In many parts of the world, water in the amounts needed can only come from irrigation systems developed on a regional or national basis. And fertilizer has to be obtained from distant sources and is manufactured on a large scale by sophisticated processes. The introduction of elements of modern farming systems into self-contained agrarian systems has great promise for substantially raising food production, but it also carries with it considerable difficulties and risks.

There may be serious dangers involved in using new strains of corn, wheat, oats, or rice; they have not gained a natural immunity to the diseases of a region nor adapted to its unique vicissitudes. Being newly developed strains, often hybrids, there is a danger that they do not have the built-in resistance of age-old varieties. For example, when hybrid corn grown in the American Midwest was attacked by a leaf blight in 1970, 10 percent of the crop was lost. What would happen to the world food supply if almost all of some major crop in the Midwest were lost some year? The introduction of new varieties into self-contained agrarian systems in other parts of the world, in an attempt to increase production, may carry with it even greater dangers, because in those countries there may not be the technical and research support services to cope with such problems. Also, insects and other pests, as well as weeds, tend to develop a resistance to pesticides and herbicides. Farmers use stronger doses, and researchers develop new biocides. But, what if we are unable to find a way to control some pest, and the plants and animals that we depend upon are overwhelmed?

Then, there is concern over the long-term effect on the environment of one species, man, who introduces tremendous amounts of energy and materials into ecosystems to radically modify them so that the human population can grow far beyond the level that can be supported by the natural ecosystem. What will happen to the other species in the ecosystem? If the populations of some organisms are destroyed or their numbers drastically reduced, will the human population also become more vulnerable? These kinds of questions are being examined, discussed, investigated, and sometimes argued about heatedly, but not even the most ardent advocate of a position can be absolutely certain about the answers. Students have a great stake in the answers, and they will probably see many of them unfold in their lifetimes.

Many environmental effects of modern farming systems can be kept to a minimum. Modern soil conservation practices, for example, have minimized many of the effects of intensive cultivation of the land. It should be possible to return manure from the feedlots back to the land where the feed was grown. It should be possible to apply commercial fertilizer in such a way that little of it will be washed into rivers, lakes, and reservoirs. The use of biological controls and biodegradable pesticides will limit the impact of these chemicals upon the environment. However, one of the lessons of modern technology is that the introduction of new techniques and substances often has unpredicted consequences. As modern farming practices evolve to feed growing populations, we will have to continue to monitor our systems to be able to detect unexpected consequences in time to devise countermeasures.

The development of the modern farming system has already had a profound impact upon American society. Where once more than 90 percent of the population was directly involved in agriculture, now only 6 percent is, and this 6 percent produces food for a much larger population than that of the United States. This development was one of the important causes of the migration of people from rural areas to the cities and of the decline of some rural institutions. Further, it was, at least in part, a contributing factor to some of the nation's most critical social problems. In the 15 years from 1954 to 1969, 10 million people moved from rural areas into the cities, the majority of them ill-prepared for the transition. Difficult social and economic problems were generated in the cities, and communities and institutions in the rural areas were weakened by the exodus. This was one of the great migrations in history, and it went relatively unnoticed. However, it drastically changed the lives of many and probably affected almost the entire population in one way or another.

The displacement of people from the rural areas and their migration to urban and suburban areas as modern farming systems develop appear to be a worldwide phenomenon. In a few countries, such as Tanzania, attempts are being made to build viable relationships between rural and urban areas; but in most places the migration to industrialized urban systems takes place without much planning, preparation, or apparent concern, and the human price paid is sometimes high indeed.

CITIES AND INDUSTRIALIZED URBAN SYSTEMS

The concentration of populations in relatively small areas appears to be a feature of developing industrialized societies, and this has had considerable social and environmental impact.[11] The first cities probably originated 7 or 8 thousand years ago in the Middle East or South Asia. They were probably made possible by the development and improvement of agriculture, and they became centers for trade, manufacturing, government, defense, religion, education, and recreation. Even at that time there was probably some migration from the land to the city. However, the cities were not large. Rome was unusual, with a population of perhaps 1 million; but as late as the Middle Ages a city of 10,000 was considered large.

While there may be a general understanding of what is meant by "urban" and "rural," a moment of reflection will indicate that it can be difficult to classify the people living in some small hamlets. In the United States, the definitions of the U.S. Bureau of the Census are the ones usually used. An *urban population* refers to the persons residing in places of 2,500 or more population, except for those living in rural portions of extended cities. Included under this definition are persons living in both incorporated and unincorporated areas. A *rural population* refers to persons living in areas that are not considered as being urban. Obviously, there are marked differences between a small town of 2,500 and a large metropolitan area. A metropolitan area, including a central city and the nearby areas that relate to it, is termed a *standard metropolitan statistical area* (SMSA). An SMSA typically includes a city of 50,000 or more people, the county in which the city is located, and adjoining counties that meet certain criteria of metropolitan character and are closely integrated with the central city, as through commuting. (In New England SMSAs include towns rather than counties.)

Large cities require sufficiently efficient agriculture to grow the food and other essentials needed by large numbers of people and a transportation and distribution system that can convey goods from the agricultural areas to the cities and vice versa. Harnessing energy in the form of the internal combustion engine, the ability to distribute energy widely in the form of electricity, transportation systems that can handle large quantities of goods and people, and effective communications and information systems have all contributed to the growth of cities. Large industrial cities are a relatively recent arrival on the stage of human history, but they are growing rapidly. While world population is increasing at a rate of about 2 percent per year and doubling in about 35 years, the population living in urban systems of more than 1 million is increasing at a rate of 4 percent per year and, therefore, doubling in about 18 years. Increasingly, people in the more advanced developing regions of the world are coming to live in urban systems.

Exercise: The Location of Cities   Why are cities located where they are? Students who live in a city may be able to find out what factors led to their city being located where it is. Following are some of the factors that influence the location of cities. Which might have been operative in the location of your city?

Near a harbor where ships can dock
The farthest point upstream that ocean-going vessels can go
At a pass through a mountain
Near important natural resources
A place where goods have to be loaded and unloaded
Near an important energy source, such as a waterfall
At the crossing of important land transportation routes
Desirable climate

It may be that urbanization and the development of large cities are features of social, economic, and industrial development. Prior to 1850, probably no nation was primarily urban, and even by the turn of the century many would have classified only Britain as largely urban. However, once a large proportion of the population is no longer needed in agriculture, there tends to be a flow of people into urban areas. Some kinds of manufacturing require a large labor force, and the workers have to live within reach of the plant. Various kinds of health, educational, governmental, and recreational services also tend to be located in cities, where they can be more accessible to many people. While Western Europe and North

America are already very urbanized, urbanization is also continuing at a rapid rate in many other regions, particularly in the developing nations. In Brazil, for example, over 34 percent of the people live in cities of over 100,000 population, and, with a population in the neighborhood of 100 million, Brazil has 6 cities with populations probably over 1 million. Other South American nations such as Uruguay and Argentina are even more urbanized. Similarly, as economic development continues throughout much of the world, the percentage of the population that lives in urban areas is growing.

There are a number of very large cities in the world. The following are the ten largest in order of size. All of these cities have more than 4 million people:

> Tokyo, Japan
> New York, U.S.A.
> London, England
> Moscow, U.S.S.R.
> Shanghai, China
> Sao Paulo, Brazil
> Bombay, India
> Cairo, Egypt
> Rio de Janeiro, Brazil
> Peking, China

Large cities tend to be surrounded by suburban areas that share the cities' dependence upon other areas for food and other essentials. It has been predicted that the entire strip along the Atlantic shore from Boston to Washington, D.C., will soon become one continuous urbanized area — sometimes referred to as a megalopolis. Other likely megalopolises are along the West Coast, around the southern shores of the Great Lakes, and along the coast of Florida.

Changes revealed by the 1970 U.S. census may be indicative of some of the population shifts taking place in industrialized urban systems.[12] Almost 74 percent of the American population lived in urban areas, an increase of about 4 percent in the 10 years since 1960. In fact, almost all of the population growth during the 1960s took place in metropolitan areas, with the rural population remaining about the same. The growth of the metropolitan areas was partly due to a natural increase resulting from more births than deaths and partly (about 25 percent) due to migration from rural areas to urban.

Part of this migration was the continuing movement of the black population from the rural areas of the South. By 1970, the black population was 60 percent urbanized. In the rural areas, higher birth rates tended to offset losses of population through migration.

While almost all the population growth in the United States in the 1960s took place in urban areas, within many of these areas there was a movement of people away from the central cities to the suburbs. This process has sometimes been called "suburbanization." Of the ten largest metropolitan areas, eight had central cities that lost population. By 1970, there were more Americans living in suburbs than in the central cities.

Cities are centers of culture, recreation, and specialized activities that require the support of large populations. Museums, zoological and botanical gardens, large libraries, and other cultural institutions are usually located in or near cities, where there are many people to use and support them. Professional baseball and football teams, for example, require a certain size of population to support them. Professional societies such as academies of medicine and science, organizations of hobbyists such as stamp collectors and photographers, and musical associations such as symphonies and choral groups are likely to be found in cities; this is where there will be enough people of like interests to band together to pursue such interests. Thus, when people live relatively close together in cities, they are able to participate in a variety of cultural activities that would be more difficult to organize if they lived farther apart.

However, large concentrations of population can lead to environmental problems. Urban systems have to be constructed, and in many cases they represent almost complete landscape alteration. There are apartment buildings and streets, houses and driveways, factories and shopping centers, railroads and highways. One of the little-realized effects of this landscape alteration is its effect upon runoff (from rain and snow) and groundwater. It has been estimated that as much as 10 percent of the surface of the eastern United States is covered with concrete, macadam, or some other hard, impermeable surface from which water runs directly into sewers, rivers, and streams and cannot soak into the soil. Another effect of a "constructed" environment is that, since it has been built by man, many of those who live in such an environment may not realize that it is ultimately subject to the same ecological principles that hold for other ecosystems.

As populations become more concentrated, the amount of atmosphere, water, and land surface available per person for the dispersal and disposal of wastes decreases. Students of mathematics and biology will recognize the similarity between this statement and the relationship between the volume and the surface area of a sphere. (The volume of a sphere is proportional to the cube of the radius, but the surface area, which is the interface with the environment, is proportional to the square of the radius. Therefore, volume increases much faster than surface area.) Mythical Island City, for example, has only the same amount of atmosphere above it to absorb the soot and sulfur dioxide of its homes and industries when its population is 1 million as it had when its population was 100,000. Space for sanitary landfill becomes difficult to find and expensive to pay for. A river can carry away sewage, but the condition of a river that served as sewer for a few sleepy villages will be quite different when it has to carry away the wastes of a dozen urban systems. The nightmare of a waterborne communicable disease such as cholera or typhoid in a densely populated area can spur even the most economy-minded legislator to vote the money needed to pay for sewage treatment facilities.

Discussion: Some Consequences of Urbanization There may be a maximum size for urban systems beyond which the environmental problems become so complicated and so expensive to deal with that it becomes more efficient and effective to limit population concentrations. From his analysis of the problems of large concentrations and the trends shown by the 1970 U.S. census, Philip M. Hauser has suggested that, for effective operation, the maximum size of a city may be about 3 million.[13]

What are some of the consequences for people of the shifts of population from rural areas to urban and suburban areas? Following are some of the possible effects of these population shifts. Students might discuss which apply to them, their families, and their community.

- Economic status is usually improved when people leave the rural areas and move to the city.
- As time goes on, the ties between the people who move to the city and the rural community they left behind weaken.
- Population in the rural areas does not grow and may even decline.
- People in cities tend to have smaller families than those in rural areas.
- Families in cities tend to be nuclear, that is, composed only of parents and their children.

- There is a greater variety of educational, recreational, and social services available in a city.
- People in a city tend to have less contact with the natural environment.
- There are more housing and recreational opportunities for unmarried people in a city.
- As people move to the suburbs and the suburbs spill out into the countryside, valuable farmland may be used for housing.
- People in the suburbs spend more time and money commuting to work.
- People living in metropolitan areas tend to move more often than do those who live in rural areas.
- In metropolitan areas, much of the land is covered with buildings, roads, and parking lots.
- Metropolitan areas have to develop special systems for the disposal of wastes.
- People in metropolitan areas have easier access to colleges and universities, hospitals and specialized medical services, museums and other cultural institutions.

What will become of our cities? Will suburbanization lead to endlessly sprawling SMSAs that have little or no central core? Los Angeles, for example, is sometimes described as a city without a downtown. As happened in agriculture, will fewer people in the future have to be involved in manufacturing and other industries that depend on concentrations of population? Then, will it be possible for populations to spread more evenly over available lands? Of course, it is quite likely that the future of cities will depend upon technological, economic, and natural resource developments. The automation of industry, the development of efficient mass transportation, the cost and availability of energy, the extent of decentralization of industry and recreation, and our success in handling environmental problems will all affect the future of our cities.

A few decades ago, a distinguished student of urban civilization, Lewis Mumford, suggested that cities pass through cycles of growth and decay. They start as village communities, grow into large megalopolises, and decay into empty shells.[14] The young people who live through this century and beyond will have a chance to see what will happen to our cities.

The coming decades may see a continuing movement toward a "postindustrial society."[15] Just as mechanization and improved production techniques in agriculture have led to a smaller fraction of the total population being engaged in working on the land, so automation and improved production techniques in manufacturing will lead to a smaller fraction of the population being engaged in semiskilled manufacturing jobs. This will mean more people will be engaged in highly sophisticated technical and professional services, which, in turn, will require more education. Already, by the early 1970s, 60 percent of the U.S labor force was involved in service occupations, and the percentage was increasing. This transition will probably have profound implications for populations. Society will have to invest more in the education and development of people. Not only will educational institutions be challenged by growing populations, but the individuals who make up those populations will probably need more and better education. Doctors, scientists, artists, technologists, and teachers will be more typical of the postindustrial society than will semiskilled workers, and their preparation will require a correspondingly heavier investment in "human capital."

Discussion: Education for the Future If we are moving into a postindustrial society, with an increase in highly technical and professional occupations, this carries important implications for schools and colleges and for young people planning for their futures. Your students might wish to discuss the following questions.

• Do you believe our society is becoming a postindustrial society?
• What will be the implications for schools and colleges of the transition to a postindustrial society?
• What will happen to individuals who formerly held unskilled or semiskilled jobs?
• How can you best prepare for living in a postindustrial society?

THE GLOBAL SYSTEM

Spaceship Earth may be the most fundamental system for considering both population and the environment.[16] Viewed from space, Earth is a very bright planet, with sunlight brilliantly reflected from the atmosphere and the clouds that surround it. Much of the planet is covered with clouds, and about two-thirds of its surface is water. The few who have had a chance to view this planet from outer space have described the experience—a truly religious experience—of seeing the planet as a whole and recognizing the features that make it "home." All of us have had a chance to see in a new way that ours really is "one world." Earth is the home of Homo sapiens, the only place in the universe as of now where we *know* there is life. Within this global system, the family of man exists and grows. The eventual size of the population and the future quality of the lives of its members will depend on how we care for our planet home.

It is unlikely that the effects of rapid population growth will be localized to a particular city, state, or nation. Extreme population pressures leading to hunger, social strife, and human suffering are unlikely to be contained by a cartographer's lines on a map. Nor, is pollution a respecter of national boundary lines. It seems likely that the mean temperature of the entire globe is being influenced by air pollution, and this may affect both the Stone-Age Tasaday in the interior Philippines and the steel worker in Gary, Indiana. Mercury discharged by chemical plants in North America may be concentrated in the flesh of tuna caught by Scandinavians and eaten by Russians. Traces of pesticides used for agricultural and public health purposes have been detected in animals near Antarctica. Many of our environmental problems must be viewed in global terms.

Population Distribution[17] If the population of the earth were spread evenly over all the continents except Antarctica, there would be about 70 people per square mile. However, the population, whether of the world or of the United States, is not spread evenly. Instead, people tend to be concentrated in relatively small areas.

Over 80 percent of the world's population lives on less than 20 percent of the land, and about 50 percent lives on about 5 percent of the land. In fact, over 70 percent of the earth's population is concentrated in four great clusters. One of these clusters is in East Asia and is composed of part or all of China, Japan, the Koreas, and Taiwan. A second cluster is in South Asia and includes India, Pakistan, Bangladesh, and Sri Lanka. A third cluster is in Western Europe, including European Russia. The smallest cluster is in Eastern and Central North America.

When we analyze population distribution in terms of land, we find that about 60 percent of the land is inhabited by only about 5 percent of the earth's people. Over 30 percent of the land has practically no human population. This includes such areas as the Greenland ice cap, the great deserts, some very rugged mountain areas, and such tropical rain forests as the Amazon and Congo basins. While the trend is probably toward ever greater population concentration, the areas of extremely low population density are also being reduced. The discovery of important natural resource deposits in the Arctic and in Antarctica may lead to some population even in these forbidding regions.

Another important way of analyzing population distribution is in terms of developed and developing regions. Figure 6-1 shows the distribution of population in various years, with projections to the year 2000. Perhaps, the most striking feature of this figure is its indication of how the proportion of population in the developing regions is likely to grow. The basic reason is the much higher birth rate in those regions as the following figures indicate:

	Birth rate per thousand	Death rate per thousand	Rate of change per thousand
Developing regions	40	18	22
Developed regions	20	9	11

Thus, some of the most important problems associated both with population and with economic development have their major locus in the developing regions.

Exercise: Distribution of the World's Population The problems associated with rapid population growth are compounded by the uneven distribution of population and of population growth rate. Table 6-1 shows the distribution of population in 1977 and as projected for the year 2000. Students can gain some feeling for the impact of these unequal distributions through the following simulation.

On a classroom or gymnasium floor, mark with chalk or masking tape areas that are proportionate to the land areas of the various continents and the U.S.S.R., as shown in Figure 6-1. Students should note the comparative size of the continents—for example, that Europe is considerably smaller than any of the other continents.

The 1978 population of each of the continents can be simulated by assigning proportionate numbers of students to stand in the "continents." If there are 30 students in the class, each student will represent about 136 million people and they should be assigned as follows:

Africa	3 students
Asia	17 students
Europe	3 students
Latin America	3 students
North America	2 students
U.S.S.R.	2 students

The fact that over half the people in the world live in Asia should be noted. Do the students "living" in Asia feel crowded?

Now, make a simulation of what the population of each continent will be in the year 2000. (This time, more students will be needed. If none are available, the continents can be inhabited one at a time.) Note that the amount of space available remains the same.

Africa	6 students
Asia	26 students
Europe	4 students
Latin America	5 students
North America	2 students
U.S.S.R.	2 students

Perhaps this will give students some impression of what it might be like to be an inhabitant of each of the continents in the year 2000.

In Chapter 7, this point will be pursued further with an exercise demonstrating the distribution of food and income in these six regions of the world.

Table 6-1
Distribution of World Population in 1978 and in the Year 2000

	Area (in millions of square miles)	1978 Population (in millions)	Projected population in 2000 (in millions)
Africa	11.6	436	811
Asia	10.6	2,433	3,584
Europe	1.9	480	539
Latin America	8.7	344	608
North America	7.5	242	294
USSR	8.6	261	314
World	52.3	4,219	6,182

SOURCE: 1978 population derived from Population Reference Bureau, *1978 World Population Data Sheet*, Washington, D.C.: Population Reference Bureau.

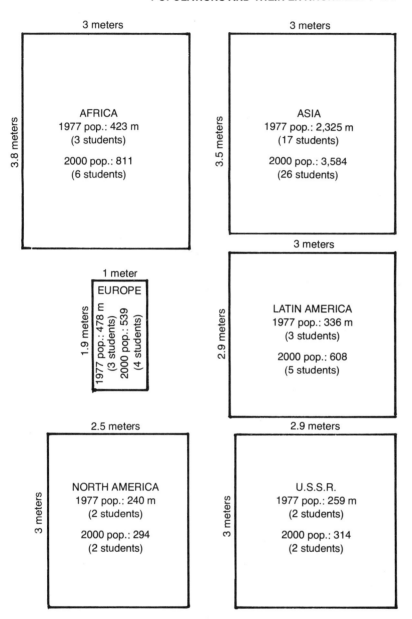

Figure 6-1 Continental floor plan showing current distribution of world population and growth projections for the year 2000.

Global Environment   In addition to a rapidly growing human population and unequal distribution of this population, there has been a sharp rise in the "ecological demand" made on the environment. A partial measure of the ecological demand is the gross domestic product (GDP) (minus services).[18] This statistic has been increasing at a rate of 5 to 6 percent per year, compared with the world population rate of increase of 2 percent, which means that the ecological demand is doubling in 13 years. This rapid rise in ecological demand stimulates a sense of urgency among those who are concerned about the quality of the global environment.

In two spheres of the global environment, the atmosphere and the oceans, the effects of environmental pollution can be worldwide.[19] For example, DDT washed into the oceans by the Mississippi, or dust and vapor trails over the Sahara, can affect conditions everywhere. We are on Spaceship Earth, but, as one Cassandra put it, "Ships can sink, and, if we sink beneath the weight of global pollution, we all sink together."

Part of the difficulty in dealing with problems in the global system is that there has not been a strong, effective unit to deal with problems at the world level. For example, the oceans are a very important source of fish and other food, and it is in the best interests of everyone that the number of fish not be depleted to the point where the fish population cannot replace losses. However, individual fishing vessels and independent nations that depend on fish construe their interests to be best served by maximizing their catches ("After all, if we don't catch the fish, someone else will."). As a result of this intensive fishing, some of the most productive ocean fisheries may soon be "fished out," and there will no longer be any fish for anyone. Too often, there has been no agency or political unit to take the global view and deal with problems that might affect many peoples and nations. As a UN delegate once said, "Everybody's business too often becomes nobody's business." To help build a world view can be an important goal of education.

The United Nations has undertaken a variety of steps to help people gain a better understanding of world population and population growth so that they may be better able to deal with problems related to population. It collects basic information about populations on a worldwide basis.[20] It has sponsored such international conferences as World Population Year. And its various agencies have carried out a great deal of development work related to population and population education. For example, UNESCO has been the sponsoring agency for the development of regional source books for population education[21] and has set up a clearinghouse for population education. The Food and Agriculture Organization (FAO) collects information about food production and attempts to stimulate improved and increased food production. The World Health Organization (WHO) and other agencies carry out similar services in their fields. These are all important steps in the direction of caring for "everybody's business."

Migration from the Global System

Man has dreamed of living among the stars, and it has been suggested that one of the solutions to a rapidly growing population on Planet Earth is migration to some other place in the universe — some other planet orbiting some other star. Migration to the Western Hemisphere provided an escape valve when the death rate declined and the population of Western Europe began to grow. Now that the population of the global system is growing so rapidly, why not find an escape valve through migration to some other planetary system?

Two questions arise in relation to extraterrestrial migration: Is it possible, and, if possible, is it desirable? A first reaction often is that such migration is fraught with so many difficulties that it approaches the impossible and consideration of it distracts us from tackling difficult population problems here on earth.[22] Certainly, the obstacles to such migration are formidable. The nearest star is over four light-years away; it would take many human generations to reach this star system at any speeds that seem conceivable now, and we still do not know what kind of conditions those who arrived would find when they reached there. Even the most optimistic tend to agree that it will be impossible for many to leave the earth and colonize outside of the solar system.

But it has been suggested that it might be possible for a small number of humans to set up a colony on the moon — after all, men have lived on the moon for short periods of time. When we begin to think about such a colony, we can gain a better understanding and appreciation of our own home on earth. In a sense, a moon colony would have to recreate to a large extent the environmental conditions of the global system. First, the colony would probably have to live underground to be protected from harmful solar radiation and to maintain tolerable temperatures. Almost all the necessities for life, such as nitrogen, oxygen, carbon, and water would have to be recycled, much as they are on the earth. If there were occasional losses, most of the necessities might be replenished from materials on the moon. Without going into detail, it seems conceivable that man might set up a small colony on the moon.

Discussion: Would Migration to Outer Space Be Desirable? Since it may become possible for man to emigrate from the earth, the next question is, would it be desirable? This question can lead to a consideration of purpose and to some fundamental beliefs concerning man, his place in the universe, and what may be his destiny.

Would extraterrestrial migration provide an "escape valve" for the global system's growing population? About 76 million people are added to the world population every year. It is difficult to believe that even a small percentage of this yearly increment could migrate.

Would it be desirable for some people to have the experience of living under radically different conditions? If we and our ideas are at least in part the products of our experiences, then there might be arguments in favor of giving some people opportunities for radically different experiences.

Would it be desirable to have some humans living elsewhere in case some great cataclysm should threaten earth's human population? Cataclysms of such magnitude can be conceived of. Do we have a responsibility to our species to try to make certain that some survive even the unthinkable?

Should the resources of the vast majority who would not migrate be taxed so that a few can experience a radically different environment and, in case of a global holocaust, survive to perpetuate the species?

Should we begin to think seriously about such questions?

IMPACT OF POPULATION GROWTH

Population growth, technology, and economic development are inextricably interrelated and have a combined impact upon environmental and social systems. It can be argued that population growth is not the major contributor to environmental deterioration, and no one can say with absolute certainty whether or not this argument is valid. It may be that technology and high standards of living are greater villains. But, neither has as much impact with a small population as with a large one. A small population can operate a highly technologized civilization and enjoy a high material standard of living without putting any great strain upon the environment. However, the world population even now is not small; and it is growing rapidly. It is questionable whether a large human population could sustain itself at all without the use of sophisticated technology.

Then there is the even more serious question, would people, after having tasted or at least become aware of the possibility of a higher material standard of living, curb their aspirations or actually reject the possibility of an improved standard of living?

Technology has been a major contributor to human population growth. Pest and weed control agents, the sanitation of water supplies, public health services and facilities, better nutrition, improved pre- and postnatal care of children, and, perhaps most important of all, more efficient agriculture and industry, which has freed talented people for research and service in all of these areas — these have been among the major contributors to the very rapid population growth of the past century. This technology contributes to the ecological demand. But, it is an upward spiral, for there is little hope of supporting a rapidly growing population without the increasing use of an ever more sophisticated technology.

Not only the earth's population is growing but also the aspirations of its peoples. The strident calls for faster development and the suspicion that discussions of population planning and environmental concerns are really attempts to curb economic development in developing countries are symptomatic of the almost universal desire for a higher standard of living. Higher standards of living place a correspondingly greater demand on the environment. But the developing nations are apparently willing to pay the environmental price for economic development. Indeed, where are the people, in rich or poor nations, who do not want a higher standard of living? The populations of developing countries are growing considerably faster than those in developed countries. If these large and growing populations are to achieve the standards of living to which they aspire, a much greater ecological demand will inevitably be made on the global environment.

As human population grows, the complexity of the environmental problems increases. While it is true that many environmental problems are the result of the technology man uses, a growing population will call for even greater use of technology if larger populations are to be fed, clothed, housed, heated, cooled, and transported. The Green Revolution, for example, requires much more intensive use of fertilizer, irrigation water, and pesticides, and this intensification of agriculture will almost inevitably increase the rate of pollution of the environment. A larger population — and there are many reasons for believing that the proportion of this population that will aspire to higher material standards of living will grow rather than decline — will require more energy and materials. To obtain these, lower grade ores will have to be mined, dirtier fuels will have to be burned, and all of this will place an ever greater burden on the environment. No one knows whether we can deal with the increasing complexity of environmental problems. As man increases the degree of his alteration, manipulation, and control of the environment, the natural checks and balances and the resilience of natural ecosystems that provide insurance against ecological disaster are reduced. There is the gnawing fear that sometime, some perhaps unrecognized factor may prove to be "the straw that breaks the environmental camel's back."

A central thesis of this discussion of environmental and social impact is that it is most important and helpful to consider the combined effects of population, technology, and economic growth. While there may be purposes for which it is useful to try to focus upon and deal with only one of these factors, to understand what is happening in our environment it is important to consider all three. It is something like the age-old question of "Which is of greater importance in the development of the child — nature or nurture?" In terms of the child, both nature and nurture are important. In terms of the environment, population, technology, and economic growth are inextricably intertwined, and, to understand what is happening to our environment, we have to deal with all three. Therefore, it is suggested that it is more fruitful to consider population along with the other causative factors of environmental deterioration in the various systems — natural ecosystems, self-contained agrarian systems, modern farming systems, industrialized urban systems, and the global system.

Changes in the size and distribution of populations have impacts upon many of our social institutions. Growth in population necessitates more schools, hospitals, libraries, and government services. If adequate institutions and services are not developed before or during population growth, personal hardships and social difficulties can result. A loss of population, as has occurred in many rural areas, can lead to the waste or underutilization of such services as schools, parks, playgrounds, roads, sidewalks, water and sanitary systems, and lighting and heating systems. Unfortunately, the people who leave such communities often move to another where such services are not available or are seriously inadequate. The movement of people may leave such institutions as churches almost empty in some areas, as in the inner city, and greatly overcrowded in others, as in some suburbs.

One of the outcomes of population growth and change is its possible effects on representative government.[23] Plato held that the state should be small enough so that all citizens could know one another. Aristotle believed it desirable to be able to assemble all citizens in one place so that they could be addressed by one speaker. (It would be interesting to have Aristotle's reaction to broadcast fireside chats or nationally televised reports.) Other theoreticians, such as Rousseau, have expanded on the advantage of governmental units that are small enough so that citizens can actively take part. One form of government, which many would consider to be the truest example of representative government in America, the New England town meeting, does call for every citizen to take part annually in such a meeting.

With the growth of population and, often, the concomitant increase in the size of government units, this kind of citizenship participation becomes impossible. Obviously, it would be impossible for the more than 210 million people in the United States to assemble in one place and decide issues that are important to them. Instead, cities, states, and nations have representative governments. Citizens elect representatives to express views, cast votes, and generally represent them in government.

As the population of a governmental unit grows, either the number of representatives must increase or the number of people that each represents will become larger. In the United States, the number of senators is fixed at 2 per state; California with a population of more than 20 million is represented by the same number of senators as Alaska with its population of a little more than 300,000. The House of Representatives is apportioned according to population, but the total number of representatives is now fixed at 435. Each congressman now represents over 470,000 constituents; in 1920, each represented about one-half as many constituents. It can be argued that a growing population also increases the number and complexity of the issues with which our representatives must deal; there seems little doubt that, with growth, it becomes more difficult for representatives to learn their constituents' views and thereby represent them adequately in the legislature.

Increasing the number of representatives leads to greater complexity of government without necessarily improving the quality of representation. In the 435-member House of Representatives, much of the substantive research, hearings, and drafting of legislation is done by committees. Thus, it becomes difficult for most legislators to become deeply involved in proposed legislation except through the particular committees on which they serve. Also, in large legislatures a hierarchical organization often develops. Legislators who have seniority are chairmen of important committees; they are wise in the politics of legislatures and wield great power. Citizens represented by a legislator of low seniority serving on relatively insignificant committees may have some justification for feeling that they and their representative have little say in government.

In addition to their legislative tasks, representatives must also serve the people of their states or districts. They may arrange for groups of constituents to meet specific government officials, seek and provide information, and strive to eliminate the inequities and hardships caused by governmental action or inaction. As constituencies grow, much of this service must, of necessity, be handled by staff members or be referred to governmental bureaus. Studies of how legislators handle these service functions seem to indicate increasing bureaucratization, and some citizens feel more and more removed from their government.

Technology can be used in representative government, and it helps with some of the problems. Sophisticated data-gathering and processing systems are available to governmental officials. Also, somewhat like Aristotle's orators addressing the populace under a tree, it is possible for legislators to speak directly to their constituents via radio and television. However, much of this communication is one way. While the citizen can in theory make it two-way by picking up a telephone and calling his or her congressman, the likelihood of actually reaching the ear of the legislator diminishes as the size of the constituency grows.

Discussion: Implications for Government Population changes undoubtedly have profound implications for government. Students might debate the following topics:

1. How does population growth potentially affect representative government and the democratic process? (One side might argue that population growth makes for a decrease in democracy for various reasons, including those cited in the foregoing section; the other might argue that it makes

democracy more essential and more likely, e.g., because of the need for citizen cooperation in dealing with population and environmental problems.)

2. What kind of government would be most effective in dealing with population and environmental problems and at the same time best serve and satisfy the individual needs and social aspirations of citizens? (One side could argue for democracy and full citizen participation in the decision-making process; the other for extensive government intervention and the imposition of solutions by decree.)

OPTIMUM LEVELS OF POPULATION

An optimum level of population is one in which, indefinitely into the future, individuals can strive to approach their potential for development and achieve what they consider to be a high quality of life.[24] While it is difficult to state categorically what an optimum level of population would be, the limits within which an optimum level would fall can be roughly defined. The upper limit would be dictated by the need for food and the other essentials required by the individuals in a population to enable all of them to achieve a certain minimum quality of life. However, there is also a lower limit of population, below which a society cannot maintain its schools, universities, hospitals, museums, and the various other social institutions that many individuals would judge necessary to a reasonable quality of life. These requirements provide some boundaries, however imprecise, for setting optimum levels of population.

There is also an ecological dimension to the concept of optimum levels — that it should be possible to maintain the optimum level indefinitely. A level that enabled one or a few generations to enjoy "the good life" but that, in the process, consumed all available resources would preclude future generations attaining a reasonable quality of life and could not be considered optimum. Instead, an optimum level would be akin to a climax ecosystem, where there is a balance between various populations and this stable condition can continue indefinitely. In its study of the American population, the Commission on Population and the American Future found that no substantial benefits would accrue from continued population growth and recommended "that the nation welcome and plan for a stabilized population."[25]

The stabilization of population levels somewhere within the optimum limits may make it possible to work toward universal participation in "the good life," for example by ensuring that all children receive the amount and quality of education that will help them to reach their full potential. This necessitates, among other things, high quality teaching and good schools. In contrast, a rapidly growing population often can provide only large classes, inadequately prepared teachers, double sessions, and poorly equipped schools.

The optimum level should make possible a variety of life styles. Some individuals enjoy the hustle and bustle of big city life and thrive in an environment that has great universities, a diversity of clubs and organizations, and a variety of cultural institutions. Others want a chance to be close to nature, to be able to sit alone with their thoughts on a rock ledge and not see another human being all day. The optimum level should make possible both such life styles.

It may be that optimum levels differ for different societies and cultures. Some may value a wide variety of social interactions and place less emphasis on material things. For such a society the optimum level of population might be higher than for one in which individuals treasure material possessions and make greater ecological demands. Of course, important ethical question might arise if population levels in those societies where ecological demands were high continued to rise and impinged upon the opportunities of individuals in other cultures to lead the kind of lives they desired.

Optimum population levels would leave options open to future generations. However, severe environmental damage may make it impossible for future generations to enjoy certain kinds of options. Although most environmental systems have great resilience and recuperative powers, there are limits beyond which they cannot recover. Some of the hillsides in Tennessee have been completely denuded by smelter fumes, and it will be a long time before trees grow there again. There is fear that the contamination of some lakes, such as Lake Erie, will reach such critical levels that they will never again be able to support certain kinds of life. If wilderness areas are opened up to grazing, future generations will never have a chance to see natural ecosystems like the primeval forest or virgin grasslands. The too heavy demands of too large a population may effectively close out certain options for future generations.

Discussion: What Would Be an Optimum Level of Population? Optimum levels may be considered in terms of different systems. Students can begin by considering the problem in relation to their local community:

- What proportion of space is needed for housing, recreation, roads, factories, stores, and government buildings? Do children have enough room for play?
- Is there enough food and water for everyone? If not, is it possible that with better planning they could be provided?
- Are there adequate employment opportunities—a job for everyone who wants one? If not, is it possible that more could be provided?
- Is it possible to treat and dispose of the wastes of the community without causing too much harm to the environment?
- Do people of the community have access to hospitals, universities, museums, and the other institutions that people need or want?
- Do people of the community have the opportunity for a wide variety of experiences? For example, are they within reach of cultural, sporting, and other events, that depend upon the support of large crowds of people? Do they have access to areas where they can be alone?

CONCLUSION

A consideration of populations and their environments raises profound questions about how we live and and what we want for the future. No one has a greater stake in the future than students. Can we and they really begin to become actively concerned about the future? If there is to be a future, the answer will have to be yes. If a primary goal of education is to help individuals prepare to live in the future, then population, the environment, and our social systems would seem to rate some attention for some of the hours in some of the years we all spend in school.

FOOTNOTES

1. For a sophisticated analysis of such systems, see Howard T. Odum, *Environment, Power, and Society* (New York: Wiley-Interscience, 1971). Odum approaches questions of economics, law, and religion, as well as ecology, through a systems approach and suggests that, "A general systems view of the world is possible and preferable in the orientation and education of man."
2. Most books on ecology contain a discussion of the ecosystem concept. One such discussion is "Principles and Concepts Pertaining to the Ecosystem" in Eugene P. Odum, *Fundamentals of Ecology*, 3rd ed., (Philadelphia: Saunders, 1971), pp. 8–85.
3. Odum, *Environment, Power, and Society, op. cit.,* p. 136. All estimates of the number of people that can be supported in different systems are derived from this source.
4. For a technical discussion of some of these societies, see Colin M. Turnbull, "Demography of Small-Scale Societies," in *The Structure of Human Popula-*

tions, ed., G. A. Harrison and A. V. Boyce (New York: Oxford, 1972), pp. 283–312; Turnbull's books *The Forest People* (Garden City, N.Y.: Doubleday, 1962) and *The Mountain People* (New York: Simon and Schuster, 1972). See also Peter Matthiessen, *Under the Mountain Wall* (New York: Ballantine, 1962) for descriptions of life among the Kurelu of New Guinea before they had any contact with "civilization."

5. Perhaps, the clearest statement of this point of view is that developed by a group of British scientists and published as "Blueprint for Survival," *The Ecologist* 2, no. 1 (January 1972).

6. There is a school of thought that suggests that major changes in man's ways of living are the result of necessity, arising in part from population pressure, rather than of cultural evolution. Reay Tannahill, *Food in History* (New York: Stein and Day, 1973), has suggested that the ape-into-man transmutation was set in motion by shortages of food in the forests, which led to foraging in the grasslands. Ester Boserup, in *The Conditions of Agricultural Growth: The Economics of Agrarian Change under Population Pressure* (Chicago: Aldine, 1965), has suggested that agricultural development was a consequence of population pressure.

7. Among the many books describing life in such villages are those by the anthropologist Oscar Lewis: *Village Life in Northern India* (New York: Random House, 1965); and *Life in a Mexican Village: Tepoztlan Restudied* (Urbana, Ill.: University of Illinois Press, 1951). For a comparative study, see Robert Redfield, *Peasant Society and Cultures* (Chicago: University of Chicago Press, 1956).

8. There are many descriptions of life in North American self-contained agrarian systems. Among the classics is Hamlin Garland, *A Son of the Middle Border* (New York: Grosset and Dunlap, 1917).

9. For a discussion of the environmental impact of modern farming systems, see William W. Murdoch, ed., *Environment, Resources, Pollution, and Society* (Stamford, Conn.: Sinauer, 1971). For a discussion of some of the environmental and social implications of the Green Revolution, see Lester R. Brown, *Seeds of Change* (New York: Praeger, 1970).

10. See Roger Revelle, "Food and Population," *Scientific American* 231, no. 3 (September 1974): 161–170.

11. For an extensive discussion of population distribution trends in the United States, see Sara Mills Mazie, ed., *Population, Distribution, and Policy* (Washington, D.C.: U.S. Government Printing Office, 1972).

12. Two analyses of the 1970 census are: Philip M. Hauser, "The Census of 1970," *Scientific American* 225, no. 1 (July 1971): 17–25; and Conrad Taeuber, "Population Trends of the 1960s," *Science* 176 (19 May 1972): 773–77.

13. Hauser, *op. cit.,* p. 20.

14. Lewis Mumford, *The Culture of Cities* (New York: Harcourt, Brace, 1938), pp. 282–92.

15. Probably, the most sophisticated discussion of the "postindustrial society" is Daniel Bell, *The Coming of Post-Industrial Society* (New York: Basic Books, 1973). Also, see Kenneth Boulding, *The Meaning of the Twentieth Century* (New York: Harper & Row, 1964). Boulding uses the term "postcivilization" rather than "postindustrial."

16. For a more extensive discussion of population and the global system, see such sources as John D. Durand, ed., "World Population," *Annals of the American*

Academy of Political and Social Science 369 (January 1967); John P. Holdren and Paul A. Ehrlich, eds., *Global Ecology* (New York: Harcourt Brace Jovanovich, 1971); Roger Revelle, Ashok Khosla, and Marie Vinovskis, eds., *The Survival Equation* (Boston: Houghton Mifflin, 1971); and Study of Critical Environmental Problems (SCEP), *Man's Impact on the Global Environment* (Cambridge, Mass.: MIT Press, 1970).

17. For a discussion of global distribution of population, see Glen T. Trewartha, *A Geography of Population: World Patterns* (New York: Wiley, 1969). Population distribution in the United States is discussed in Commission on Population and the American Future, *Population Growth and the American Future* (New York: New American Library, 1972), Chapter 3. See also Irene B. Taeuber, "The Changing Distribution of Population of the United States in the Twentieth Century," in *Population, Distribution, and Policy, op. cit.*

18. United Nations, *Statistical Yearbook,* 1972, p. 50.

19. One of the best and most comprehensive discussions of environmental problems at the global level is Study of Critical Environmental Problems (SCEP) *op. cit.*

20. United Nations, *Demographic Yearbook* (New York: UN Publishing Service, issued annually) is a basic source for world demographic information.

21. For example, *Population Studies for Population Education in Asia: A Source Book,* trial ed. (Bangkok: UNESCO Regional Office for Education in Asia, 1973).

22. This point of view has been expressed by Garrett Hardin in "Interstellar Migration and the Population Problems," reprinted in his *Population, Evolution, Birth Control* (San Francisco: Freeman, 1964), pp. 93–99.

23. For a more extensive discussion of this subject, see Roger H. Davidson, "Population Change and Representative Government," in *Governance and Population: The Governmental Implications of Population Change,* ed. A. E. Keir Nash (Washington, D.C.: U.S. Government Printing Office, 1972).

24. For a collection of papers dealing with optimum population and environmental and resource factors, education and health services, and life styles and human values, see S. Fred Singer, ed., *Is There an Optimum Level of Population?* (New York: McGraw-Hill, 1971).

25. Commission on Population Growth and the American Future, *op. cit.,* p. 192.

SELECTED REFERENCES

Brubaker, Sterling. *To Live on Earth.* New York: New American Library, 1972. 253 pp.
A "Resources for the Future" book that focuses on the possible effects of man's accelerating use of the environment, primarily in the United States; it identifies 5 major environmental threats and suggests some of the problems involved in dealing with them.

Commoner, Barry. *The Closing Circle.* New York: Knopf, 1971. 326 pp.
Probably the most cogent statement of the thesis that our environmental problems are primarily due to changes that have taken place in our technology.

Ehrlich, Paul R., and Ehrlich, Anne H. *Population, Resources, Environment.* San Francisco: Freeman, 1970, 383 pp.
A major work, in which the environmental effects of a rapidly growing human population are explored.

Hinrichs, Noel, ed. *Population, Environment, and People*. New York: McGraw-Hill, 1971. 225 pp.
A Council on Population and Environment book containing 24 original essays by leading scholars on the basic problems, human factors, and possibilities for action.

Holdren, John P., and Ehrlich, Paul R., eds. *Global Ecology*. New York: Harcourt Brace Jovanovich, 1971. 295 pp.
A collection of essays, many of which deal with population and the environment on the global level.

Meadows, Donella H.; Meadows, Dennis L.; Randers, Jørgen; and Behrens, William W. III. *The Limits to Growth*. New York: Universe Books, 1972. 205 pp.
A Club of Rome report, which is an ambitious analysis of the limitations to growth. Analyzes problems related to resources, population, food, industrial output, and pollution; it concludes that all of these factors must be dealt with.

Mesarovic, Mihajlo, and Pestel, Deuard. *Mankind at the Turning Point*. New York: New American Library, 1974. 210 pp.
The second Club of Rome Report, in which attention is devoted to regional differences and the concept of "organic growth" is developed.

Murdoch, William W., ed. *Environment, Resources, Pollution, and Society*. Stamford, Conn.: Sinauer, 1971. 440 pp.
A collection of papers that generally take an ecological approach to environmental problems. There are sections that deal with population and resources, environmental degradation, and environment and society.

Nash, A. E., ed. *Governance and Population: The Governmental Implications of Population Change*. Washington, D.C.: U.S. Government Printing Office, 1972, 342 pp.
Prepared for the Commission on Population Growth and the American Future. Discusses the impact of population change upon government.

Odum, Howard T. *Environment, Power, and Society*, New York: Wiley-Inter-Science, 1971. 331 pp.
A systems approach to the problem of survival in the complex systems of nature and man. The possible ramifications of this approach have probably not yet been fully explored.

Revelle, Roger; Khosla, Ashok; and Vinovskis, Maris, eds. *The Survival Equation*. Boston: Houghton Mifflin, 1971. 508 pp.
A collection of papers that deal with "Population—Humanity's Problem," "Resources, Food, and Development," and "The Environmental Crisis." In general, a global view is taken of these problems.

Ridker, Ronald G., ed. *Population, Resources, and the Environment*. Washington, D.C.: U.S. Government Printing Office, 1972.

Smith, Robert L. *The Ecology of Man: An Ecosystem Approach*. New York: Harper and Row, 1972. 436 pp.
A collection of papers in which the conceptual framework of the ecosystem is developed to discuss man and the systems in which he lives. While all parts of this book are relevant, Part I, "The Ecosystem and Man," and Part III, "Man and His Habitat," are especially germane.

Study of Critical Environmental Problems (SCEP). *Man's Impact on the Global Environment*. Cambridge, Mass.: MIT Press, 1970. 319 pp.

The report of a study and conference involving a large coterie of eminent scientists and other professionals. It is probably one of the best sources of data on various global environmental problems.

Ward, Barbara, and Dubos, René. *Only One Earth.* New York: Norton, 1972. 288 pp.
This is a report prepared with the assistance of 152 consultants from 58 countries for the United Nations Conference on the Human Environment. Among the many contributions of this important book is that it reveals the wide divergence in the views of distinguished experts on problems related to man and the environment.

CHAPTER 7

Population and Resources

> Through the animal and vegetable kingdoms, nature has scattered the seeds of life abroad with the most profuse and liberal hand. She has been comparatively sparing in the room and nourishment necessary to rear them.
>
> *Thomas Malthus*

WHAT RESOURCES are needed to support a population and to maintain at least a minimum quality of life? What is the state of adequacy of the world's supply of essential resources, and how will possible shortages affect future populations? What are some proposals for increasing the supply of essentials and desirables? How are population and resources interrelated?

Populations consist of individuals, and when we study populations we eventually become concerned with individual human beings. During their sojourn on earth, all human beings are utterly dependent upon their environment for the food, water, and other resources needed to maintain life. If there is not enough water, crops will fail. If there is not enough food, some will starve. If there is not enough fiber for clothing or shelter, some will suffer. As we study population, examine population policies, and consider our possible actions, it becomes essential to analyze the nature and adequacy of our resources. But, while doing this, it is well to keep in mind the possible impact upon individual human beings. One may read of populations starving or prospering, but it is individual human beings, each with hopes and concerns, who are suffering or achieving fulfillment, living or dying.

APPLICATION OF UNIVERSAL LAWS

In a generalized approach to problem situations, it is desirable to identify universal laws or principles that may apply. In the study of resources, it is easy to become lost in minutiae and to be overwhelmed by an avalanche of statistics. But the minutiae and statistics, while interesting and important, are quickly out-of-date and often as quickly forgotten. Broad generalizations or principles are more useful. They can be used to interpret the welter of information, and students can carry these distillates of experience with them as they approach other problem situations in the future.

Also, broad generalizations, because they summarize a tremendous amount of experience and because their validity probably will persist, provide us with a perspective with which we can view problematic situations, evaluate information, and judge proposals for action. Among the most basic generalizations in our consideration of population and resources are the first law of thermodynamics and the law of tolerance levels. They are among the generalizations that are sometimes called "limiting laws" because they place limits on what is possible. These two laws have to be kept in mind for responsible consideration of most matters relating to resources.

First Law of Thermodynamics *In a closed system the total amount of matter and energy remains constant.* Under almost all conditions related to the study of populations and their environments, this law can be restated as, "Energy can be neither created nor destroyed; matter can be neither created nor destroyed." In the words of a young student, "What this law really says is that you can't get something for nothing." It is true that under special circumstances, such as in atomic particle accelerators, energy can be converted into matter. In atomic piles, matter is converted into energy, and this will probably be one of our major sources of energy in the future. However, under almost all circumstances in our environment and in our daily lives, this law holds, and can be expected to hold in the future.

An application of this law can be seen in any garden or farm. When vegetables or any other crops are grown and harvested, material is removed from the soil. If this process is continued for a number of years, the soil will eventually be depleted, and the crops will deteriorate. The rate of soil depletion can be slowed by returning to the soil as much as possible of plants that have been harvested and manure from the animals that eat the plants. But some enriching material must eventually be added to the soil. As we shall see, enriching materials such as fertilizers are needed to increase food production for a growing population.

Law of Tolerance Levels   *Too little or too much of any one of several elements can critically affect our well-being and possibly our survival.* All organisms, including man, can live only within certain tolerance levels. This is a very basic concept in ecology, sometimes called "Shelford's law of tolerance." It is an extension of "Liebig's law of minimum," which states that organisms have to have minimum amounts of critical substances to survive. Some fish, such as trout, will continue to live only in streams or lakes where temperature and oxygen levels remain within certain limits. Although man is very ingenious, he too can probably exist only within certain levels of tolerance. One of the central ideas in the Club of Rome report, *The Limits to Growth,* and one that has not been seriously questioned, is that it is not enough to provide *some* of the critical factors for survival; *all* must be present, and they must be present within their respective tolerance levels. To illustrate how the principle of tolerance levels might affect man, phosphorous and phosphates are essential materials whose supply might become depleted; a serious shortage could have dire results for the human population.

An interesting characteristic of our biosphere is that most of the essential elements for life—hydrogen, carbon, nitrogen, oxygen, and sulfur—are naturally recycled. While there are dangers that growing populations and increased industrialization may alter the nature of these cycles, the total supply of these critical elements will probably remain essentially the same.

Is there a phosphorous cycle? The phosphates that are used in agriculture or in detergents are eventually washed into the oceans, and the oceans become the ultimate sink for this critical material. Some of the cycled materials are carried back to the land from the atmosphere, for example, water in the oceans evaporates and falls on the land as rain. However, except under infrequent and unusual conditions, there is no phosphorous in the atmosphere. There is a cycle of sorts, though; it involves the guano bird, which feeds on anchovies and other sea life and deposits its phosphate-rich droppings on some Pacific islands. These guano deposits are an important source of phosphate. Could it be that the droppings of the guano bird are one of the links that hold the chain of life together?

Phosphate is almost always in short supply in the environment. Phosphate is an essential ingredient of most fertilizers. In fact, there are those who say that depleted or "worn out" soils are basically lacking in phosphate. Asian farmers who have no access to commercial sources of phosphates have been advised to grind up animal bones and spread them on the soil. As the pressure on food supplies increases and as agriculture becomes more intensive, certain areas of the world may suffer from serious shortages of phosphates.

Are there other such links? Although we may not wish to face it, there is the danger of weak links, which might snap as the human population increases and, with it, the consumption of nonrenewable resources. At the very least, some of the complex environmental factors involving critical materials should be subjected to more intensive study and more careful monitoring. It is desirable — in some cases vital — to become aware of possible threats to tolerance levels before they become critical.

FOOD—A NECESSITY OF LIFE

Every individual needs a certain quantity and quality of food in order to live, grow, and approach optimum physical, emotional, and intellectual development. Every individual needs food to keep the body functioning, to maintain constant body temperature, for movement, for growth, for repair of tissue, and for the regulation of body functions. Food is the fuel that provides the energy needed to maintain the body and whatever activity we undertake. The amount of energy we have, how we feel, and, to a certain extent, our personalities are dependent upon the food that we take into our bodies. Also, all the tissue in our bodies is derived from the food we have eaten. Since much of this tissue is continuously being replaced, we continue to be dependent on the quality of the food we eat. If an individual eats too little or too much or cannot get all the nutrients that she or he needs, growth, health, and general body efficiency will be affected.

A certain amount of energy is needed to keep the body operating. The heart beats, the lungs move, blood flows, and a fairly constant

196 / POPULATION EDUCATION

body temperature has to be maintained. The energy needed to keep the body operating is called the basal metabolism. The amount of energy needed for basal metabolism varies with age, weight, height, and sex. While there are individual differences, we can gain an appreciation of the amount of food needed to keep the body operating by noting that the average energy requirement to maintain basal metabolism is about 1,500 kilocalories per day. (The kilocalorie is the "calorie" referred to in discussions of nutrition and diet. A kilocalorie is the amount of energy needed to raise by 1° C the temperature of one kilogram of water.) The body must have this energy. If it does not get it from the food that is eaten, body tissues—starting with body fat and going on to body proteins—are metabolized to provide the energy needed to keep the body operating.

In addition, individuals need energy for all of their activities, and this energy also comes from food. The total amount of energy needed by an individual depends upon basal metabolism, weight, age, sex, and amount of activity. However, in making calculations of the amount of food needed by populations, 2,800 kilocalories is often used as the average energy requirement of individuals—3,200 for males and 2,300 for females.[2] This averages out to approximately 2,800 kilocalories per individual.

A lack of food energy can lead first to irritability and then to general lethargy. Some children who seem "totally apathetic" may actually be lacking in nutrition. Clinicians have noted the amazing change that can take place in children and adults when they are placed on a diet that provides sufficient nutritional energy. If population pressure, natural calamities, or other causes lead to inadequate food supplies, the effect can be debilitating—individuals have less and less energy with which to improve their situation. Thus, in a famine, conditions tend to deteriorate unless help comes from outside, because individuals have less energy to help others and eventually not enough to help themselves.

Food is also needed for the growth and repair of body tissue. A 7-pound baby may eventually grow to become a 170-pound adult. The material used in this growth comes from the food that is eaten. Also, it has been estimated that most of the cells in the human body are replaced every 7 years. This replacement material, needed especially when the body is injured in any way, also comes from the food that is eaten. Nutritionists sometimes say, "We are what we eat." In a physical sense this is true, which makes it essential that the body receive the kinds of food that can be used for growth and repair.

Proteins are the food material used for growth and repair. However, the foods that are rich in proteins, such as meat and milk, are often scarce and expensive; thus, the poor and underprivileged throughout the world often suffer a lack of protein — a deprivation that is particularly critical for children.

Foods derived from animals — meat, milk, and eggs — are excellent sources of protein, but as we shall see, they are usually more expensive than those derived from plants. It is possible to obtain the necessary protein from such plant foods as soybeans, lentils, and peanuts, but more careful dietary planning is necessary because usually a larger quantity of food is needed to supply sufficient protein if only vegetable sources of protein are used. The debilitating protein deficiency disease kwashiorkor, which afflicts many children in Central and South America and in Africa, is generally caused by the absence of certain nutritional essentials in diets based on cereals such as corn. When these essentials are missing, children are weakened and become very susceptible to disease. One of the world's more serious problems with regard to food is to produce sufficient protein for everyone's needs.

In our diet we must also have such minerals as calcium, potassium, sulfur, sodium, chlorine, iron, and iodine. These are sufficiently widely available so that they will probably not be factors limiting human population size. However, many of our minerals come from foods that are rich in protein and usually relatively expensive. In most diets, for example, milk and milk products are the best sources of calcium. There are important regional deficiencies of certain minerals. Iodine, for example, is lacking in some Central American areas, and it was a common dietary deficiency in the Midwest until corrected with iodized salt.

If we close our eyes and picture a group of children, we would like to envision healthy, happy, lively youngsters bursting with energy and with no physical limitations upon their development. This picture holds true for some children, but for more than two-thirds of the world's children it does not. In many parts of the world, children are weakened by malnutrition, and more than 50 percent die before the age of 5. Those that survive to become adults do not grow as tall and as strong as they should. (Comparisons of children with their parents and grandparents, in the United States and in Japan, have shown the potentialities for growth with adequate nutrition.) They do not run and play as the children we envision on our cerebral TV; they are weak, lethargic, and sickly. This is the physical condition of the majority of the world's children.

Of equal importance for the future of the world is the effect of malnutrition upon intellectual development. As with so many other aspects of population study, there is multiple causation. Where there is malnutrition, there is usually poverty and all the other physical, social, and cultural factors associated with poverty. All of them probably have an impact upon the intellectual development of children. However, a brief description of one of several studies will indicate the kind of evidence that is beginning to indicate a relationship between malnutrition and intellectual development.

In a study of 20 children who were grossly undernourished in infancy, investigators found that, "Severe undernutrition during the first 2 years of life, when brain growth is most active, results in permanent reduction of brain size and restricted intellectual development."[3] The 20 children were matched with 20 other children with similar physical characteristics and of the same race and socioeconomic background. However, in the case of the experimental group, living conditions were much worse during the period of infancy. The children were followed for 11 years. The most striking physical difference between the two groups was that the undernourished children had a substantially smaller head circumference. There were significant differences between the groups on a variety of intelligence tests; 60 percent of the undernourished children fell below the level of the lowest child in the control group. The pattern of responses of the undernourished children to items on nonverbal subtests resembled those of brain-damaged children.

It has been estimated that about 70 percent of the world's population suffers to some extent from undernourishment. Studies of the effects of undernourishment among very young children show the importance of ensuring that infants receive adequate nutrition. However, studies of populations facing starvation conditions indicate that young children are among the first to be deprived of food. Fortunately, under less severe nutritional stress, infants may benefit during the crucial early months of their lives from being fed nutritious mothers' milk. If urbanization and other sociocultural changes lead to a decrease in breast feeding in societies where there is a serious shortage of food, the detrimental consequences for young children could be very serious.

While short-term undernourishment later in life has effects that seem to be reversible, it appears that the effects of severe malnutrition on a developing fetus during pregnancy and on young children in the first year or two of their lives are probably irreversible. This fact, of course, carries with it profound consequences for societies as well as for the individuals involved. If, as a result of population pressure, serious crop failures, breakdowns in food distribution, or ignorance, young children are seriously malnourished, they will carry the effects with them for the rest of their lives. They will be ill-equipped to deal with the problems and obstacles that face the world, particularly the developing countries.

Exercise: The Foods We Eat   Eating tends to be such a habitual act that many people are not aware of the kinds of food they eat or the quantities. A useful exercise is to have students record all foods (including snacks) that they eat for a period of 3 days, with one of these days being part of a weekend or a holiday. The students can then compare what they eat with the daily dietary plan suggested by the U.S. Department of Agriculture (USDA).[4] Following are the USDA suggested amounts from each of the four basic food groups:

1. Milk and milk products—milk, cheese, and ice cream. Three or four cups of milk a day for children. (Source of energy, minerals, and vitamins.)
2. Meat—beef, veal, pork, lamb, poultry, fish, and eggs. Two or more servings a day. (Major source of protein.)
3. Vegetables and fruit—dark green and deep yellow vegetables, citrus fruit, and other fruits and vegetables. Four or more servings a day. (Source of vitamins and minerals.)
4. Bread, breakfast cereals, wheat, rice, and oats. Four or more servings a day. (Source of energy and minerals.)

Sources of Food[5]   *We are ultimately dependent upon solar energy that has been utilized by green plants for the food that we and other organisms consume.* The plant and animal life in a balanced aquarium can exist for months without any food from the outside because green plants are the source of food — as they are for almost all the animals and plants in the biosphere.

However, a balance must be maintained between the population of plants and that of all the other organisms. If the number of snails, fish, and other animals becomes so great that they consume too much of the green plants, there will not be enough food to maintain the animal population or for the plant population to be able to renew itself. On the other hand, if there are too few animals and other organisms in the aquarium to convert a sufficient amount of the plant material into fertilizer, then plant growth will be limited. There are similar interrelationships in natural ecosystems, and they affect the food supply available to man.

The green plants on the land and in the sea use energy from the sun to combine carbon dioxide from the air with water and minerals to form food and release oxygen. In the simplest photosynthetic reactions, carbohydrates such as sugar and starch are formed, and these are our most important sources of energy. Such important sources of food as cereals, potatoes, and various root crops are composed largely of carbohydrates. Legumes such as clover, alfalfa, soybeans, and peanuts have nitrogen-fixing bacteria on their roots that make nitrogen from the air available to plants. The legumes use nitrates to manufacture proteins, and they contain two to four times as much protein as the grasses. Also, it is largely the proteins in legumes that are concentrated by the domestic animals that feed upon these plants to yield such protein-rich foods as meat, milk, and eggs. In considering food and man, it is important to emphasize the critical importance of this process of photosynthesis—it is the source of almost all of our food and much of our oxygen.

In some ways, photosynthesis may be considered an inefficient process. Only about .1 percent of the solar energy reaching the earth is utilized in the photosynthetic process. Moreover, about half this energy is used immediately by plants for their own respiration. Some of the plant's food is transported to and stored in the fruit, stem, or root. It is this stored food that can be utilized by man and other animals. Although at first glance the photosynthetic process may seem inefficient, total annual world production is estimated at 150 to 200 billion tons of dry organic matter. This is the material available as food for all the living organisms in the biosphere. About 5 percent, about 10 billion tons, of dry organic matter is produced in agricultural ecosystems and is available for use by man. As the human population grows, it may be possible and necessary to increase the amount of this basic raw material. Undoubtedly, it will be necessary to use it more efficiently.

Exercise: Example of a Balanced System Students can set up an aquarium that contains sand, green plants, two or three fish, and two or three snails, to demonstrate how food is produced and cycled in a balanced system. The aquarium should be placed near a window where it will be in bright sunlight. Once a week, or more often, students can record any of the following changes that appear to be taking place in the aquarium:

- Are the plants growing?
- Are green plants (algae) beginning to grow on the sides of the aquarium?
- Are the animals growing? Are their numbers increasing?
- Are there bubbles on the plants?
- Is there dark waste material on the bottom of the aquarium?
- What happens to plants or animals that die?

After several weeks the aquarium should be moved to a place where it receives very little light, with the students continuing to record changes that take place. What happens when the aquarium is deprived of sunlight?

Food Pyramids

Green plants form the base of the food pyramid; the further removed consumption is from the base of the food pyramid, the smaller is the percentage of the original energy that is utilized. Some of the food that is manufactured by green plants enters food chains or webs. A steer grazes on grass; when it is slaughtered, man eats the meat. This is a way humans can utilize the solar energy fixed by green plants, even though they do not eat much of them directly.

Energy conversion in food chains roughly follows the "10 percent law." A steer is able to convert only 10 percent of the energy in the grass into energy for its own body functioning and activity. A person, in turn, is able to convert only about 10 percent of the meat that he or she consumes into energy. This means that when you eat a steak, you are using only 1 percent of the energy that was fixed by the grass.

An examination of the food pyramid (see Figure 7-1) indicates that we use the original solar energy more efficiently when we eat plant materials. This, of course, is what vegetarians do. In regions where there is limited food supply, people tend to depend largely on such plants as rice, wheat, and corn. As we move up the food pyramid, much of the original energy is lost, and, of course, meat and other animal products become expensive. It has been said that we may pay more to feed a steer that eventually becomes a steak than the poor pay to feed themselves.

It is more difficult to obtain all dietary essentials, particularly proteins, if we restrict ourselves to eating the various parts of plants. However, soybeans, peanuts, and other legumes do contain considerable amounts of protein, and many vegetarians lead healthy and energetic lives while eating only plant products. If the pressure on food supplies becomes great and foods higher up the food pyramid become prohibitively expensive, our diets will, of necessity, contain a higher percentage of plant foods.

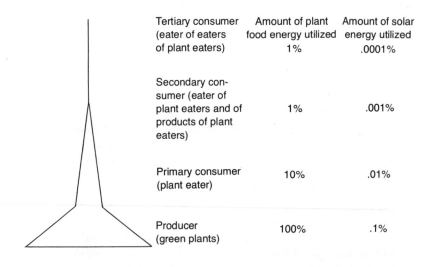

	Amount of plant food energy utilized	Amount of solar energy utilized
Tertiary consumer (eater of eaters of plant eaters)	1%	.0001%
Secondary consumer (eater of plant eaters and of products of plant eaters)	1%	.001%
Primary consumer (plant eater)	10%	.01%
Producer (green plants)	100%	.1%

Figure 7-1 Energy conversion in the food pyramid.

Spokesmen from developing nations have severely criticized people in the developed nations for the amount of meat they eat. As people improve their economic status, they tend to eat more meat; this has occurred in North America, Europe, and Japan. To produce this meat, a great deal of the original plant food is used. If everyone were to eat foods that are nearer the base of the food pyramid, such as cereals and tubers, more food would be available for everyone.

Exercise: Where on the Pyramid Are the Foods We Eat? Have students analyze the record of all the foods they have eaten for 3 days (as suggested on pp. 199 and classify each as to the level of the food pyramid it represents.

Food pyramid level	Number of servings
Producer	
Primary Consumer	
Secondary Consumer	
Tertiary Consumer	

About what percentage of the foods eaten are green plants (producers), that is, at the first level of the food pyramid?

World Food Requirements[6]

Population growth will make it increasingly difficult to provide all individuals with the food they need. There has been a shift in food production and consumption patterns, and a major factor contributing to this shift has been rapid population growth, particularly in the developing countries. In the early 1950s, many developing nations, such as India, were actually food-exporting nations. In 1967, the President's Science Advisory Committee Panel on World Food Supply published a 3-volume report, *The World Food Problem;* it suggested that (at that time) there was no worldwide shortage of food but that very serious nutritional problems were arising from uneven distribution among countries, within countries, and among families with different levels of income. In 1967, William and Paul Paddock, two students of food production and consumption, wrote a book with the shocking title *Famine 1975!* It stated that by 1975 major famines would occur in different parts of the world. As a harbinger of what might lie ahead, in 1966 and 1967 there were two successive monsoon failures on the Indian subcontinent. Tens of millions of people were saved from starvation by an armada of over 600 ships carrying one-fifth of the U.S. wheat crop to India. In 1973, another long-time student of food production and consumption, Georg Borgstrom, in *The Food and People Dilemma,* wrote that if all the food produced in the world were distributed equally, everyone would be malnourished. In 1974, J. George Harrar, president emeritus of the Rockefeller Foundation, stated:

> The world food picture from today's vantage point is not encouraging. A minimum of a 4 percent annual increase in food production is necessary to feed the present population, the 75 million new individuals who

join the world each year (200,000 each day) and to provide for reasonable reserves with which to guard against periods of deficit which occur all too frequently. We have not reached this 4 percent figure worldwide and in consequence, the poorer nations have become increasingly dependent upon North America and Australia.[7]

Also in 1974, Roger Revelle, a noted student of population and food supply, suggested that the planet could conceivably support a population of 40 to 50 billion if all the cultivated acreage in the world were farmed in the way that agriculture is carried out in the state of Iowa, that is, with intensive use of fertilizer, pesticides, and energy. However, he acknowledged that there was little chance of this happening.

Food production has increased in most parts of the world. In the 1950s, an annual increase of about 2.5 percent was achieved, largely by increasing the amount of land devoted to agriculture. Now, there is less new land that can be brought under cultivation. However, the introduction of improved strains of rice, wheat, and other cereals—the so-called Green Revolution—raised the annual increase in food production to about 4 percent during the 1960s.

It is believed that at least two-thirds of the world's population is undernourished or malnourished. The Food and Agriculture Organization (FAO) has suggested 2,800 as the average number of calories required daily by individuals. While North America and most countries of Western Europe have an average calorie intake of over 2,900, none of the mainland South and Southeast Asian countries has an average intake of over 2,200 calories. In spite of rationalizations to the effect that people with smaller body weights and living in warm climates may not need as many calories to maintain a reasonable energy level,[8] there must be hundreds of millions of people in South and Southeast Asia who are not getting enough food. Similar conditions exist in parts of Latin America, Africa, and the Middle East. In all these regions there are appalling numbers of people who lack the energy to work as hard they might and to achieve their full potential as individuals, simply because they do not get enough to eat.

Exercise: How the World's Food Supply Is Distributed Using the floor plan of population and land distribution given in Figure 7-2, it is possible to provide students with a practical demonstration of how discrepancies in world food distribution affect the daily life of people living on the various continents.

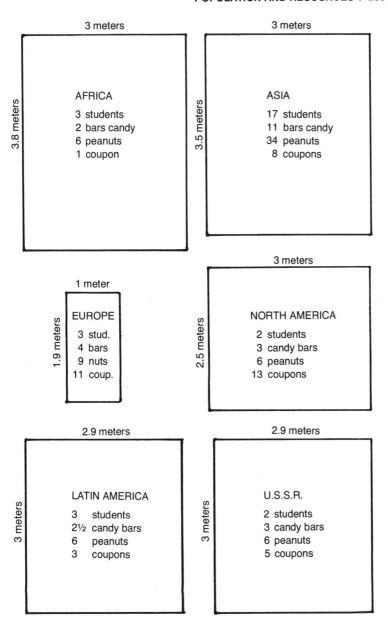

Figure 7-2 Continental floor plan showing world distribution of land, population, food, and income.

Distribution of daily calorie intake: Column 1 of Table 7-1 shows the average number of calories consumed by individuals on each of the continents. In this simulation, one chocolate bar will represent 3,000 calories, which is approximately the average daily allowance recommended by the FAO. The candy bars should be distributed among the continents and 30 students as follows:

Africa	3 students	2 bars
Asia	17 students	11 bars
Europe	3 students	4 bars
Latin America	3 students	2½ bars
North America	2 students	3 bars
U.S.S.R.	2 students	3 bars

However, this simulation is based upon the *average* amount of food eaten daily by the inhabitants of each region; that is, some inhabitants consume considerably more than others. The candy bars should, therefore, be *unevenly* distributed among the "inhabitants" of each continent.

What is the reaction of students who receive a comparatively small amount of candy? Of those who receive a comparatively large amount?

Distribution of daily protein intake: Protein is one of the essential types of food substances, and the one most often lacking in the diet of the poor.

Table 7-1
World Food Distribution

	Calories (average daily intake per person)	Protein (average daily intake per person, in grams)
Africa	2,190	58.4
Asia	2,170	60.0
Europe	3,200	93.7
Latin America	2,530	65.0
North America	3,320	105.2
U.S.S.R.	3,260	99.3
World	2,480	69.0

Abstracted from: Joseph J. Willett, ed., *The World Food Situation, Problems and Prospects to 1985* (Dobbs Ferry, N.Y.: Oceana, 1976), p. 162

Column 2 of Table 7-1 shows the average amount of protein consumed daily by individuals on each of the continents. In this simulation, three peanuts will represent an adequate daily intake of protein. Any student receiving less that three peanuts can be considered to be suffering from protein deficiency. The peanuts should be apportioned among 30 students as follows:

Africa	3 students	6 peanuts
Asia	17 students	34 peanuts
Europe	3 students	9 peanuts
Latin America	3 students	6 peanuts
North America	2 students	6 peanuts
U.S.S.R.	2 students	6 peanuts

Again, distribution should be unequal among "inhabitants" of a continent; some should receive four peanuts while others receive none.

Have the students consider and discuss the effect on people's daily lives—in terms of health, energy, and productivity—of the discrepancies in food distribution illustrated by this exercise. What can and should be done to make distribution more equitable?

Serious malnourishment and even starvation exists also in the United States.[9] The preliminary results of the first health and nutrition examination survey indicated that 95 percent of all preschool children and women of childbearing age receive less than the recommended amounts of iron. Inadequacies in other nutrients are found among such groups as preschool children and the low-income elderly.[10] In the United States, malnourishment is more likely to be due to ineffective distribution, inadequate income, and ignorance than to overall lack of resources to feed the population. Such programs as food stamps and school lunches are designed to bring food to those who need it, but these also can fail when those who need the programs are too proud to use them or where goodwill is lacking to implement programs locally.

In the early 1970s, there were serious famines in Afghanistan, Bangladesh, parts of India, Ethiopia, and in the Sahel region of Africa. There were also grain shortages in the U.S.S.R. The only countries with sizable food surpluses for export were Australia, Canada, and the United States. If a drought or major plant infection should occur in these countries, there would be no reserves to meet emergency food shortages in other areas of the world. Thus, the line between bare sufficiency and catastrophic famine is a dangerously thin one.

In addition to trying to slow population growth, we can lessen the risk of famine by increasing food production in a number of ways.

Since distribution has always been a problem and there is further safety in having agricultural production spread throughout the world, it would seem desirable to increase food production in the areas where the greatest need exists.

Increasing the Production of Food   *Food production can be increased through greater use of resources and improved efficiency in resource utilization.* Food production can be augmented by increasing the amount of land under cultivation; by improving the productivity of plants and animals; through increased use of fertilizers; through irrigation, mechanization, and the chemical control of weeds and pests; and possibly by farming the oceans. All these are important ways to provide the increased food supplies needed to feed a growing population and to improve overall standards of living. However, all these have environmental and social consequences that need to be carefully considered. And all require a fairly sophisticated level of technology and a fairly high general level of education.

INCREASING ACREAGE   It is estimated that there are about 3.5 billion acres of land now under cultivation and that another 5 billion acres are used for grazing. Since the world's population is a little over 4 billion, that represents less than 1 acre of cultivated land and 1.5 acres of grazing land per person. It has been estimated that a little over 5 acres of agricultural land per person are needed to maintain the standard of living enjoyed by many people in the United States.

One of the ways to support a growing population is to bring more land under cultivation and grazing. It is estimated that the total amount of land that might be brought under cultivation is 8 billion acres and, under grazing, another 8 billion acres. Then, the earth could produce the food to support a population of 10 to 12 billion at the level of about 2,800 calories per person. Much of the land that could be brought under cultivation is in South America and Africa; in South and Southeast Asia, where population density is the greatest, there is very little new land available for food production. Therefore, in the future we are likely to continue to have a geographical imbalance between food production and the need for food.

There are often climatic and ecological factors that must be considered in bringing new lands under cultivation and grazing. A warning is provided by the difficulties encountered by the U.S.S.R. in its attempt to bring virgin lands under cultivation in Siberia. There, undependable and usually inadequate rainfall has led to crop failures on a wide scale. Worldwide, there are problems and risks in bringing under cultivation lands on mountainsides, in marshes, swamps, and deserts, and in the far north and south, where growing seasons are short and erratic. Much of the new land will be on hillsides, which will increase the danger of excessive soil erosion. Erosion, in turn, can lead to the rapid silting up of reservoirs used for irrigation and hydroelectric power. To illustrate the complexities of ecosystems, some ecologists fear that cutting and clearing the tropical rain forests in the Amazon Basin might lead to a depletion of the oxygen supply in the atmosphere. While we cannot predict all the possible consequences of tampering with natural ecosystems, it is important that a concerted effort be made to forestall the most undesirable consequences that can be foreseen.

One of the very important ways that food production can be increased is through intensive gardening.[12] Britain, for example, during World War II, raised its food production remarkably through victory gardens; these were planted not only in family backyards but on vacant lots, by the roadsides, and even on cricket fields. Where there is plenty of water and a warm or temperate climate, a great deal of food can be grown in a relatively small area. However, in some of the poorest regions of the world, water is a limiting factor. Much agriculture in these regions is already very intensive, but it is utterly dependent upon the availability of irrigation water.

Exercise: Growing More Food Students can gain first-hand experience and make a direct contribution to increased food production by undertaking to cultivate a garden. In many cases they will have access to small plots of land near their homes. Even in large, densely populated cities, gardening is possible using vacant lots or plots provided by schools or botanical gardens. A great deal of information about gardening is available from state agricultural extension services, the U.S. Department of Agriculture, and the many garden books available in almost any library.

IMPROVING PLANT AND ANIMAL STRAINS Remarkable progress has been made in increasing plant and animal productivity since 1940. In the United States, yields per acre of corn and potatoes have more than tripled, and wheat and soybean yields have more than doubled. Until 1940, average corn yields were 22 to 26 bushels per acre; now, yields of up to 300 bushels per acre have been achieved, and yields of 400 bushels per acre are considered possible. Milk and egg production have increased even more dramatically. Similar kinds of increases in productivity are being striven for in developing countries through the Green Revolution.

The improvement of seeds has been a major factor in this increased production. Almost all corn in the United States is now grown from hybrid seeds, and this has been largely responsible for the dramatic rise in corn production. Hybrid corn that can mature within a shorter growing season has been developed; as a result, corn is now also being grown in Canada. New varieties of wheat, rice, and other food plants have been developed that give much higher yields. As a consequence of the development of short-stalked, nonlodging wheat (wheat that remains erect), with more kernels per stalk, Mexico has been able to triple its wheat production. Development of the "miracle" rice varieties in the Philippines has led to a quintupling of yields. Concerted efforts are under way to adapt these high-yield varieties, or to develop similar ones, for use in developing countries around the world.

However, using new high-yield varieties of plants entails problems and dangers. A farmer can no longer depend on using the best of his own crop for seed. Instead, he is dependent upon an outside source — which means dependence upon a fairly sophisticated technology for something as basic as the seeds he plants. There is also the danger that a planting of one particular kind of hybrid seed might succumb to some kind of disease or insect. In 1970, a substantial part of the U.S. corn crop was attacked by corn blight, and the crop yield was reduced by 10 percent. In 1971, however, the corn crop was not affected by corn blight, and production outstripped corn storage facilities. The danger of having an entire crop threatened in regions that do not have any stored reserves is something to be concerned about. Similar dangers exist for new, improved strains of livestock.

MECHANIZATION One of the major contributions of mechanization is that it makes available a greater proportion of farm produce for use by humans — no longer is a substantial part of the produce consumed by the horse, mule, or bullock. Since the energy for mechanized farming almost always comes from fossil fuels, mechanization can be viewed as the use of stored solar energy, that is, solar energy that was trapped long ago to form oil and coal deposits, making it possible for us to use a larger fraction of the total solar energy reaching the earth.

Mechanization of agriculture often reduces waste. Even in societies where labor is very cheap, it has been found economical to introduce threshing machines and even tractors. The tremendous losses to wind, insects, birds, and rodents when threshing is done in the old, traditional way—with patient bullocks plodding round and around on the piles of grain and the chaff removed by gusts of wind—are largely eliminated with the use of mechanical threshing machines. Although there may be long periods when work can go on at a leisurely pace, in agriculture, there are periods when it is critical that certain kinds of work be completed rapidly. For example, when grain or grape is ripe, it is critical that it be harvested before hail or wind storms strike and before the crop becomes overripe, spoils, or falls to the ground. In these and other ways, mechanization can make more food available.

INCREASED USE OF FERTILIZER Another major way of increasing food production is through the extensive use of fertilizer. At the present time it is estimated that at least one-fourth of the world's food supply is dependent on the use of fertilizer. It is not uncommon for a Midwestern farmer, following increased yields, to double the investment he makes in fertilizer. In regions such as Japan, where very intensive agriculture is practiced, suitable fertilizers are essential.

Nitrogen, potash, and phosphates are the most common materials supplied through fertilizers. It may turn out that one of the greatest inventions of all time is the Haber process and its refinements, by which nitrogen from the air can be fixed and utilized for fertilizer. Since the atmosphere is about 80 percent nitrogen, the resources available for agriculture by this process are very large. However, considerable energy, often in the form of fossil fuels, is needed to manufacture nitrogen fertilizer. Similarly, there seems to be ample resources of potash. The potash deposits in Canada alone are probably large enough to supply the world's needs for centuries. However, phosphate resources are limited, and unfortunately there are practically no deposits on the Asian mainland.

IRRIGATION Where there is limited rainfall, or where rainfall is concentrated in a very short rainy season, irrigation can make it possible to carry on agriculture. In fact, some of the most populous regions on earth are arid, or almost all their rainfall is concentrated during one season. Thus, irrigation can be a very important way of increasing food supply. Even in areas that are being farmed intensively, production can often be increased through irrigation. The new breeds of plants used in the Green Revolution require a dependable water supply for their most effective use. In much of Asia, implementation of the Green Revolution will depend upon the extended use of irrigation.

Undoubtedly, more land will be brought under cultivation through irrigation, and irrigation will increase the productivity of some land already under cultivation. The Science Advisory Committee Panel predicted that the amount of irrigated land throughout the world may double by the year 2000. It is especially important that irrigation development be speeded up in South Asia — that continent of thirsty lands and hungry people. However, the development of large irrigation systems requires regional development and, often, international cooperation. For example, use of the waters of the Colorado River requires cooperation between Mexico and the United States; use of the Indus River, cooperation between Pakistan and India.

CONTROL OF WEEDS AND PESTS   Many other organisms compete for the same resources that humans use. In agriculture, we try to control the growth of various plants so that the plants we favor — be they corn or wheat, rice or oats — can grow while weeds are controlled. Weeds compete for the water, soil nutrients, light, and space that are needed by food plants; we try to control the growth of weeds with methods ranging from hacking with a hoe to spraying with industrially produced fungicides and herbicides. Animals, ranging from insects to rodents and others, eat the same foods that we do. We try to reduce the populations of such competitors by direct killing — with fly swatter, shovel, or trap — or the use of chemical and biological insecticides and rodenticides. It is estimated that in the United States at least 30 percent of agricultural production and 10 percent of livestock production are lost to pests. In developing countries the losses are undoubtedly far higher. Since these losses are very significant, an important approach to increasing food production is to try to improve the control of weeds and pests.

Much food is lost to insects and rodents, or through spoilage, during storage and transportation. This is especially true in developing nations, where a third of the food may be lost in these ways.

Construction of insect-, rodent-proof storage facilities will make that much more food available to humans.

FOOD FROM THE SEA About three-fourths of the earth's surface is covered with water, and the seas receive solar energy at the same rate as the terrestrial surface. To look to the seas for food may be considered a way of increasing the acreage devoted to food production.

In the oceans, the major limiting factor for food production is the supply of mineral nutrients. Obviously, there is ample water, and cold ocean currents, such as the Labrador Current that chills the beaches of the east coast of North America, carry in dissolved air a great deal of carbon dioxide. But mineral matter is essential, and it comes from the rivers that empty into the sea and from the ocean bottoms. Primarily because of a lack of mineral matter, about 90 percent of the oceans — the great open sea — must be considered a biological "desert." The open sea produces little food and has little or no potential for producing any more. This chilling fact, that almost three-fourths of the earth's surface cannot produce much in the way of food is a major limit to the biotic potential of Planet Earth.

The 1968 yield of about 69 million metric tons of food from the sea may eventually be increased to between 150 and 160 million metric tons. This will be done by tapping potential fisheries, such as those that may exist off Antarctica, improved fishing technology, and, hopefully, wiser harvesting of the fish crops of the great Atlantic and Pacific fisheries. But if world population at the turn of the next century is 6 to 7 billion, only about 3 percent of human energy requirements will come from food from the sea. Fish is, nevertheless, a very important source of animal protein. Many cereal-based diets are enriched with protein from fish meal. Incaparina, the synthetic food used to provide needed protein in diets in Central and South America, has fish meal as an important ingredient. It has been estimated that about 23 percent of the minimal protein needs of the human population can be met from present fish production. But if fish production could be increased to 150 or 160 million metric tons, it would mean that about 37 percent more protein per person would be available, even if population were to increase to 6 billion.

IMPROVING TECHNOLOGY AND EDUCATION Almost all approaches to increasing world food supplies involve more sophisticated technology. Growing two or three crops where only one was grown before calls for more careful soil culturing and a greater knowledge of the characteristics of the various crops that can be grown. To increase acreage, heavy equipment is often necessary. Irrigation farming is one of the more complicated forms of agriculture. The use of hybrid seeds requires the technology to develop the seeds and the know-how to use them. Tractors, motors, threshing machines, mechanical harvesters, and other mechanized equipment call for a modicum of skill to use and considerable expertise to maintain and repair. The modern farmer needs simultaneously to be an agronomist and animal husbandryman, mechanic and technician, businessman and, hopefully, ecologist. To increase our food supplies significantly, the requisite skills and knowledge will have to be acquired by many more people.

Increasing food production will require a higher level of general education among those who work the land, raise the animals, and harvest the oceans. There are stories of peasants who neglected to put oil in tractors, and one case at least of precious hybrid seed, the product of several years of development, being sold to a local baker. Not all problems can be foreseen; it is the hand on the plow and the finger on the button of the irrigation gate that is critical for increased food production. Farmers the world over will need the general educational background that will make it possible for them to use the technology judiciously and to anticipate and cope with the problems that often follow in its wake.

BUT ... GREATER SOPHISTICATION, GREATER RISK As world population grows and agricultural systems become more sophisticated, the risks increase and the possibilities for catastrophic breakdowns become more stark. In early agriculture, when man domesticated the plants and animals in his local ecosystem, there was little risk of complete failure of the system. But with just a few varieties of highly productive breeds of plants and animals being used, the risk is increased that disease or some other catastrophe will destroy a significant portion of a year's crop. What would happen to the world food supply if 90 percent of the U.S. corn crop were destroyed by some disease such as the 1970 corn blight? (This is feared by some experts.) Natural disasters can also occur. In 1815, Mt. Tambora in Indonesia exploded a massive amount of material into the atmosphere. The amount of solar energy received on the surface of the earth apparently was significantly reduced: snow fell in New York

City in June, and the 1816 growing season throughout the world was seriously affected. Central North America is one of the most productive agricultural areas in the world and regularly produces food surpluses. However, it does experience occasional droughts and may have a periodic drought cycle of about 20 years. Now that the earth's population is over 4 billion, what would happen if a substantial part of one season's crop were lost? The world's cushion of food reserves is very unsubstantial. A world food bank containing food reserves from those regions that have surpluses might provide a partial buffer against disaster in the future.

MATERIALS AND LIFE STYLES

While a certain minimum of material is essential for life, the amounts and kinds of materials we use depend largely upon our style of life. In addition to food and water, we also need fiber for clothing and various kinds of material for shelter, household goods, and cooking utensils. The need for essential materials varies somewhat, with needs being somewhat greater in colder climates. However, there is an irreducible minimum of material needed, and, as the population grows, the total amount of the basic, essential material required increases.

Exercise: The Kinds of Materials We Use   People in different societies and cultures use varying amounts of various materials. It is useful for students (and others) to become aware of the kinds of materials they use, and one way to do this is to keep a "materials diary."

In a materials diary, students might try to list all the different kinds of materials they use during the course of one day. When the diaries are completed, they can be compared with those kept by a 12-year-old student in New York City and a student of the same age in an Asian village.

The materials diary of a 12-year-old student in New York City:
A. Home:
     1. Wood (floors, furniture, etc.)
     2. Plaster (walls and ceiling)
     3. Copper (electrical wires and utensils)
     4. Steel (building framework, utensils, etc.)
     5. Bricks (building)
     6. Cement (building)
     7. Cotton (clothes, furniture)

     8. Wool (clothes, furniture)
     9. Glass (windows, dishes)
   10. Ceramics (plates, lamps, etc.)
   11. Tungsten (light bulbs)
   12. Mercury (fluorescent light, electrical switches, thermometers)
   13. Plastic (furniture, dishes, etc.)
   14. Synthetic fibers (clothes, furniture, etc.)
   15. Rubber (electrical insulation, furniture, etc.)
   16. Silver (tableware)
   17. Brass (doorknobs and fixtures)
   18. Silicon, germanium, etc. (radio and television)
   19. Graphite (pencils)
   20. Aluminum (television antenna, siding, window sashes)
   21. Paper (books, newspapers, etc.)
   22. Leather (shoes, etc.)

B. Bus and subway:
     1. Steel
     2. Copper
     3. Vanadium
     4. Chromium
     5. Nickel
     6. Lead
     7. Mica
     8. Plastics
     9. Glass
   10. Rubber
   11. Graphite
   12. Aluminum
   13. Paper

C. School and playground:
Many of the same materials as in the home.

The materials diary of a 12-year-old student in an Asian village:[13]

A. Home:
     1. Clay (house and water containers)
     2. Steel (cooking utensils)
     3. Aluminum (cooking utensils)
     4. Cotton (clothes)
     5. Synthetic fibers (clothes)
     6. Leather (shoes)
     7. Wood (furniture, roofing, etc.)
     8. Plastics (buttons, etc.)

B. School:
1. Paper
2. Chalk
3. Clay
4. Cement
5. Wood

After completing their own materials diaries, students might consider the following questions:

- Which materials in your diary do you consider absolutely essential? Which materials do you believe it would be possible to do without?
- In what ways is your diary like that of the student in New York City? In what ways is it like that of the student in an Asian village? In what ways does it differ from both of them?

The United States, with about 6 percent of the world's population, uses about 30 percent of the materials consumed in the world. (However, it also produces about 26 percent of the world's materials.) Because of the rate at which people in the United States use materials, it has been suggested that it is especially important that population growth in the United States be limited. During the course of a lifetime, a child born in the United States will probably use much more of the earth's material resources than a child born in one of the developing nations.

However, aspirations for higher material standards of living are found not only in the United States and other developed nations. "Developing" in the developing nations often *means* achieving a higher material standard of living—more food, clothing, bicycles, automobiles, radio and television sets, schools and hospitals, and better quality homes. Even the poorest peasant in the fastest-growing population is likely to strive for things she or he hears about over the omnipresent transistor radio, catches a glimpse of in an occasional newspaper or magazine, or sees displayed by the infrequent visitor from the outside. As with many other aspects in this problem area, it is not fruitful to try to separate population growth and the other variables that lead to burgeoning aspirations for material things. We appear to live in a world where there are not only more people, but where more people want more things. If the rest of the world's population were to use material resources at the same rate as the population of the United States, the drain upon the world's natural resources would be 100 to 200 times as great and, perhaps, could not be supported.

Changes in life style can reduce the demands made on material resources. It would be possible, for example, to stress such forms of recreation as music, art, and those hobbies and sports in which there is very little need for materials. Sometimes materials that are plentiful can be substituted for those that are scarce; for many uses, relatively abundant aluminum can be substituted for less abundant copper and silver. The optimum use of mass transportation requires less material and energy expended per passenger than do automobiles carrying only their drivers. Deliberate programs of recycling make it possible to use the same materials over and over again.

More affluent life styles increase the demand for material substances and so does population growth. Together they make us more dependent on distant sources, narrow our choices, increase the costs, enlarge the risks, and amplify the deleterious impact upon the environment. Even though modifications in life style may reduce the amount of materials each individual uses, every individual has to have certain minimum essentials. Thus, an increase in population leads to an increase in demand. Some materials — mercury and tin, for example — are found primarily in a few deposits in faraway countries; as we use up our limited deposits, we become more and more dependent upon those distant sources. One way to meet the demand for materials is to mine less concentrated deposits, but this almost invariably means handling, processing, and disposing of larger amounts of waste materials and using a great deal of energy to do it — all of which can have considerable adverse effect on the environment.

Some nations have very little choice with regard to materials — they have to strive to obtain those that are essential for life. For them, increases in population make the struggle for necessities that much more desperate. Nations that have choices will probably find their options diminishing as their populations grow. Of course, population growth, with resultant greater demand for materials, increases risks — there is the risk that some critical material will become in short supply, that some proposed solution to a materials problem will be tried before it has been adequately tested, or that some "solution" will have a critically deleterious effect upon the environment.

Material Resources in Limited Supply[14] *Populations need minerals and other substances of which there is a limited supply available.*[15] Anyone who keeps a materials diary will be im-

pressed by the range of materials that we use in our daily lives. Starting with breakfast, in the average kitchen one may find aluminum and nickel from Canada, copper from Chile, iron from Minnesota, silver from Mexico, and tungsten from Nevada. Some of the essential materials used are not so clearly in evidence: phosphate, potash, and nitrates were needed to grow our breakfast cereal, and uranium may have been used to generate the electricity needed to brew our coffee. As we proceed through the day, we use many other materials made from minerals. Some of these are absolutely essential for life; others help provide a certain standard of living. (Material standard of living is often expressed in terms of the consumption of raw materials and the use of energy.) Since it is individuals who use materials and energy, and there is a basic minimum required for each, the amount used tends to grow as population grows. It is, of course, possible for some individuals to reduce the amount of materials and energy they use, but this is not often done by choice.

Although estimates of existing materials are fraught with difficulties and inherent inaccuracies, policies have to be developed and plans executed on the basis of the best evidence that we have. In discussing this topic, we will draw upon the terminology commonly used in discussing material and mineral supplies.[16]

Reserves are known deposits from which minerals can be extracted with existing technology and under present economic conditions. We know, for example, that there are rich deposits of nickel near Sudbury, Ontario, and this district has been producing more than half of the world supply since about 1905. Reserves can be compared to money in the bank; it is known to be there and can be withdrawn at almost any time. We know the location and approximate size of some deposits and can mine them whenever we wish.

Resources include not only reserves but also deposits that can be recovered with improved technology or when economic conditions make it feasible and profitable. *Identified resources* are those whose existence and location are known. *Hypothetical resources* are those that can reasonably be expected to exist in areas where finds have been made. *Speculative resources* are those that are undiscovered but thought to exist because of geologic similarities with areas that contain known deposits. In the financial analogy, resources as a whole would be represented by the money one has in a bank plus all that one can expect to earn in the future. Just as we cannot be sure how much we will earn in the future, we cannot be certain what resources will actually become proven reserves. Whether resources actually become reserves depends not only on proven existence but also upon the state of extractive technology, the availability of energy, and the level of economic demand.

Estimates of the extent of the world's critical resources that are in limited supply are obviously crude, dependent upon the assumptions made and justifiably subject to criticism from both optimists and pessimists. However, some notion of the availability of materials is necessary if intelligent policy decisions are to be made. The Commission on Population Growth and the American Future estimated that worldwide reserves of the following minerals are inadequate through the year 2020:[17]

Aluminum	Sulfur
Copper	Tin
Lead	Titanium
Manganese	Tungsten
Molybdenum	Zinc

Other analysts have added such minerals as phosphates, mercury, and nickel.

It is important to recognize some of the complications involved in making such estimates and developing policies based on them. Some critics have remarked that while there have been many predictions of impending shortages, we have never actually "run short" of anything. Copper is still being mined in King Solomon's copper mines in the Middle East; when new technology is developed or economic conditions change to make mining profitable, old mines can be reopened. Aluminum is on the list of elements in short supply, but aluminum is one of the most common elements in the earth's crust. It is found in low concentrations in ordinary clay. Extracting it would involve handling tremendous quantities of clay and would consume a great deal of energy—all of which would have monumental environmental impact. But the aluminum is there, and it could be obtained. There are very large deposits of phosphates, but few are located in South Asia, which is one of the regions of greatest need. Because of their bulk, phosphates are expensive to ship, but it can be done. Then, there is the nagging concern that a shortage may occur of some critical mineral for which we can find no adequate substitute, for example, mercury. Might there be some mineral link in the chain of life which, if it should break, would snap the chain? Although survival, or at least survival of ways of life, are at stake, policy decisions will probably have to be made on the basis of data about which no one can be very certain.

Discussion: Limited Resources and Future Policy It is important for young people to consider some of the implications of limited resources for future policy. Following are some proposals that you and your students may wish to discuss:

Limit population growth: As Sterling Brubaker has said, "It is hard to make a positive case for increased population."[18] In general, a growing population places growing demands upon limited resources and reduces the number of options we have. It might be better to limit population growth at a level that is still supportable.

Change our style of life so that we use fewer of the materials that are in limited supply. Preston Cloud has estimated that, if all of the peoples in the world were to use mineral raw materials at the rate the people of the United States use them, the annual production of such minerals as iron, lead, zinc, and tin would have to be multiplied 100 to 200 times present annual production.[19] This would indeed place a heavy strain on the world's resources that are in limited supply.

Increase the price of materials so that they will be used with greater care and so that it will be economic to mine lower grade ores. Hans H. Landsberg has pointed out that, "When one speaks of increasing scarcity, one refers properly not to an absolute running out of material as such, but of materials possessing characteristics that enable them to be sold at a price that will attract buyers."[20]Increasing the price may increase the supply and ensure that the supply will be more wisely used.

Carry out aggressive research and development to produce substitutes for scarce materials. The National Materials Advisory Board has recommended that, "The search for substitutes should be encouraged wherever positive benefits might be achieved, as in improved product durability, disposability, recyclability, or the elimination of toxic materials, [and] the use of relatively abundant rather than less abundant materials should be encouraged wherever that is practicable."[21]

Monitor supply and demand of essential materials, so that action can be taken before shortages become critical. The Committee on Resources and Man recommended that "action should be taken to reduce the lag between the recognition of probable mineral-resource shortages and investigations intended to alleviate them."[22] There is the danger that a shortage of some essential material could have critical consequences.

Keep avenues of supply open: No nation or region is completely self-sufficient with regard to natural resources. In the words of the National Materials Advisory Board, "All signs point to a growing world need for materials. For most countries, there will be an increasing interdependence on sources of raw materials. The United States, as one of the world's major industrialized nations, will continue to need broad access to varied sources of supplies."[23]

Access to Material Resources *Essential resources are not evenly distributed; populations everywhere need to have access to vital supplies.* Essential materials are not found everywhere, but they are needed by everyone. There are large phosphate deposits in North America, North Africa, and the U.S.S.R., but there is a need for phosphate fertilizer everywhere. Canada has been producing about 80 percent of the nickel in the free world. The largest known reserves of petroleum are in the Arabian peninsula. Perhaps most important of all, only three countries (Australia, Canada, and the United States) usually have surpluses of food. Unfortunately, the essential resources are often not located where the populations are growing the fastest and where the needs are greatest.

One of the challenges in the future will be to find ways of ensuring the distribution of essentials. The logistical difficulties involved in transporting large quantities of bulky materials from point of production to point of use are considerable. The huge supertankers and the long, wide-diameter pipelines across frozen tundra and barren deserts are examples of the tremendous investment in effort, capital, and technology required to transport such commodities. But, the political difficulties are probably even greater. On the one hand there are tariffs, import and export quotas, and the intricacies of monetary and commodity exchanges. Perhaps inevitably, control over vital commodities tends to be used for political, economic, and military purposes. However, this can threaten the welfare of those who need the materials. In the future it may become necessary to ensure that "those in need will receive."

ENERGY AND STANDARDS OF LIVING[24]

Higher material standards of living are in large part dependent upon the availability of energy. Populations are growing and so are the aspirations of many of the individuals who make up these populations. Perhaps, the single most important resource that can be used to attain and raise material standards of living is energy. It is possible for families to survive frigid winters with a charcoal burner under a low table covered with blankets, with all members of the family inserting as much of their bodies as possible into this blanket tent. (One difficulty is that the head freezes while the toes are charcoal toasted.) However, if given a choice, most people would probably prefer the extravagance of space heating. Most peoples of the world probably do most of their traveling on foot; but when a choice becomes possible, automobiles proliferate. The sight of a multitude of women pounding clothes on a smooth rock at the river's edge is an excellent subject for tourist photographers, but if given a chance, the women will usually opt for a washing machine. The devices that enable people to raise their standard of living usually require energy.

The world's use of energy is increasing much faster than the human population. Energy doubling time is estimated to be 20 years, as contrasted to population doubling time of 35 years. This rapid increase in the use of energy is at least partly a function of the worldwide struggle for improved material standards of living. Since this struggle will undoubtedly continue, we can expect the use of energy to continue to increase.

The United States probably has one of the highest average material standards of living. With about 6 percent of the world's population, it uses about 35 percent of the energy consumed annually. As others strive for higher standards of living, they will certainly increase their consumption of energy. Thus, it is important to survey the ways in which energy is used and the energy resources that may be available to populations in the future.

Exercise: The Ways We Use Energy One way for students to gain an awareness of the ways we use energy is to keep an "energy use diary," a list of the kinds of energy they use during the course of a day and the ways they use it. When the diaries have been completed, they can, as previously, be compared with those kept by a 12-year-old student in New York City and a boy of the same age in an Asian village.

The energy use diary of a 12-year-old student in New York City:
A. Fossil fuel oil for heating home and school.
B. Electricity from coal, hydropower, or nuclear power:
    1. For lighting home, school, and city
    2. For the subway system
    3. For water pump

    4. For such household appliances as refrigerator, stove, washing machine, dishwasher, air conditioner, vacuum cleaner, television, radio, toaster, clocks

    5. For such gadgets as motion picture and slide projectors, tape recorder, hi-fi set, etc.

C. Gasoline for automobile

D. Diesel oil for bus

In addition, large amounts of energy were used to grow and process this student's food, to manufacture the fibers for his clothes, the steel and other materials used in construction of his home and the subway system, and the quantities of aluminum and other materials listed in his materials diary (see pp. 215-6).

The energy use diary of a 12-year-old student in an Asian village.[25]

A. Electricity from coal or hydropower, kerosene, or gasoline for lighting home and village

B. Wood or dried dung for cooking

C. Electricity from dry cells for radio.

    In addition, a little energy was used to grow and process this student's food and in the manufacture of his clothes, cooking utensils, and other items listed in his materials diary (see p. 216).

    After completing their own energy use diaries, students might consider the following questions:

• What form of energy do you use most often?

• Which energy uses would you consider to be absolutely essential? Which could you possibly do without?

• In what ways is your diary like that of the student in New York City? In what ways is it like that of the student in an Asian village? In what ways does it differ from both of them?

    The per capita daily use of energy is 23 times greater in the United States than it is in India. The annual growth rate in per capita energy demand is about 1 percent in the United States and about .3 percent in India. However, about one-third of the energy used per capita in the United States is in the form of petroleum to fuel the relatively inefficient internal combustion engine that powers automobiles. The automobile is a very significant contributor to our high per capita energy use.

The largest source of energy used in the United States and many other countries (1978) is oil and natural gas. Both are fossil fuels in which solar energy received eons ago is stored. The United States is among the nations, both developed and developing, that are dependent upon other nations, particularly those in the Arabian peninsula, for this essential commodity. Withholding or raising the price of oil and natural gas can have dire consequences for national economies. The search for more oil continues, but drilling under the waters covering the continental shelves and obtaining oil from the far north are difficult and expensive. Always there are environmental problems. And, of course, there will be a limit to the amount of oil that can be extracted from the earth. We can reduce our consumption of fossil fuels, but this will require the cooperation of most energy users. Rational energy policies should also be developed, and the students of today should prepare themselves to contribute to the development of such policies.

It has been said that each year there are more people wanting more things, and choices may have to be made between population growth and continued improvement in material standards. Unless abundant and inexpensive sources of energy become available, it may be difficult for everyone in the world to achieve a material standard of living comparable to that of those who live in North America or Western Europe and difficult for people in North America and Western Europe to maintain such standards. This is another area of decision making in which students of today will probably have to make choices tomorrow. Perhaps students should begin to consider ways in which the total amount of available energy can be increased and in which the energy that is currently available can be more fairly shared.

Exercise: Income Per Person Throughout the World The ability of people to fulfill their needs, whether for food, materials, or energy, depends upon their income. Incomes vary widely throughout the world—not only among continents but also within each continent. Table 7-2 shows the gross national product (GNP) per person in the various continents. The total GNPs of nations in a continent is divided by the total population of the continent. The total GNP, usually, is not divided equally among the population.

Using the floor plan of land and population distribution already established in Figure 7-2, discrepancies in income can be graphically illustrated to students. Make paper coupons, each of which represents $1,000 annual per capita income, and distribute the coupons among 30 students as follows:

Africa	3 students	1 coupon
Asia	17 students	8 coupons
Europe	3 students	11 coupons
Latin America	3 students	3 coupons
North America	2 students	13 coupons
U.S.S.R.	2 students	5 coupons

Once again, the distribution among each continent's "inhabitants" should be unequal.

Have the students who represents the various continents think about and discuss what could be purchased with their individual shares of annual income—some will have insufficient income to meet even their bare subsistence needs, others will have the means to secure for themselves many luxuries. What are the implications of these glaring discrepancies in purchasing power?

Table 7-2
Distribution of World Income

	Gross national product per capita (in dollars)
Africa	440
Asia	610
Europe	4,420
Latin America	1,100
North America	7,850
U.S.S.R.	2,760
World	1,650

SOURCE: 1978 Gross National product per capita derived from Population Reference Bureau, *1978 World Population Data Sheet* (Washington, D.C.: Population Reference Bureau)

CONCLUSION

Population is one of several factors related to the demand for resources; a continuing growth in population will almost inevitably lead to a greater demand for many resources. It has been argued that developments other than population growth have placed great drains upon resources. Developments in technology have led to much greater use of natural resources. As more people begin to use automobiles for transportation, the demands upon available resources are increased manyfold. Affluence and the desire for affluence has also greatly increased the drain upon natural resources. A family who lives in a centrally heated/air-conditioned house, has one or more automobiles, radios, television sets, vacuum cleaners, refrigerators, and cooking ranges — in addition to the level of skill and education needed to be able to earn these material accoutrements — certainly uses much more of the earth's resources than a family who has none of these. There is value in trying to analyze the factors that lead to the use of resources — it may lead us in the direction of a technology that would place less strain upon resources and the environment and perhaps curb somewhat the universally voracious appetite for more material goods.

But the attempt to pinpoint the factors that lead to resource depletion can also be misleading. Many factors, not just population growth, have an impact upon resource use. In fact, they are often synergistic, in that growth in one factor has an impact upon the other factors. A growth in population, for example, will probably require an acceleration in technological development in order to feed many more people; it will also increase the number of individuals who aspire to higher levels of affluence. Not only is the whole greater than the sum of its parts, but changes in any one of the parts lead to changes in many of the other parts and to much greater changes in the whole.

Exercise: Seeing the "Whole" as Well as the "Parts" The necessity to see the "whole" and the interaction between the "parts" poses difficult intellectual problems for students. The tendency in many sciences is to be reductionistic, that is, to analyze the whole into its component parts. But in many modern problem areas this can be misleading. In literature and the arts, and a few of the sciences, such as ecology, the emphasis is on the interrelationships that make up wholes. It is important to view the world's problems from this perspective as well as using the analytical-reductionistic approach.

One of the ways to do this is to try to place oneself in a different time/space frame. For example, how might a novelist writing in the year 2050 describe the living conditions of various individuals in developed and developing nations in the 1970s? How might an artist or ecologist equipped with "X-ray vision" view the lot of humankind today from a perspective outside our planet?

Population growth will tend to exacerbate many of man's problems and limit his choices. It is likely to call for more rather than less technology (How else will we be able to grow more food and process the lower-grade ores necessary to support larger populations?) and it is likely to increase the number of people who desire to become affluent. Continued population growth may also generate powerful social and international tensions. What will happen if large segments of the world's population cease to believe they have a chance to acquire the food and other resources that they need or the artifacts of affluence to which they aspire? If they give up hope and become desperate, the tensions could conceivably affect every individual everywhere. The futures of students in the classrooms of Boston and Bangkok are linked with what happens in Chicago and Calcutta. One of the objectives of population education is to foster an awareness of how "close to home" the problems of world poverty and world hunger really are. The future of our students and of young people throughout the world will depend on their ability to make wise decisions about the world's resources.

The study of population and resources raises very profound questions about people, purposes, and the kind of future we want. This has been stated very clearly and succinctly by Bernard Berelson.

> What are people for? That is the profound question underlying the problems of population. The question is of course unanswerable in any definitive or final sense, but it serves to remind us that quantitative answers are not acceptable. And contrary to common belief, population problems do not deal at bottom with quantities — with numbers or rates or densities or movements — but with the qualities of human life: prosperity in place of poverty, education in place of ignorance, health in place of illness and death, environmental beauty in place of deterioration, full opportunities for the next generations of children in place of current limitations. Population trends, if adverse, exacerbate and aggravate other social problems and relieve none. Population trends, if favorable, open man's options and enlarge his choices. Thus population policy is not an end, but only a means — a means to the better life. That is what concern about population is about, or ought to be.[26]

This is what students are about when they study population and resources. They are considering what people are for and preparing themselves to deal with the future — their future. They have the most at stake!

FOOTNOTES

1. Donella M. Meadows et al., *The Limits to Growth* (New York: Universe Books, 1972).
2. Food and Agriculture Organization (FAO), "Calorie Requirements," *FAO Nutritional Studies No. 15* (Rome, 1957).
3. Mavis B. Stoch and P. M. Smythe, "Undernutrition during Infancy, and Subsequent Brain Growth and Intellectual Development," in *Malnutrition, Learning, and Behavior*, ed. Nevin S. Scrimshaw and John E. Gordon (Cambridge, Mass.: MIT Press, 1968) pp. 278–288.
4. For more detailed information on how foods can be classified and diets analyzed, see National Research Council, *Recommended Daily Dietary Allowances* (Washington, D.C.: National Academy of Sciences, 1974), p. 129, summary table.
5. Additional references for this and the following section are Arthur S. Boughey, *Ecology of Populations*, (New York: Macmillan, 1968); and George M. Woodswell, "The Energy Cycle of the Biosphere," *Scientific American* 223, no. 3 (September 1970): 54–74.
6. Additional references for this section are Georg Borgstrom, *The Food and People Dilemma* (North Scituate, Mass.: Duxbury Press, 1973); Joseph Hutchinson, ed., *Population and Food Supply* (Cambridge: Cambridge University Press, 1969); William Paddock and Paul Paddock, *Famine 1975! America's Decision: Who Will Survive?* (Boston: Little, Brown, 1967); President's Science Advisory Committee Panel on the World Food Supply, *The World Food Problem*, 3 vols. (Washington, D.C.: U.S. Government Printing Office, 1967); and Roger Revelle, "Food and Population," *Scientific American* 231, no. 3 (September 1974): 160–70.
7. J. George Harrar, "Nutrition and Numbers in the Third World," Sixth Annual W. O. Atwater Memorial Lecture at the 140th Meeting of the American Association for the Advancement of Science, San Francisco, February 28, 1974.
8. Japanese and American experience suggests that small body size may be at least partially a *function* of insufficient food intake. In both countries children have tended to be larger than their parents and grandparents, probably because of more adequate nutrition. Also, recent research seems to indicate that people in warm climates may need almost as much food to do work as those working in colder regions.
9. Jean Meyer, "Toward a National Nutrition Policy," *Science* 176, (21 April 1972): 237–41.
10. U.S. Public Health Service, *Preliminary Findings of the First Health and Nutrition Examination Survey, United States, 1971–1972* (Rockville, Md.: National Center for Health Statistics) p. 11.
11. Additional references for this section are Daniel G. Aldrich, Jr., ed., *Research for the World Food Crisis* (Washington, D.C.: American Association for the Advancement of Science, 1970); Lester R. Brown, *Seeds of Change* (New York: Praeger, 1970); David M. Gates, "The Flow of Energy in the Biosphere," *Scientific American* 224, no. 3 (September 1971): 88–100; Walter H. Pawley, *Possibilities of Increasing World Food Production* (Rome: Food and Agriculture Organization of the United Nations, 1963); David Pimental et al., "Food Production and the Energy Crisis," *Science* 182 (2 November 1973): 443–49; and John

H. Ryther, "Photosynthesis and Fish Production in the Sea," *Science* 166 (October 1969): 72–76.

12. Almost all agricultural production statistics are admittedly unreliable. For example, no nation has an accurate record of foodstuffs grown in small family gardens or of the food consumed or bartered by farmers.

13. I am indebted to Dr. Ramesh Sharma for help with the materials diary from an Asian village.

14. Additional references for this section are Alan M. Bateman, *Economic Mineral Deposits* (New York: Wiley, 1950); Peter Brobst and Walden P. Pratt, eds., *United States Mineral Resources* (Washington, D.C.: U.S. Government Printing Office, 1973); Preston E. Cloud, Jr., "Realities of Mineral Distribution," in *The Survival Equation*, ed. Roger Revelle et al. (Boston: Houghton Mifflin, 1971); Hans H. Landsberg, *Natural Resources for U.S. Growth* (Baltimore: Johns Hopkins University Press, 1964); Thomas S. Lovering, "Mineral Resources from the Land," in *Resources and Man: A Study and Recommendations by the Committee on Resources and Man of the National Academy of Science —National Research Council* (San Francisco: Freeman, 1969) pp. 109–55; Meadows et al., *op. cit.;* National Materials Advisory Board—National Research Council, *Elements of a National Materials Policy* (Washington, D.C.: National Academy of Sciences—National Academy of Engineering, 1972); and National Commission on Materials Policy, *Material Needs and the Environment Today and Tomorrow* (Washington, D.C.: U.S. Government Printing Office, 1973).

15. The term "limited supply" is used rather than the more common "nonrenewable." Although not involved in natural cycles, most of these materials can be deliberately recycled and in this sense are "renewable." Unlike water, oxygen, carbon dioxide, and nitrogen, minerals and other materials are for practical purposes not naturally renewed, and thus their supplies are limited.

16. The definitions and the explanatory analogy are adapted from Brobst and Pratt, *op. cit.*

17. Ronald G. Ridker, *Population, Resources, and the Environment* (Washington, D.C.: U.S. Government Printing Office, 1972).

18. Sterling Brubaker, *To Live on Earth: Man and His Environment in Perspective* (New York: New American Library, 1972) p. 203.

19. Cloud, *op. cit.*, p. 203.

20. Landsberg, *op cit.*, p. 199.

21. National Materials Advisory Board, *op cit.*, pp. 33–34.

22. Committee on Resources and Man, *op cit.*, p. 14.

23. National Materials Advisory Board, *op cit.*, p. 56.

24. Additional references dealing with energy are M. King Hubbert, "Energy Resources," in *Resources and Man, op cit.*; Sam H. Schurr, *Energy Research Needs* (Washington, D.C.: U.S. Government Printing Office, 1971); A. R. Ubelohde, *Man and Energy* (New York: Braziller, 1955); U.S. Dept. of Interior, *United States Energy: A Summary Review* (Washington, D.C.: U.S. Government Printing Office, 1972); "Energy and Power," *Scientific American* 224, no. 3 (September 1971), entire issue.

25. We are indebted to Dr. Ramesh Sharma for assistance with the energy diary from an Asian village.

26. "World Population: Status Report 1974," *Population/Family Planning*, no. 15 (January 1974): 47. Reprinted with permission of the Population Council.

SELECTED REFERENCES

Aldrich, Daniel G., ed. *Research for the World Food Crisis*. Washington, D.C.: American Association for the Advancement of Science, 1970. 323 pp.
A collection of excellent papers dealing with food supply and how food production can be increased.

Bateman, Alan M. *Economic Mineral Deposits*, 2nd ed. New York: Wiley, 1950. 916 pp.
A classic textbook on mineral geology, including an especially good description of how mineral deposits have been formed.

Borgstrom, Georg. *Too Many: A Study of the Earth's Biological Limitations*. New York: Macmillan, 1969. 368 pp.
A warning to man that this planet has definite limitations, which we may soon approach.

Brobst, Donald A., and Pratt, Walden F., eds. *United States Mineral Resources*. Washington, D.C.: U.S. Government Printing Office, 1973. 722 pp.
Probably the most comprehensive survey of mineral resources, on both a national and worldwide basis, that is available.

Brown, Lester R. *Seeds of Change*. New York: Praeger, 1970. 205 pp.
Perhaps the best description of the Green Revolution and discussion of some of its possible consequences.

Cloud, Preston E., Jr., "Realities of Mineral Distribution." In *The Survival Equation*, ed. by Roger Revelle et al. Boston: Houghton Mifflin, 1971. pp. 187–207.
Discusses mineral distributions and finds them "neither inconsiderable nor limitless." Suggests that world population will probably reach 6 to 7 billion by the turn of the century and that this is probably about the maximum number of people that can be supported at a standard of living comparable to that now enjoyed in Western Europe.

Hutchinson, Joseph. *Population and Food Supply*. Cambridge: Cambridge University Press, 1969, 144 pp.
A collection of short, but good, papers on the world's human population and its food supply.

Lovering, Thomas S. "Mineral Resources from the Land." In *Resources and Man. A Report of the Committee on Resources and Man of the National Academy of Science, National Research Council*. San Francisco: Freeman, 1969. pp. 109–134.
A technical discussion of the world's mineral resources: the estimated reserves, consumption demands, trends in mineral production, and outlook for the future.

——"Non-Fuel Mineral Resources in the Next Century." In *Global Ecology*, ed. by John P. Holdren and Paul R. Ehrlich. New York: Harcourt Brace Jovanovich, 1971, pp. 39–53.
Suggests that our main hope for avoiding, or at least minimizing, scarcity is through technical advances. Calls attention to the importance of "lead time" for technology to work out answers to problems.

Ridker, Ronald G., ed. *Population, Resources, and the Environment.* Washington, D.C.: U.S. Government Printing Office, 1972. 377 pp.

A collection of papers prepared for the Commission on Population Growth and the American Future. The chapters "Resource and Environmental Consequences of Population Growth in the United States" and "Adequacy of Non-fuel Minerals and Forest Resources" are especially good.

Smith, Robert L., *The Ecology of Man: An Ecosystem Approach.* New York: Harper & Row, 1972. 436 pp.

Part II, "Man and the Food Chain," and Part VI, "The Prospect before Us," are especially useful for further consideration of topics developed in this chapter.

U.S. Panel on World Food Supply. *The World Food Problem,* 3 vols. Washington, D.C.: U.S. Government Printing Office, 1967.

Very long, but perhaps the most authoritative discussion of the world food problem.

CHAPTER 8

Population, Values, and Education

Determination of the good must be prior to determination of what is right, since the justification of action depends on the desirability of its contemplated results.

Clarence Irving Lewis

EDUCATION CAN BE a profound and powerful undertaking in which students address critical issues, struggle with consequential ideas, and probe into problems that will affect their lives and the lives of others in the future. By the year 2000, world population will probably be 6 to 7 billion. If the fertility rate is reduced to replacement by the end of this century, world population could stabilize at about 8 billion. If reduction in the fertility rate to replacement level is delayed 100 years, until the last quarter of the twenty-first century — which appears likely from UN population projections — world population will probably reach 14 to 15 billion by then. Our students' children could live in a world of 8 billion people if world population were stabilized in our lifetime. If nothing is done, they may have to face a world with more than three times as many human beings as there are today. Which will it be? If students go to school to prepare to live in and improve the future, then certainly these demographic "facts of life" are among the matters that should constitute a part of their education.

There is accumulating evidence that the returns from any particular aspect of education are clearly related to the amount of time, materials, imagination, and energy devoted to it.[1] More directly, "If you want students to learn something, teach it!" If we want our young people to be better prepared to deal with the very difficult issues related to population, then we should include consideration of these difficult issues in the curriculum. Fortunately, students have also shown concern for such issues, and the experience of teachers attests that this can be challenging and productive education.

Proposals for ways to deal with population growth, discussions of actions that can be taken by individuals and families to plan family size, and many aspects of population education touch some of our most deeply held values — values that many people never discuss, question, or even consciously consider. And it is not strange that this is so. Reproduction and the struggle for the survival of the individual and of the species may be among the strongest of drives. For 3 million or more years most children died in the first few years after birth, a small fraction lived to the age of reproduction, very few lived beyond the age of 30 or 40. A high reproduction rate was absolutely essential for the security of the individual, the welfare of the family, and the survival of the species. Over the generations, rituals and taboos, cultural mores, and values have developed that provide powerful directives for thought and action. Now, in just a minute in the time span of our species, conditions have changed dramatically and, instead of being menaced by death and rapid population decline, our well-being is threatened by a too rapid growth of population. It is little wonder that when we begin to contemplate actions to deal with this radically different situation, we encounter deeply held beliefs of what is right and what is wrong. Even to question and discuss some of these beliefs is difficult, often threatening.

However, if we believe in rational and intelligent discussion, planning, and action, then it is critical that young people learn to examine and discuss values and to consider the relative "value" of values. Perhaps, they should begin by attempting to clarify what their ideals and goals are and by analyzing how various values are related to these goals and ideals. Possibly the fraction of our population who can examine issues, inquire into problems, and weigh values related to population will never be as large as we might wish, but population education certainly should aim to enlarge the size of this important fraction.

CLARIFYING TERMS

One aspect of population education is clarification of the meanings of various terms so that communication and understanding are facilitated.

Exercise: Differences in Meaning A possible approach to studying differences in meaning, *semantic clarification,* involves juxtaposing two or more items that are often misconstrued. Have students consider and discuss the following terms:

> *family planning* and *population limitation*
> *fecundity* and *fertility*
> *contraception* and *birth control*
> *population regulation* and *population control*
> *prediction* and *projection*
> *population size* and *population density*
> *causation* and *multiple causation*
> *arithmetic progression* and *geometric progression*

APPROACHES TO VALUATION

Our values are related to our view of what is of most worth; ideas and proposals can be evaluated as ends-in-view contributing to the achievement of what is desired.[3] Values are the criteria by which we make judgments of worth, of right and wrong, and of the actions that should be taken to deal with a situation. Judgments of worth involve not only moral and ethical considerations but also discrimination among conflicting ideas. For example, students of population need to make judgments as to the value or relevance of animal crowding experiments. Some believe such experiments to be of great worth and suggest that we ought to heed the results of these experiments in developing population policies and planning our arrangements for living. Others, while expressing interest in the experiments, believe that the differences between man and other animals are so great and fundamental that the results are not of great worth.

We judge what is right and wrong in terms of our values. Some value very highly the right to life of the fertilized egg, and they condemn any proposals or actions that might threaten this right. On the other hand, some value very highly the right of women to exercise control over their own bodies and to make decisions as to whether or not to have a baby, and they condemn proposals or actions that might threaten this right.

Many are concerned about the rapid growth of the human population, and they value proposals and actions that might tend to reduce the rate of growth. Others, however, are more deeply concerned about the future and relative standing of a particular nation, or group within a nation, and they place greater value upon proposals and actions that might tend to promote the growth of that nation or group.

Valuation is the process by which we examine and clarify the values that we and others hold — the sources of these values, the possible inconsistencies among them, and the likely consequences of actions based on them. The study of population is permeated with problems of valuation; at the very least it is important to become aware of some of the values that we and our neighbors on this planet hold.

General Goals

One approach to valuation that has been suggested is to articulate and try to agree upon one or more very general goals. Once agreed upon, values and proposals for action can be evaluated in terms of those agreed-upon general goals. Direct comparison of specific values can be valuable, but if there is no generally agreed-upon approach to analyzing the values, direct comparison is more likely to lead to conflict than to rational valuation.

One of the general goals that might be quite readily agreed upon is that of *survival*. It can be argued that without survival nothing else has meaning; neither economic affluence nor political liberty, for example, have much meaning if no one survives to benefit from them. However, survival can be interpreted in terms of the individual, the family, the group, the nation, or the species. Most individuals value individual survival very highly; yet we have many examples of individuals laying down their lives for others. Patriotism is often interpreted as loyalty to the nation, and many have sacrificed their lives in the belief that their sacrifice would make it more likely their nation would survive. Some students of population are concerned about survival of the species, and it has been suggested that one of the arguments for the exploration and colonization of other regions of space is that it would enhance the possibilities of species survival. Survival, then, is a goal that is generally highly valued.

But it is necessary to clarify the term. What some mean by survival is survival of a way of life — often a way of life characterized by a preoccupation with technological affluence and not really related to survival in the physical, biological sense.[4] On the other hand, there are many who feel concern for the survival of large segments of the human population. Widespread famine, for example, can threaten the survival of millions. In the foreseeable future, the United States will probably have the world's largest stocks of food surpluses, but they may not be enough for all. It has been speculated that those who control food surpluses may be put in a position of deciding who will live and who will die and of watching the dying on their color television sets. Some have proposed that, in such a situation, the moral act would be for all to starve together. But others have argued that the more ethical path would be to ensure that some individuals, groups, and civilizations survive. These may become real dilemmas that will test our power of valuation.

If we agree that the goal of survival is generally desirable, then it can be used to evaluate other values and ends-in-view in terms of how they contribute to survival. For example, the following was a major recommendation of the Study Committee of the National Academy of Sciences:

> To serve national objectives of economic development, public health and welfare, and environmental conservation, we recommend that all nations establish policies to influence the growth of their populations and to adopt politically and ethically acceptable measures toward this end that are within their administrative and economic capability. For most nations of the world, the major goal of population-influencing policies should be a reduction in fertility.[5]

This recommendation clearly recognizes the relationships between population growth and such values as economic development, public health and welfare, and environmental conservation. Are these values, in turn related to or essential for survival? It should be noted that the recommendation is made to nations—that "most nations" should follow policies that will lead to a reduction in fertility. Presumably, it is for individual nations to make the decision as to whether such policies would be consistent with national survival. Suppose that some nations decide that it is not in their interest to reduce fertility? Then, can the policies and actions of these nations and the likely responses of other nations be evaluated in terms of the broader goal of survival of the species?

Another broad general goal is that of the *greatest overall good*. When questions of value arise or disparate courses of action are proposed, they can be evaluated in terms of their possible contribution to the greatest overall good. Although it has a slightly different meaning, the phrase "greatest good for the greatest number" is also sometimes used. This general goal goes beyond the goal of survival, and obviously there are important valuations that have to be made that are not closely linked to the primordial goal of sheer survival. For example, population policies may be influenced by the desire to provide a good education to every child who is born—this is judged to be in the direction of the greatest good.

One of the difficulties with this concept is that measures purported to promote the greatest overall good may threaten what some individuals or groups consider their basic, fundamental rights. For example, it may be for the greatest overall good to limit the number of children a family can have to two or less. However, this would directly conflict with the right of couples to decide freely and responsibly the number and spacing of their children. One of the fundamental issues in ethical valuation is whether there are basic human rights not necessarily related to broad general goals and, if so, what these rights are and how they should be ranked in importance if different rights come into conflict.

Exercise: Analyzing Issues in Terms of General Goals Once there is agreement upon a broad, general goal, it can be used in the analysis of issues, to decide upon less comprehensive goals, and to evaluate various proposals for action. Some of the recommendations of the Commission on Population Growth and the American Future can be analyzed in this way.

As our work proceeded and we received the results of studies comparing the likely effects of continued growth with the effects of stabilization, it became increasingly evident that no substantial benefits would result from continued growth of the nation's population. This is one of the basic conclusions we have drawn from our inquiry.

Recognizing that our population cannot grow indefinitely, and appreciating the advantages of moving now toward the stabilization of population, the Commission recommends that the nation welcome and plan for a stabilized population. [6]

What is the general goal implied here? How is the commission's recommendation related to this goal?

In addition, the commission recommended:

[That] states eliminate existing legal inhibitions and restrictions on access to contraceptive information, procedures, and supplies and ... develop statutes affirming the desirability that all persons have ready and practicable access to contraceptive information, procedures, and supplies [p. 168].

A national policy and voluntary program to reduce unwanted fertility, to improve the outcome of pregnancy, and to improve the health of children [p. 185].

That birth control information and services be made available to teenagers in appropriate facilities sensitive to their needs and concerns [p. 189].

That present state laws restricting abortions be liberalized along the lines of the New York State statute, such abortions to be performed on request by duly licensed physicians under conditions of medical safety [p. 178].

Changes in attitudes and practices to encourage adoption, thereby benefiting children, prospective parents, and society [p. 148].

That immigration levels not be increased and that immigration policy be reviewed periodically to reflect demographic conditions and considerations [p. 206].

That this nation give the highest priority to research in reproductive biology and to the search for improved methods by which individuals can control their own fertility [p. 182].

Enactment of a Population Education Act to assist school systems in establishing well-planned education programs so that present and future generations will be better prepared to meet the challenges arising from population change [p. 125].

How would each of these recommendations contribute to population stabilization? What other actions might contribute to the overall goal of population stabilization?

Basic Values [7]

It has been suggested by many philosophers that there are basic values that are important in and of themselves. Three values that are related to population issues and can provide important guides to human conduct are: freedom, justice, and survival.

Callahan suggests that "survival" is a value; earlier we have called it a "general goal." In a sense, these values are concepts; different individuals and societies may have quite different understandings as to their meaning. Also, the values themselves are often in conflict, and choices must be made among them.

Freedom is the opportunity to make the decisions and take the actions that an individual believes to be in his or her interest. In a sense, freedom is "self-determination." In another sense it is "liberty" in that the individual is free from excessive societal limitations. A very basic freedom might be for families to have the number of children they want, which in turn would imply that they should have access to the information and services necessary to enable them to limit the size of their family if they so wish. Access to information and services, unrestricted by the lack of economic means, is usually considered a basic freedom. Another freedom that is often suggested is a woman's freedom to choose, often with the counsel of her physician, whether or not to have a baby. Most nations jealously guard their freedom to develop and carry out their own population policies. Here, of course, the policies of the society may impinge upon the freedom of the individuals in the society. A national policy of population stabilization, for example, may exert at least psychological pressure upon families that might otherwise want many children.

Justice is equality of treatment and opportunity. Justice implies that families should have equal opportunities to plan the nature and size of the families they want and have equal access to the means to implement their family plans regardless of their economic status. Universal education is an expression of justice, in that it is supposed to provide a way for all children and young people to develop their capacities. However, there may be inequalities, because children are born into families, communities, and nations that place varying amounts of stress on health care and education and have varying economic means to provide them. Justice also implies equal access to important resources; yet, realistically, the place and circumstances of a child's birth will affect the access that she or he has to the resources he or she wants or needs.

Survival is, in a sense, fundamental to all human values. We have said it is a broad general goal. Without survival at a certain minimum level, freedom and justice probably have very little meaning. What do freedom and justice mean to someone who is starving to death?

However, there are serious dangers in applying survival as a value ethic. Survival is not always viewed as sheer physical survival but as survival of a way of life or a balance of power. Murder has been committed to try to ensure the survival of ethical codes in which "Thou shalt not kill!" is a central tenet. Population policies that encourage and promote population growth have been advocated on the grounds of survival when the actual goal was greater power.

There can be perplexing conflicts between these values. It can be argued that a woman should have the freedom to choose whether or not to have a baby, but this can be viewed as conflicting with the unborn baby's basic right to survive. We may agree that sheer physical survival is basic; but of what worth is survival without some kind of human dignity, such as that associated with freedom and justice? The freedom to procreate is viewed by many as essential, but what if this freedom is exercised to the point that there is not enough food and other essential resources to sustain everyone? Then, if there is not enough for everyone, should there be equitable distribution or should everyone be free to use his physical or economic power to appropriate for himself whatever he needs to develop his capacities? Those who base their ethics upon one or more of these values will usually encounter exceptions that are difficult to handle, and conflicts between the values that can be confounding.

It has been suggested that when there are conflicts between basic values, we can make rankings or judgments in terms of their comparative contributions to a general goal.

> *Put formally, it can be understood to mean that one is obliged to act in such a way that the fundamental values of freedom, justice and security/survival are to be respected and, in case of conflict, that one or more of these values can be limited if and only if it can be shown that such a course will serve to increase the balance of good over evil.*[8]

In the field of population, freedom is usually ranked as the highest of the values. The accepted primacy of freedom underlies the policies that urge that families should have the freedom to plan the number and spacing of their children and that nations should have the freedom to develop their own population policies.

Exercise: Analyzing Proposals in Terms of Basic Values The following are some policy proposals. Have students analyze them in terms of the basic values we have been discussing and then answer the questions that follow each.

The economist Kenneth Boulding has suggested a system of "marketable licenses to have children."

Each girl on approaching maturity would be presented with a certificate which will entitle its owner to have, say, 2.2 children, or whatever number would ensure a reproductive rate of one. The unit of these certificates might be the "deci-child," and accumulation of ten of these units by purchase, inheritance, or gift would permit a woman in maturity to have one legal child. We would then set up a market in these units in which the rich and the philoprogenitive would purchase them from the poor, the nuns, the maiden aunts, and so on. The men perhaps could be left out of these arrangements, as it is only the fertility of women which is strictly relevant to population control. However, it may be found socially desirable to have them in the plan, in which case all children both male and female would receive, say eleven or twelve decichild certificates at birth or at maturity and a woman could then accumulate these through marriage.[9]

- Which of the three values (freedom, justice, survival) seem to have primacy in this proposal?
- Is one or more of the values restricted in this proposal? If so, which ones?
- Does the restriction contribute to the greater overall good?
- What is your view of this proposal? What seems to be *your* primary value in reaching this view?

Another proposal depends upon the development of a reliable method of sex determination of a child before birth and a shift to polyandry as a family system. This proposal has been discussed by Garett Hardin, among others:

It is quite likely that a reliable way of determining the sex of a child soon after conception will be developed. In population limitation it is the number of female babies born that is critical. With prenatal sex determination, families might have as many babies as they wish, but they would be limited in the number of girl babies that they could have. For example, each mother might be limited to having only one girl baby. If the population needs and policies should change in the future, the number of girl babies permitted could be altered. This would provide a means of controlling population size so that every one might have access to the resources needed to develop his innate capacities.

It has been argued that this would lead to societies in which there would be more men than women. It has been suggested that family structures be changed so that women would have several husbands. This would lead to larger families which might make for better child care. It might also lead to female dominance in the human species. Throughout the biotic world male dominance tends to be perilous for the species. Perhaps, female dominated societies would be less bellicose and less likely to undertake ventures that might threaten the survival of the species. It is conceivable that this kind of society might also be a happier society.[10]

- What are some other possible ramifications and consequences of such a proposal?
- What seems to be the general goal that is implicit? Would the proposal contribute to this goal?
- Would this proposal threaten one or more of such values as freedom, equality, and survival?
- Some students of social systems believe that it is generally unwise to make radical changes in such a basic institution as the family and the ways in which we bring children into the world and rear them. Are the two proposals described here too radical to be considered as ways of controlling population growth?

ISSUES RELATED TO POPULATION

An important element of population education is to develop a deeper understanding of some of the issues and dilemmas related to population and to use our approach to valuation in examining them. The key descriptors of this approach are *clarification* and *exploration* — clarification in that we try to bring into clearer focus the values that are involved; exploration in that we try to explore the possible consequences of various viewpoints or proposed solutions and relate them to such general goals as survival and the greatest overall good, and to such basic values as freedom, justice, and survival.

Several other issues are presented in the remainder of this chapter. Some proposals or viewpoints may seem quite plausible, even commonsensical. Others may appear abhorrent, and there may be the temptation to reject them without thought. However, considering a wide range of views on each issue will broaden our understanding of the possible, raise significant questions about views that may have been unexamined, and possibly, give us a greater sense of certainty as to what may be desirable. We suggest that all the issues be analyzed and considered from a variety of standpoints, using such questions as the following to clarify ideas and explore differing views:

1. What is the value framework out of which the proposal or viewpoint seems to originate?

2. How is the proposal or viewpoint related to a broader goal such as survival or the greatest overall good?
3. Does the proposal or viewpoint tend to negate one or more of such basic values as freedom, justice, or survival? If so, what rationale is there for negating that basic value?
4. What might be foreseeable as possible consequences if the proposal were implemented or if the viewpoint were acted upon by many individuals, groups, or nations? Would these consquences be desirable?

Should Population Control Be *Imposed*? *Does society have a right to take steps to control population growth that go beyond depending on the cooperation of individuals and their families?* When societies promote voluntary fertility control and family planning, they are helping individuals to achieve their goals. Implicit in this approach is the hope that the goals of individuals, families, and the broader society are congruent. But, suppose they are not?

Many developing nations have population growth rates of over 2 percent, and even the most valiant efforts at socioeconomic development are frustrated by the needs of an ever-growing population. Some of the most imaginative and ambitious family planning and fertility control programs have been instituted in such nations, but in some cases population continues to grow. The more educated and accessible segments of the population are reached, but it has proved difficult to reach the uneducated, who often live in remote villages and are not easily contacted through mass communication systems. Even if voluntary programs were eventually to work, the fear is that there is not the time for them to do so — some nations just cannot support populations that will double in 35 years and double again in the next 35 years. Do such societies have the right to take steps that go beyond depending on voluntary cooperation in order to curb population growth?

The citizens in such a society might agree that steps beyond voluntary fertility control are necessary. This might involve "mutual coercion, mutually agreed upon." Most societies limit the freedom of individuals to engage in acts that will harm their neighbors. Would they be justified in limiting the freedom of families to have more children than they or the society can support? The issue is a very complex one, and an analysis of it will need to involve a careful assessment of the rate of population growth, experience with attempts at voluntary control, the gravity of the socioeconomic situation, and the nature of the particular kind of control that is proposed.

Discussion: Population Control In the analysis of the issue whether or not population control should be imposed, we will assume that voluntary approaches have been tried and will be continued, but that they have not reduced the population growth rate significantly; that socioeconomic problems associated with continued rapid population growth are grave; and that the proposed method of population control is technically, administratively, and politically feasible. We will limit our proposals to two, but it should be kept in mind that a number of other possible approaches have been suggested.[12] Students should consider the merits and demerits of each proposal, with the aid of the questions that follow.

The first proposal is that a positive decision to have a child be required before pregnancy is made possible. One suggested way of implementing the proposal is the temporary sterilization of the male or female. When a decision to have a child is made, sterilization could be reversed and the female could become pregnant. After having given birth, the mother or father would again be sterilized until a positive decision were made to have another child. This proposal depends upon the development of reversible sterilization.

Is this a desirable approach to population limitation? Should the society be involved in the decision to have a child? Is such an approach morally right?

A second proposal is to require the sterilization of men and women after they have had three children. Since many would have fewer than three, this might lead to an average family size of about two, which is approximately the family size needed for a stabilized population.

What drawbacks, if any, do you see in such a program? Should families be free to have as many children as they wish? Would a society ever be justified in requiring compulsory sterilization?

The element of compulsion involved in these proposals clearly points up a conflict between the values of freedom and survival. It could be argued that a very clear case would have to be made that survival was threatened by rapid population growth before people would be willing to relinquish much freedom. But suppose the case *is* convincingly made or that what is at stake is survival at a level at which some human dignity can be maintained? Should we be willing to relinquish some freedom for this?

Would compulsory population limitation programs such as these contribute to the greatest overall good and tend to enhance the chances and conditions of survival? Can you conceive of situations in which you might advocate such proposals for your community or society?

Should Young People Be Taught Birth Control   *Should young people be taught various methods of birth control? Should they have access to birth control materials and services?* Proposals to include instruction on birth control procedures in educational programs have been very controversial in many communities and societies. Even more controversial have been proposals to give all young people, both poor and well-to-do, ready access to birth control materials and services. These proposals apparently touch values that are deeply held.

There is the belief among people in many societies, that sexual intercourse should take place only after marriage. The information, materials, and services essential for effective birth control, according to this view, should be made available only to people who are married or about to be married. Many who hold these views believe that early instruction in and ready access to birth control measures would imply social approval of premarital sexual intercourse and general promiscuity. In many societies there have been severe moral strictures against premarital sex, and girls have been ostracized for bearing a child out of wedlock. The values associated with this view of sex and marriage have been highly cherished in many cultures around the world.

However, several developments have led to a questioning of these values. Empirical studies have shown that there is and long has been a great deal of premarital sexual intercourse. A number of thoughtful experts in this field, as well as policy study groups, have recommended that young people should have access to birth control instruction, materials, and services.

Discussion: Access to Birth Control Methods   It would seem important for young people, as well as those who work with young people, to examine proposals for making birth control available to young people. Using the approaches to valuation that have been suggested, students might consider and discuss these questions:

In the community in which you live, and in terms of the values you hold, do you believe that teenagers should have access to birth control education and services?

Following are two recommendations made by the Commission on Population Growth and the American Future:

> Toward the goal of reducing unwanted pregnancies and childbearing among the young, the Commission recommends that birth control information and services be made available to teenagers in appropriate facilities sensitive to their needs and concerns.
>
> The Commission therefore recommends the development and implementation of an adequately financed program to develop appropriate family planning materials, to conduct training courses for teachers and school administrators, and to assist states and local communities in integrating information about family planning into school courses such as hygiene and sex education.[13]

Do you believe that these recommendations should be implemented on a nation-wide basis?

Group Interests and Population Policies

How should groups within a society react to population policies and changes in population? A nation may have very limited resources and lack the means to support a larger population. However, the goals of different groups within the society may be in conflict with those of the broader society.

Religious, ethnic, racial, and socioeconomic groups within a society may be concerned about relative balances of power. A minority may view with alarm a high birth rate among the majority, fearing that eventually they will be completely overwhelmed by it. The majority, on the other hand, may fear that rapid population growth among a minority will disturb established relationships and balances of power. While the members of each group may see that they have a stake in the welfare of the broader system, their fears of competing groups may be overriding—"We know we should be concerned about the greater good, but we have to be concerned with our own interests first."

There may also be conflicts among groups that hold different values to be paramount. Those who esteem freedom the most highly will struggle mightily against any proposals viewed as a threat to the freedom of the individual or the group to make their own choices, even if these choices be inconsistent with the general welfare of the broader system of which they are a part. Groups who are most strongly committed to justice will be willing to have everyone surrender some freedom and even run the risk of nonsurvival in order to achieve greater justice for all. Survival may be judged the paramount value by yet other groups, and they will be willing to surrender some freedom and risk some injustice to enhance the chances of survival.

This struggle between groups who have a stake in a broader system but are inhibited from working toward the greater good by fears of competing groups or what are viewed as threats to cherished values is sometimes called the "prisoner's dilemma." Groups caught in this dilemma are impeded by their fears of what others may or may not do, and, in a sense, they become "prisoners" of these fears. Groups within nations may sense that they have a great stake in what happens to the national population but have great difficulty in overcoming old fears and animosities. Nations may recognize global population problems yet judge their primary concern to be the welfare of their own nation. While patriots may say, "We must all hang together or we will most assuredly all hang separately," patriots are among those who become concerned if the suspicion and fear develops that only they will "hang."

Exercise: Role Imagining   One way of analyzing situations in which competing group interests make it difficult to act for the greater good is through a process of role imagining. In each of the following situations, have students imagine that they are members of the designated group. What would they do? Is there a way out of the "prisoner's dilemma"?

Role A: Member of the ruling majority. In the following situation, imagine that you are a member of the ruling majority group. Your nation is very poor and has very limited natural resources so that further economic development is difficult. The quality of life of all the people is deeply affected by a population growth rate that is considerably higher than the world average. The majority group has lived for a long time in this region and tends to be better educated and to hold most of the important positions in government and business. The minority group migrated into the area but still maintains ties with the "mother country" and does not seem to be as concerned with the problems of the nation and the economic welfare of all as is the majority. The majority group and some of the intellectual leaders of the minority group agree that a curbing of the explosive population growth is absolutely essential for the welfare of everyone in the nation. When voluntary birth control programs were tried, they were quite successful among the majority ruling group, but the minority group continued to reproduce at the same rate. If they were to continue, many in the majority group fear, the minority would become an even larger segment of the population and eventually gain control of the nation through the sheer force of numbers.

If you were a member of the majority group, how would you react? What policies would you favor? What might you do to further these policies?

Role B: Member of the minority group. In the following situation, imagine that you are a member of the minority group, which is of a different race and has a quite different cultural background from the majority. The nation is largely controlled by the majority group; it dominates government, business, and the most important social institutions and holds most of the best jobs. There has been a great deal of discrimination against the minority. Lately, your minority, largely through its own efforts and with a little help from the majority, has made substantial social and economic progress, but it still has a long way to go. The proportion of your minority of the total population has remained about the same for a long time. Now, there is a recognition that population growth represents a problem, and the majority, with the concurrence of a few members of the minority, has decided that efforts should be made to stabilize population size. Many members of your group believe that this would relegate your group to a position of permanent minority, forever more or less dependent upon the goodwill of the majority. Some find this degrading and see it as the ultimate discrimination.

As a member of the minority group, what position would you take? What would you consider to be the most important factors supporting your position? Would you try to convince others? If so, how?

Role C: Citizens of a wealthy nation. Imagine that you are a citizen of a relatively wealthy nation that for a long time has had a large foreign aid program for which you and your fellow citizens have been taxed. The reports you read and a quick trip through several developing nations seem to indicate that economic conditions, instead of improving, are becoming worse. You are shocked by the extreme poverty you have seen. Some of your fellow citizens are urging that the aid program be increased, to "stem the tide of starvation." Others say that no aid will help very much as long as population in these developing countries continues to grow at an explosive rate. In fact, some say that to increase aid is merely to ensure that there will be more people who will eventually starve. They urge that further aid be made contingent upon progress, or at least plausible plans, toward reduction of the population growth rate. Your nation has succeeded in stabilizing its population. Still, it is hard to eat knowing that there are others who are starving.

What values do you believe should be considered in analyzing such a situation? If you were a citizen of such a nation, what position would you take? Why? Would you try to persuade your fellow citizens to your viewpoint?

It can be helpful to try to imagine how population issues are viewed from different frames of reference. It is especially important that an attempt be made to view issues from the perspective of the broader system—the system that may include competing groups but one in which all have a stake.

Survival: A Question of Responsibility
Does everyone have a responsibility to help everyone else survive? An important maxim to be found in almost all of the great religions and codes of ethical conduct is some version of the golden rule: "Do unto others as you would have them do unto you." Most thoughtful and responsible people probably agree with this maxim and try to order their lives accordingly. If we follow this maxim, we will certainly try to help everyone survive—and survive with dignity and the opportunity to develop individual potential.

Discussion: Some Ethical Dilemmas A different type of ethical dilemma is posed in each of the following three situations. Students should study each situation, then try to resolve it with the aid of the questions that follow.

Dilemma A. Perhaps the classic expression of this ethical problem involves survivors of a sinking ship who have only one lifeboat. It cannot possibly hold everyone who clamors to climb on board. Is it right for those already in the lifeboat to keep others from climbing aboard to prevent the lifeboat from sinking from the sheer weight of numbers? Or would it be more ethical to leave the lifeboat so that another might take one's place and have a chance to live?

Suppose you knew that one of those trying to climb on board intends to force everyone else off so that he and his group will have a better chance to survive. Would you be justified in keeping him off so that those of your own group might be saved? What might happen to you if you deliberately failed to save someone?

Some people have compared the earth to a lifeboat. To what extent is it like a lifeboat? In what ways is it different? The limits and resources of the lifeboat are limited and quite clear. But, humans have been inventive and resourceful in the past. Is it possible that they might find ways to provide enough for everyone? How might this be done? Does an analogy such as the lifeboat analogy help us clarify our thinking?

Dilemma B. World population has grown, but food production has not kept pace. It has been calculated that if all the food in the world were evenly distributed, we would all be malnourished. What should the people and nations that have ample food supplies do? One might answer, "We should ship all our surpluses to those who need them." But suppose this still is not enough? Should we deprive ourselves of essential food so that fewer will starve if it means that we, too, will be malnourished? (As someone has asked, "What will we do if we have to watch one another starve on color television?")

Dilemma C. The world food situation has become very serious, and two major nations are faced with catastrophic famine. We have some food that can be shared but not enough to save both nations. What should we do with our food?

Nation X, although it has made some attempts, has not succeeded in lowering its birth rate. Many statesmen believe that the people of nation X should long ago have taken drastic action to limit population, but they never did. Some believe that earlier massive shipments of food actually stimulated population growth and aggravated the problem. The nation's population is continuing to grow, and it no longer has any chance of producing enough to feed its people.

Nation Y did succeed in slowing its population growth, but it still has a very large population. In the past, it usually managed to produce enough food to maintain its population. However, a very serious drought ruined the crops, and it no longer has enough to feed its people. Some of its politicians and military men believe that they should not stand idly by as their fellow countrymen starve and die. There is some talk of taking over areas of the world that have a food surplus. "No one has a right to keep something as basic as food away from those who need it."

Should we send our food to nation X or nation Y? Or should we divide the available food between the two nations, though it will not be enough for either one?

In considering each of these situations questions such as the following need to be asked:

- Can we be sure enough of the nature of the overall situation to decide deliberately not to try to save someone? Perhaps the computer projections are wrong. (Of course, they can err in more than one direction!)
- Can we be certain that we have done all we can to try to alleviate the situation? Perhaps, if we really tried, we could provide enough for everyone.
- What would happen to us if we deliberately decided not to try to help

someone to survive? Perhaps such a decision would be so morally debilitating that we would not be able to "look at ourselves in the mirror."

Of course, there are other possible approaches to these ethical dilemmas. Some have suggested that decisions as basic as who is or is not entitled to get food should not be made by any single group or nation. Already, there is a proposal to set up a world food bank to help meet such situations. What are some other possibilities?

The conflicts posed by the dilemmas in the situations described here are not merely between values, they are also between the broad goals of the greatest overall good and survival.

The "Right" to Self-Location
Should people have a right to live where they wish? Or do communities have a right to control their growth? Population growth in a community, or the prospect of it, often leads to controversy and conflict. Different groups view growth from different perspectives, and there are often sharp differences in value preferences. In such controversies there is little value in imputing evil motives to those who hold an opposing viewpoint; it is more useful to try to understand the underlying reasons for their views.

Discussion: To Grow or Not to Grow This is another situation in which role imagining can be useful. The following arguments are often employed to support or oppose community growth.[14] Have students try to imagine themselves first as supporters of growth and then as advocates of control of growth, bearing in mind the following questions:

• What are the additional arguments that might be raised on each side?
• Which of the arguments seem to you the most important? Which do you find the most persuasive?
• Are there possibilities for compromise that might be acceptable to most of the people concerned?

Arguments for Growth
1. People have a right to a place to live.
2. We need jobs and industry. Most young people are leaving because there are no jobs for them.

Arguments for Control of Growth
1. People have a right to protect their way of life.
2. New industry almost always leads to more pollution, more traffic, and need for housing and community services.

Arguments for Growth

3. We need jobs and industry that will help reduce our tax load.

4. People should not be crowded into cities; they should have access to grass, trees, fresh air, and open space.

5. People have a fundamental right to live where they choose and not to be kept out of areas by those already there.

6. People want a better place to live and to raise their families.

7. Restrictions on population growth are used to keep out the poor and the black.

8. The poor have a right to adequate housing.

9. Everyone is entitled to a share of the good life.

10. Public policies to restrict growth and maintain environmental quality are new guises for racial, ethnic, and economic discrimination. It is the poor and least advantaged who are deprived so that the more advantaged can continue to enjoy good housing and a nice environment.

Arguments for Control of Growth

3. New industry and more people will require more of such community services as water, streets, fire protection, sewage disposal, education, and welfare.

4. If too many people move into our beautiful community, it will become overcrowded, and no one will have access to grass, trees, fresh air, and open space.

5. Communities have a right to control their growth and to decide upon an optimum population.

6. We fear that an influx of new people from the city will inevitably lead to overcrowding, more crime, and social problems we have not had before.

7. Restrictions on population growth are not discriminatory. They are necessary to preserve the environment and the quality of life in a community.

8. A community has a right to require that there be a certain amount of space around each dwelling unit.

9. The more people who come to share our good life, the less good it becomes.

10. Everyone has a stake in environmental quality. If we don't protect our environment now, then there will be less for everyone to enjoy.

If you learned that the population of your community might grow rapidly in the near future, what additional information would you want about this possible development? What factors would you consider to be most important in considering growth? What position do you think you would take? What arguments would you put forward to support your position?

A traditional source of growth (economic as well as population growth) in the United States has been immigration. Today, when concern is focused increasingly on limiting population growth, there are many who claim that the United States can no longer afford to be generous in its immigration policies.

A particular source of concern is the large numbers of illegal immigrants. Since these people have entered the country unofficially, it is very difficult to guess at the numbers involved; however, it has been estimated that there are presently more than 6 million illegal aliens in the United States. Most of them come from countries where there is high unemployment, and their earnings in the United States account for a large share of their families' incomes. Most of these people return to their homes for part of the year and make few demands upon our social services. They often fill low-skill, low-wage, and low-status jobs that many local people would not take. Probably if there were no illegal aliens to take these jobs, the cost of food and many services would rise. However, some hold quite attractive and desirable jobs.

Discussion: The Illegal Aliens Problem A number of proposals have been made to deal with the problem of illegal aliens. Students should consider each of the following proposals and then formulate their own opinions on each, giving their reasons.

Proposal 1. We are a large and rich nation, and a good part of our wealth has come from exploiting poorer countries. We therefore have an obligation to help the people from those countries, including allowing them to live and work here, especially since they fill a need in our economy.

Proposal 2. We should do our best to help improve conditions in the countries from which the aliens come so they will be able to get jobs there.

Proposal 3. We should grant amnesty to the aliens who have lived here for 3 or more years and allow them to become citizens.

Proposal 4. To make the jobs more attractive to local workers, we should force employers to pay higher wages for the jobs now done by aliens, even if this means higher prices for food and services and the possible failure of businesses that have been employing aliens at low wages.

Proposal 5. We should prosecute employers who are found employing illegal aliens.

Proposal 6. We should erect barriers that would make it virtually impossible for aliens to enter this country illegally.

Proposal 7. We should make an effort to track down all illegal aliens and send them back to their own countries.

The Use of World Resources

As world population grows, pressure on the supplies of various materials increases. *Do some people have a right to use a larger percentage of these materials?* The United States, for example, with about 6 percent of the world's population, consumes over 30 percent of the materials used each year. On the other hand, about 85 percent of these materials are produced in the United States, largely with resources found within the country.

Discussion: Basic Values and the Use of Resources The following is the central premise of this discussion: *In certain circumstances, some nations do have a right to use a disproportionate share of the world's resources.*

At this point, before they have had a chance to consider the issue fully, students might be polled on their reaction to this premise. How many are in favor? How many against?

Now have students debate the issue in detail, making use of the general goals and basic values described earlier. The following are some arguments for and against the central premise:

Arguments in Favor	*Arguments Against*
Survival	
A nation that uses a lot of materials threatens no one's survival. On the contrary, as a result of some nations developing technology and spending capital to develop material resources, everyone's chances of survival are increased.	The earth's resources are finite, and irreplaceable. As these limited resources are consumed, everyone's survival is threatened.

Arguments in Favor	*Arguments Against*

The greatest overall good

The resources were there to be developed and used. If some nations had not developed these resources, the materials produced from them would not today be available for use, and technology would not have advanced to its present level.	Overall, more people would benefit more fully if the world's available resources were more equitably divided among the peoples of the world.

Freedom

Every nation should have the freedom to develop its economy as it wishes, as long as other people are not harmed.	One nation's use of such a large proportion of the available resources limits the freedom of other nations to develop their economies and improve their standards of living.

Justice

Those who have the means, the skill, the energy, and the will to develop available resources are justly entitled to do so.	Justice requires that the world's resources be divided equally and equitably among the people of the world.

In each case, which statement, for or against, seems most persuasive? What other statements, for or against, can be made concerning each of these general goals/values as they apply to the use of resources? Which general goals/values seems most pertinent in examining this issue? Are there possibilities for compromise?

Following the discussion, a second poll of student opinion on this issue might be taken. How many now are in favor of the central premise? How many against?

The Limits of Concern *Does everyone have a stake in what happens in other places and in other societies? What should be the limits of concern about the actions of others?* In many issues related to population there is the classic conflict between the rights of individuals, communities, and nations, and the legitimate concerns of other individuals, communities, and nations.

Discussion: Rights versus Legitimate Concerns In what follows, "rights" and "legitimate concerns" related to population growth are juxtaposed. Students should carefully consider the implications of each before answering the questions that follow.

Rights. Tradition, law, and the United Nations Conference on Human Rights all tend to support the basic human right of couples to decide how many children they want. To many, any interference in this right would be reprehensible. In many societies, individuals, acting as groups or communities, are held to have a right to decide for themselves the issues in which they have the most at stake. Community size and rate of growth are certainly issues in which a community has great concern. Almost all nations jealously guard their right to determine their own population policies. Intrusion from outside is seldom welcome and is more likely to be vehemently opposed.

Legitimate concerns. Couples may have a right to decide how many children they want, but it is society as a whole that is responsible for the education, health, and welfare of those children, and it is society as a whole that will have to support the children if the family meets adversity. Therefore, everyone in a society has a right to be concerned about the number of children born. Similarly, while each community has a right to shape its own growth and destiny, if uncontrolled and unplanned growth leads to the pollution of rivers and of the atmosphere and places an overwhelming burden upon available open space and recreational facilities, other communities may feel they have a right to be concerned. Viewing the issue globally, if some nations let their populations continue to grow at explosive rates while others succeed in controlling growth, the latter may feel a justifiable concern over where the food is to come from to feed all the world's people and for the general welfare of Spaceship Earth.

After considering these conflicting rights and concerns, under what conditions do you think one should take precedence over the other? In which direction should the balance tip?

CONCLUSIONS

The issues discussed in this chapter are among those that will have to be considered, but there will certainly be many others. And they will have to be faced by each individual, each family, each community, each nation. Young people have to decide whether or not to have children and, if so, how many? Communities will have to weigh the need for jobs against environmental concerns, the advantages and disadvantages of growth and no-growth. Nations will have to decide what to do about immigrants — those who wish to come in and those who may already have entered the country illegally. And the world as a whole will have to develop better ways of dealing with global problems. Should we try to stabilize the world population? If so, how will we resolve the many conflicting viewpoints and cultural values? What weight should we give to the sometimes conflicting values of freedom, justice, and survival?

In population education we aim to prepare ourselves and young people to deal with some of these significant issues and problems.

FOOTNOTES

1. This is one of the conclusions reached from a comprehensive review of research related to the implementation of new curricula. See Decker F. Walker and Jon Schaffarzick, "Comparing Curricula," *Review of Educational Research* 44, no. 1 (Winter 1974).
2. For generally accepted definitions of many of the terms, see the glossary.
3. An eclectic method is used in discussing valuation; we have selected the approaches to valuation that seem most efficacious in dealing with population issues. The following are more lengthy and sophisticated discussions of valuation: John Dewey, "Theory of Valuation," *International Encyclopedia of Unified Science*, vol. 2, no. 4 (Chicago: University of Chicago Press, 1939); and Clarence Irving Lewis, *An Analysis of Knowledge and Valuation* (La Salle, Ill.: Open Court Publishing Company, 1946).
4. Perhaps the most cogent discussion of the uses and abuses of survival is found in Daniel Callahan, *The Tyranny of Survival and Other Pathologies of Civilized Life* (New York: Macmillan, 1973).
5. Study Committee of the National Academy of Sciences, *Rapid Population Growth* (Baltimore: Johns Hopkins University Press, 1971), p. 94.
6. Commission on Population Growth and the American Future, *Population and the American Future* (New York: New American Library, 1972), pp. 191–92. The extracts that follow are from the same report.
7. Perhaps the clearest discussion of basic values as they apply to ethical problems related to population is to be found in the writings of Daniel Callahan, *Ethics and Population Limitation*, Occasional Paper of the Population Council (Bridgeport, Conn.: Key Book, 1971). Essentially the same ideas are presented in his article "Ethics and Population Limitation," *Science* 175 (4 February 1972):487–94; and *The Tyranny of Survival, op. cit.*, particularly Chapter 7, "Population Control."
8. Callahan, *Ethics and Population Limitation, op. cit.*, pp. 14–15.
9. Kenneth E. Boulding, *The Meaning of the Twentieth Century* (New York: Harper & Row, 1964), pp. 135–36.
10. Adapted from Garrett Hardin, *Exploring New Ethics for Survival: The Voyage of the Spaceship Beagle* (New York: Viking, 1972), pp. 206–15.
11. Among the useful references related to this section are Daniel Callahan, *Abortion: Law, Choice, and Morality* (New York: Macmillan, 1970); Daniel Callahan, ed., *The American Population Debate* (Garden City, N.Y.: Doubleday, 1971);

Callahan, *Ethics and Population Limitation, op. cit.,* and Garrett Hardin, ed., *Population, Evolution, and Birth Control* (San Francisco; Freeman, 1969).

12. A discussion of many proposals for imposing population control is found in Bernard Berelson, "Beyond Family Planning," *Science* 163 (7 February 1969): pp. 533–43. This article has also been published in a number of anthologies dealing with population.

13. Commission on Population Growth and the American Future, *Population and the American Future, op. cit.,* pp. 189–90.

14. These arguments are drawn from accounts of actual community controversies and from William K. Reilly, ed., *The Use of Land: A Citizens' Policy Guide to Urban Growth* (New York: T.Y. Crowell, 1973).

SELECTED REFERENCES

Callahan, Daniel, *Abortion: Law, Choice, and Morality.* New York: Macmillan, 1970. 524 pp.
A discussion of complicated issues associated with abortion. Much of Section III, "Establishing a Moral Policy," is also applicable to other population issues.
———. *Ethics and Population Limitation.* Bridgeport, Conn.: Key Book Service, 1971. 45 pp.
An occasional paper of the Population Council that discusses the development of ethical criteria and their application to some specific population issues. The essential ideas of this paper are also available as "Ethics and Population Limitation," Science 175 (4 February 1972): pp. 487–94.
———, ed. *The American Population Debate.* Garden City, N.Y.: Doubleday, 1971. 380 pp.
A collection of papers that contribute to the discussion of population issues in the United States. The last chapter, by Arthur J. Dyck, "Population Policies and Ethical Acceptability," is especially relevant to the discussions in this chapter.
Dewey, John. "Theory of Valuation," *International Encyclopedia of Unified Science,* vol. 2, no. 4. Chicago: University of Chicago Press, 1939, 67 pp.
A highly technical but seminal work on valuation.
Hardin, Garrett. *Exploring New Ethics for Survival: The Voyage of the Spaceship Beagle.* New York: Viking, 1972. 273 pp.
A provocative discussion of ideas related to population set inside a fictional work.
Hartley, Shirley Foster. *Population: Quantity vs. Quality.* Englewood Cliffs, N.J.: Prentice-Hall, 1972. 343 pp.
A factual book about population. The last two chapters, "Political Aspects of Population Growth" and "Possibilities: Family Planning or Population Control," are especially pertinent in the consideration of population and values.
Lewis, Clarence Irving. *An Analysis of Knowledge and Valuation.* La Salle, Ill.: Open Court Publishing Company, 1946. 568 pp.
A major philosophical work that links knowledge, valuation, and action.
Reining, Priscilla, and Tinker, Irene, eds. *Population: Dynamics, Ethics, and Policy.* Washington, D.C.: American Association for the Advancement of Science, 1975. 184 pp.
A collection of articles from the journal Science dealing with various issues related to population.

Viederman, Stephen. "Values, Ethics, and Population Education." *The Hastings Center Report* 3, no. 3 (June 1973): 6–8.
One of the few available discussions of values and ethics in population education.

Glossary-Index

Terms important in population education are defined and the pages on which they are discussed are given.

abortion — the termination of pregnancy prematurely. Pp. 67–68, 75, 84, 93–94, 107, 109, 114–15, 117, 239, 258–59

age-specific death rate — the death rate for specific age groups in a population. Useful in the calculation of life expectancies. P. 20

age-specific fertility rate — the fertility rate of women of specific ages. Can be calculated by dividing the number of live-born children of mothers of an age group by the total number of women of that age in a population. P. 19

arithmetic progression — when each number in a series is increased by the same amount, e.g., 2, 4, 6, 8, 10, 12. Pp. 23–26, 33, 235

basal metabolism — the energy needed to keep the body operating. P. 196

behavioral sink — a situation in which various pathologies within a group are aggravated. Pp. 126, 130

biodegradation — the action of organisms to change materials into nutrients that can be used again by plants. Pp. 157–58, 162, 166

biosphere — that part of the earth in which life exists. Pp. 7, 194, 199–200, 229, 242

birth control — controlling the number of chidren who are born. Since it includes such practices as abortion, it is a broader term than *contraception*. Pp. 13, 29, 64, 66, 68–71, 82–83, 87–88, 91–94, 96, 107, 111, 113–15, 189, 235, 239, 246–48, 259

birth control pills — oral contraceptives that tend to simulate pregnancy in the female. This tends to suppress the release of the egg. Probably, also tends to prevent entry of sperm cells into the uterus and to make the lining of the uterus unreceptive to the implantation of an egg. Pp. 29, 84, 89– 90, 94– 95, 100, 117

births —the total number of babies born in a year. Pp. 19, 51, 60, 82, 93, 97– 98, 103– 4, 106, 109– 10, 113, 169

census —an official count of all the people living in an area. Pp. 17– 19, 45, 61, 71– 72, 134, 143, 167, 169, 171, 188

change and response —a theory of demographic change; similar to the theory of *demographic transition*, but focuses on the family as the basic social unit. Pp. 67– 68, 72, 75

climax ecosystem —a balanced interrelationship between population of different organisms and the environment. A climax ecosystem is stable and will persist indefinitely. Pp. 155– 56, 162, 185

cohort —a group of individuals in a population that have something in common. For example, individuals born in a certain year are referred to as an age cohort. P. 111

condom —a thin sheath that fits over the penis and prevents sperm from entering the female reproductive tract. Pp. 84, 88, 95

contraception —prevention of the union of sperm and egg. Pp. 29, 68, 73, · 83– 84, 87– 91, 94– 96, 100, 113– 14, 116– 17, 235, 239

critical stages of reproduction —phases of the reproductive process at which accidents or deliberate intervention can prevent conception. Pp. 83– 87, 115

crowding —the amount of space available per person. Also, often defined in terms of psychological impact. Pp. 13, 56, 118– 21, 128, 131– 34, 144, 149– 50, 235, 253

crude birth rate (CBR) —the number of births per 1,000 population in a year. Pp. 19, 22, 28– 30, 45, 55, 60, 63– 69, 90, 93, 99, 109– 10, 112, 170, 175, 247

crude death rate (CDR) —the number of deaths per 1,000 population in a year. Pp. 20, 22, 29, 34, 44– 45, 54– 55, 63– 66, 70, 72, 76, 106, 110, 157, 161, 175, 179

crude rate of natural population increase —the annual percentage of increase in population. It can be calculated by subtracting the crude death rate from the crude birth rate and dividing by ten. P. 67

demographic transition —the theory that populations pass through various stages. It begins with the lowering of the death rate, followed by a readjustment of birth rate, and eventually birth rate and death rate are balanced so that population growth rate is nearly zero. Pp. 63– 69, 75– 76

demography —a science that deals with the number and distribution of people, and the changes that take place in human populations. Pp. 28, 33, 46, 57, 63– 69, 73– 76, 115– 17, 160, 187, 189, 233, 239

diaphragm —a thin sheath that fits over the opening into the uterus and prevents sperm from entering the uterus and making contact with the egg. Pp. 84, 88– 89, 95

doubling time — the length of time it takes for a population to double in size at a given growth rate. Pp. 21– 22, 25– 27, 34, 63, 81– 82, 97, 103, 168, 223, 244

ecological demand — the demand that a population makes of its environment. A partial measure of the ecological demand is the gross domestic product (minus services). Pp. 178, 181, 185, 226

ecosystem — the living organisms and their nonliving environment in a given area. Pp. 145, 155– 59, 163, 166, 170, 182, 185, 187, 190, 200, 209, 214, 232

emigration — the movement of people out of an area. Pp. 20, 63, 66, 68– 69, 72, 78, 81, 97, 180

estrus period — the period during which the egg is available for fertilization and conception can take place. Pp. 59, 75

exponential growth — a quantity increase in which the total is multiplied periodically by a number such as a percentage and the increase is added to the original quantity. An example is the way money in a bank grows by compound interest. Pp. 24– 27, 33, 41, 45

family — the basic human social system for reproduction and nurturing of the young. Pp. xviii, 4– 9, 29, 31, 42, 44– 45, 49, 58, 62– 64, 67– 72, 74, 77– 117, 121, 128– 29, 132, 138, 146, 149, 153, 161, 171, 174, 227, 234– 36, 238, 240– 45, 247, 253– 54, 257, 259

fecundity — a woman's capacity to bear children. Contrasted with *fertility*, which is the number of children she actually bears. Pp. 81, 83, 97, 235

feedback — a small part of the output of a system is fed back into the system to regulate it. Pp. 49– 53, 55, 57, 60– 62, 66– 67, 70– 72, 74

fertility — the number of children a woman bears. Contrasted with *fecundity*, which is the number she is potentially capable of bearing. Pp. 4, 28, 34, 42– 43, 46, 64, 73, 79, 82– 83, 94, 96– 99, 102, 109– 11, 115– 18, 128, 130– 32, 233, 235, 237– 39, 242, 244

first law of thermodynamics — in a closed system the total amount of matter and energy remains constant. P. 193

food pyramids — based on green plants, which are the primary producers. The farther the food we consume is removed from green plants, the smaller the percentage of the original solar energy is utilized. Pp. 201– 3

freedom — a basic value involving the opportunity to make decisions and take the actions that an individual believes to be in his or her best interest. Pp. 12, 104, 136, 146– 48, 239– 45, 247– 48, 256, 258

general fertility rate — the number of births per year per 1,000 women aged 15 to 44. P. 19

general goals — goals most people can agree upon. They may have different meanings to different people. General goals are useful in the process of valuation. Pp. 236– 41, 243– 44, 252, 255– 56 *generalized approach* —an approach to the analysis of problematic situations that may be useful in the analysis of a wide range of problem situations. Pp. 77, 140, 193

geometric progression —a series of numbers that increases by always multiplying the preceding number by a fixed number, e.g., 2, 4, 8, 16, 32, 64. Pp. 23–26, 45, 235

gestation period —the time between conception and birth. In humans it is about 9 months. Pp. 81, 83, 93, 98

growth potential —the capacity for growth. A population that has a large number of individuals about to enter the reproductive years has a high growth potential. Pp. 29, 41

homo sapiens —a biological term for man. Sometimes interpreted as "the wise one." Pp. 1, 3, 32, 73, 174

immigration —the movement of people into an area. Pp. 20–23, 57, 78, 106, 108–9, 128, 160, 239, 254, 258

infanticide —the killing of unwanted children. P. 75

intrinsic capacity for population growth —most populations produce more young than are needed to replace the preceding generation. Pp. 36–37, 45, 48, 73

IUD (intrauterine device) —a device made of inert material such as plastic and fashioned in a variety of shapes. When inserted into the uterus, it prevents conception. Pp. 84–85, 90–91, 95–96, 100

"J" curve of population growth —a pattern, sometimes recurring, of rapid growth followed by catastrophic decline. Pp. 40–41, 43, 71

justice —a basic value involving equitable treatment and opportunity. Justice implies equal access to important resources. Pp. 239–44, 247–48, 256, 258

life expectancy —the average number of years an individual can expect to live. Pp. 1, 19–20, 55

mass production, law of —all species have the capacity to reproduce at a rate much greater than that necessary to maintain a population at a given size. Pp. 11, 80

menarche —the age at which a girl begins to menstruate and can begin to have children. Pp. 81–82, 85

migration —the movement of people. Pp. 3, 6, 19–22, 29, 39, 45, 51, 132, 146, 152, 155, 160–62, 166–67, 170, 179–80, 189, 248

modern farming system —farming systems that use the sophisticated technology and products of modern industry so that relatively few people produce a great deal of food and fiber. Pp. 21, 68, 155, 160, 163–67, 182, 188, 204, 210, 214

net reproduction rate (NRR) —the number of daughters born per woman who survive at least to the age their mother was at the time of their own birth. An approximate indicator of the rate at which a generation is being replaced by a future generation of potential mothers. Pp. 41–43, 46 *open space* —a place where people can, at least psychologically, be by themselves and have some contact with plants, animals, and geographical features. Pp. 118–19, 139–49, 185, 253, 257

pollution —that which harms or defiles the environment. Pp. 2, 43–44, 53, 111, 123, 146, 148, 156, 171, 174, 178, 181, 185, 188, 190, 253, 257

population —all of the individuals of a species. Often the definition is further limited to all the individuals that live in a geographical area. Defined, p. 12; passim

population density —the number of people per unit area. Pp. 3, 6, 10, 13, 53, 56–57, 75, 111, 118, 120–41, 144, 148–50, 152, 157–58, 171, 175, 208–9, 235

population education —the study of populations in their environments. Pp. xiii–xviii, 5–15, 67, 69, 71–74, 108, 110–12, 114–15, 140, 152–53, 161, 178, 189, 228, 234–35, 239, 243, 258, 260

population growth rate —percentage of change in population size over a period of time, usually a year. Can be calculated by subtracting the population at the beginning of the year from the population at the end of the year and dividing the result by the population at the beginning of the · year. Pp. 2–4, 8, 19, 21–22, 25, 27–28, 32–40, 46, 49, 52–54, 59–60, 63–64, 66, 69–72, 74–75, 78, 82–83, 97, 103, 107–11, 116–17, 147, 155, 165, 174–75, 178, 181, 185, 189, 203, 207, 234, 236, 244–45, 247–49, 251, 257–58

population pyramid —a bar graph showing the percentage of the population of various ages. May also show sex distribution at various age levels. Pp. 30–32, 60

population size —the number of individuals living in an area. Pp. 4, 6, 8, 13, 17–18, 21, 27–29, 31, 33–35, 39–41, 48–49, 52–53, 56–57, 59–62, 69–74, 78–79, 109, 115, 118, 121–25, 128, 132, 146, 155, 163–64, 182, 197, 235, 242, 249

problem situation —a state of affairs in which people have the feeling that something is wrong, or that the situation is not as it might be. Pp. 2–5, 7–9, 12, 48, 77, 193

prediction —a forecast of the future. In population studies, prediction connotes a greater sense of certainty than projection. Pp. 12–13, 28, 51, 220, 235

projection —using the data that are available to extend the population into the future. Often contrasted to prediction, which connotes greater certainty about what may occur in the future. Pp. 28–29, 33–34, 36–38, 41–43, 79, 106, 115, 175–77, 233, 235, 251

recycling —the reuse of materials. Pp. 43, 153, 159, 179, 194, 221, 230

renewable resources —materials that are naturally recycled and can be used over and over again. P. 230

reserves —known deposits of minerals. Pp. 211, 219–20, 222, 231

resources in limited supply —minerals and other materials that are not naturally recycled and the supply of which is finite. Pp. 2, 107, 111, 195, 209, 211, 217–22, 230, 247, 248, 255

rhythm method of birth control —a method of birth control based on abstinence from sexual intercourse during the stage of ovulation when the egg can be fertilized. Pp. 84, 87–88, 95

role imagining —to suppose one is a different person or a member of a designated group. It is a way of trying to view situations as they might be viewed by others. Pp. xviii, 248, 252

rural population —all of the population not classified as urban. Pp. 21, 124, 146, 167, 169

"S" curve of population growth —a curve in which there is rapid population growth and then a leveling off within the carrying capacity of the environment. Pp. 38–39, 41, 61, 71, 82

self-contained agrarian system —a relatively independent system in which most of the necessities of the population are produced within the system and much of the waste is recycled back into the system. Agricultural villages found throughout the world approximate self-contained systems. Pp. 99–100, 155, 159–65, 182, 188

semantic clarification —the study of differences in the meanings of terms by juxtaposing two or more terms that are often misconstrued. P. 235

standard metropolitan statistical area (SMSA) —a city of 50,000 or more, the county in which it is located, and adjoining counties that meet certain criteria of metropolitan character and are closely integrated with the central city, as through commuting. (In New England the units are towns rather than counties.) Pp. 134, 167, 172

sterilization —a surgical procedure for preventing conception. In the male, it usually takes the form of closing the vas deferens so that sperm will not be emitted. In the female, it usually involves blocking the Fallopian tubes so that sperm and egg cannot meet. Pp. 60, 68, 92–93, 95, 113–14, 245

survival —a basic value involving the continuance of life. Fundamentally, survival means the sheer physical continuance of life. However, survival can mean the continuance of a way of life, balance of power, or particular social system. Pp. xvii, 2, 19, 37, 58, 62–64, 68, 73, 75, 80, 98, 107, 140, 158, 162, 180, 188–90, 194, 220, 229–31, 234, 236–48, 250, 252, 255, 258–59

synergism —when two or more factors working together produce an effect that is greater than the sum of the two factors working independently. P. 227

system —a system is everything that should be considered when one studies a phenomenon or deals with a problem. Pp. 9, 20–21, 38, 43, 48–51, 71–72, 74–75, 77–78, 80–81, 99, 115, 122, 152–55, 159–60, 162–74, 178–80, 182, 185–88, 190, 193, 201, 214, 224

CAMROSE LUTHERAN COLLEGE
LIBRARY

HB
850
J3

27,139

territoriality —a defense of a certain geographical area. In some populations it may be a mechanism for sensing changes in population density and using that information to regulate the size of the population. Pp. 55– 58, 74

tubal ligation —sterilization of the female in which the Fallopian tubes are blocked so that egg and sperm cannot meet. P. 92

urban population —all persons residing in places of 2,500 population or more, except for those living in rural portions of extended cities. Included are persons living in both incorporated and unincorporated areas. (1970 census definition.) Pp. 21, 128, 146, 159, 167– 69

valuation —making value judgments in problematic situations. Pp. 9, 235– 38, 243, 246, 258– 59

values —the criteria by which we make judgments of worth, of right and wrong, and of what actions we should or should not take to deal with a situation. Pp. 7– 9, 43, 52, 77, 82, 99, 111, 117, 139– 41, 143, 145, 148, 150, 159, 233– 44, 246– 49, 252, 255– 56, 258– 60

value clarification —the process of becoming more aware of the values we hold. Pp. 72, 234– 35, 243

vasectomy —sterilization of males in which the thin tubes (vasa deferentia) through which the sperm move are closed. Pp. 84, 92, 114

withdrawal (coitus interruptus) —a contraceptive practice in which the male withdraws from intercourse before ejaculation of the sperm. Pp. 84, 88, 95